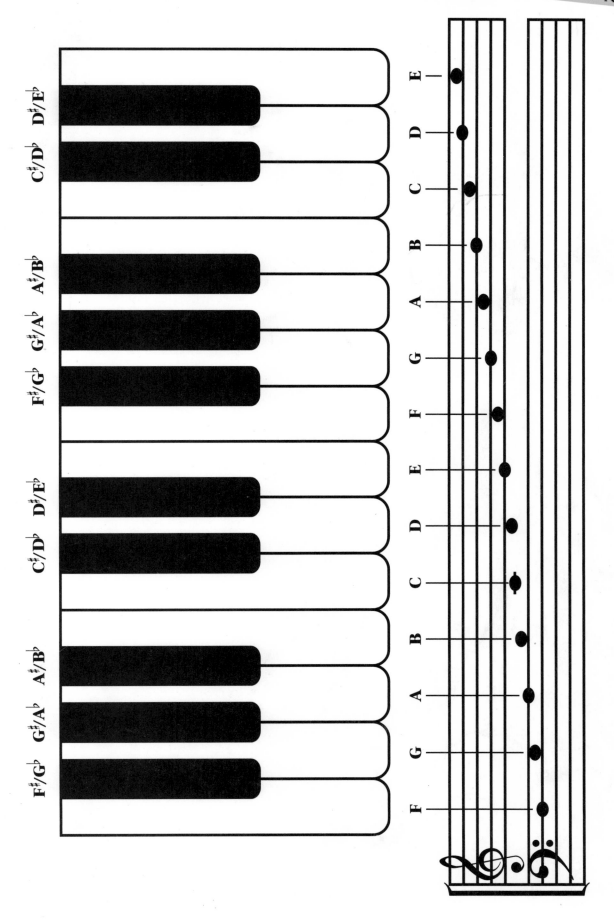

Silver Burdett MAKING MUSIC

Program Authors

Jane Beethoven
Susan Brumfield
Patricia Shehan Campbell
David N. Connors
Robert A. Duke
Judith A. Jellison

Rita Klinger
Rochelle Mann
Hunter C. March
Nan L. McDonald
Marvelene C. Moore
Mary Palmer
Konnie Saliba

Will Schmid
Carol Scott-Kassner
Mary E. Shamrock
Sandra L. Stauffer
Judith Thomas
Jill Trinka

Recording Producers

Rick Baitz
Rick Bassett
Joseph Joubert
Bryan Louiselle

Tom Moore
J. Douglas Pummill
Michael Rafter
Buryl Red, EXECUTIVE PRODUCER

Buddy Skipper
Robert Spivak
Jeanine Tesori
Linda Twine

Scott Foresman

Editorial Offices: Parsippany, New Jersey • Glenview, Illinois • New York, New York
Sales Offices: Parsippany, New Jersey • Duluth, Georgia • Glenview, Illinois
Coppell, Texas • Ontario, California

ISBN: 0-382-34348-4

Contents

Steps to Making Music

iii

Paths to Making Music

STEPS TO MAKING MUSIC

Sounds Surround

Your journey with music is like a circle—it has no end. Step into the circle and **sing** "Turn the Beat Around."

Then pass the beat around. **Clap** one beat in turn around the circle. Create different ways to do this activity.

1-1

Turn the Beat Around

Words and Music by
Peter Jackson, Jr. and Gerald Jackson

Turn it   up, turn it up, turn it up-side down.

Turn the beat _ a - round. _   Love to   hear _ per - cus - sion.

Turn it up - side down. _   Love to   hear _ per - cus - sion.

Let the Music Begin!

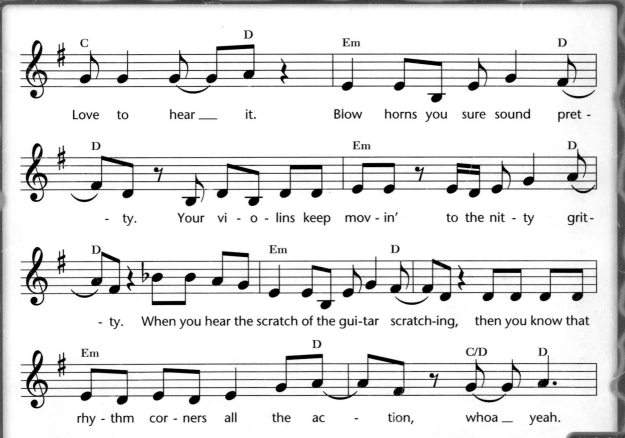

Love to hear ___ it. Blow horns you sure sound pret -

- ty. Your vi - o - lins keep mov - in' to the nit - ty grit -

- ty. When you hear the scratch of the gui - tar scratch - ing, then you know that

rhy - thm cor - ners all the ac - tion, whoa ___ yeah.

Expression in Your Music

What feeling, or emotion, do the words of this song communicate? As you **listen** to the song, do you think any other feelings are suggested, even though the words don't talk about them? One way music suggests feelings is with **dynamics.**

Dynamics are the different levels of loudness and softness of sound.

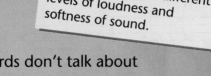

Put a Little Love in Your Heart

Words and Music by Jimmy Holiday, Randy Myers, and Jackie De Shannon

1. Think of your fel - low man, lend him a help - ing hand,
2. An - oth - er day __ goes by, and still the chil - dren cry,
3. Take a good look __ a - round, and if you're look - ing down,

Put a lit - tle love __ in your heart. _____

If

You see, it's get - ting late, oh, please don't hes - i - tate,
you want the world _ to know, we won't let ha - tred grow,
I hope when you __ de - cide, kind - ness will be __ your guide,

Put a lit - tle love _ in your heart. _____ And the world _

The Language of Expression

Musicians usually use Italian words when they talk about dynamics.

p (piano) = soft
mp (mezzo piano) = medium soft
mf (mezzo forte) = medium loud
f (forte) = loud

< *(crescendo)* = gradually louder

> *(decrescendo)* = gradually softer

Use dynamics while you **sing** "Put a Little Love in Your Heart."

_____ will be a bet-ter place, And the world _ will be a

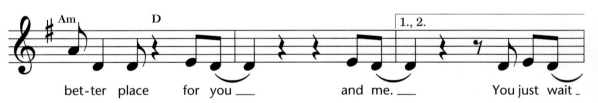

bet-ter place for you ___ and me. ___ You just wait _

_____ and see. _ You just wait _ and see. _

mf 1st time, *p* 2nd time, *f* last time

_____ Put a lit-tle love _ in your heart. _____

Video Library View and listen to another version of the song "Put a Little Love in Your Heart," as performed by the Total Experience Gospel Choir on the *Singing Styles* video.

Expressive Music

"Put a Little Love in Your Heart" has been recorded by many singers. **Listen** for dynamic contrast and style in this version by Mahalia Jackson.

 1-5
Put a Little Love in Your Heart

by Jimmy Holiday, Randy Myers, and Jackie De Shannon as performed by Mahalia Jackson

Mahalia Jackson recorded her version of the song in 1969.

Mahalia Jackson ▶

Moving with Expression

As you **sing** "Put a Little Love in Your Heart," **perform** these signs.

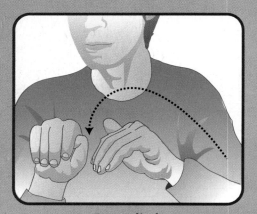

Put a little

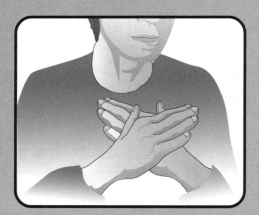

love

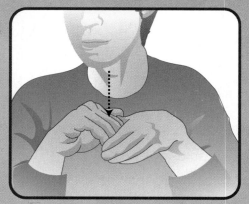

in your

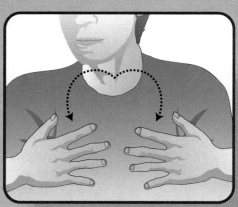

heart

A Dynamic Musician

Tony Bennett is famous for his voice and singing style.
Listen for his use of dynamic contrast as he sings *The Beat of My Heart*. When and where does he change his dynamics?

1-6

The Beat of My Heart

as performed by Tony Bennett
This song is performed in the swing style

MUSIC MAKERS

Tony Bennett

Tony Bennett (Anthony Benedetto, born 1926) is originally from Astoria, Queens, New York. He attended the High School of Industrial Arts in Manhattan. Bennett got his break in music when comedian, Bob Hope, heard him singing at the Greenwich Village Inn. Hope was impressed and asked Bennett to sing with him at the Paramount Theater. Bennett later signed a record deal with Columbia Records and recorded hits such as *Boulevard of Broken Dreams, Rags to Riches,* and *I Left My Heart in San Francisco.* Bennett remains popular, and he has performed with rock groups such as the Red Hot Chili Peppers. He has received Grammy awards for Album of the Year and Best Traditional Pop Vocal.

ON THE ROAD TO RHYTHM

Look at the rhythm patterns in these boxes. How many beats are in each pattern?

Using rhythm syllables, clap and count as you **read** your way down the rhythm road.

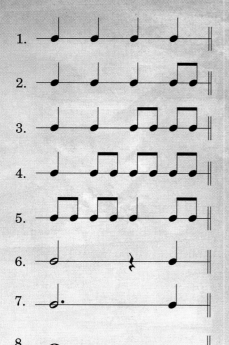

Look at the song on page 11. Find the time signature. How many beats are in each measure? **Listen** to "Soldier, Soldier" while you conduct a 4/4 pattern.

A Girl and Her Soldier

Listen to this recording of *Lazy John*, a variation of "Soldier, Soldier." Then **create** your own version.

Written and Performed by Jean Ritchie
This song is performed by Jean Ritchie, a folk singer from the Appalachian Mountains of Kentucky.

Soldier, Soldier

Traditional Song from the United States and England

REFRAIN

"Now, sol - dier, sol - dier, will you mar - ry me, with your mus - ket, fife, and drum?" "Oh, how can I mar - ry such a

rit. last time   *accel. last time*   *Fine*

pret - ty girl as you, when I've got no shoes to put on?"
when I've got no hat to put on?"
when I've got no coat to put on?"
when I've got a wife at _____ home?"

VERSE

Then off to the cob - bler _____ she did go, as
hat - ter _____
tai - lor _____

fast as she could run. She bought him a pair of the
hat
coat

D. C. al Fine

fin - est that there were, and the sol - dier put them _ on.
it _____
it _____

WORKING WITH RHYTHM

Have you ever rowed a boat or raked the leaves? What is similar about these motions? Songs like "Haul Away, Joe" are called sea shanties. They were meant for work on board large sailing ships in the 1700s and 1800s. This song has a **strong and weak beat** in each measure to fit with the work being done. What kind of work on a ship would need this type of motion?

The **strong beat** is the first beat in a measure. The **weak beat** is the second beat in a measure.

Moving with a Sea Shanty

With a partner, **create** work movements
to do while you **sing** "Haul Away, Joe."

1-10

Haul Away, Joe

Sea Shanty from England

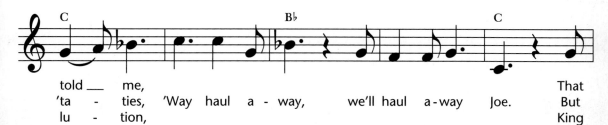

VERSE

1. Oh, when I was a lit - tle lad, or so my moth - er
2. Oh, once I was in Ire - land dig - gin' turf and
3. King Lou - ie was the King of France be - fore the re - vo -

told ___ me,
'ta - ties, 'Way haul a - way, we'll haul a - way Joe. That
lu - tion, King

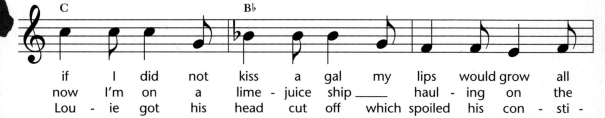

if I did not kiss a gal my lips would grow all
now I'm on a lime - juice ship ___ haul - ing on the
Lou - ie got his head cut off which spoiled his con - sti -

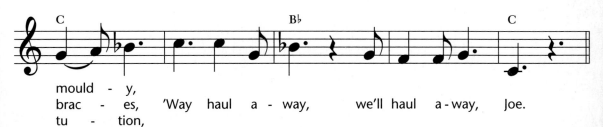

mould - y,
brac - es, 'Way haul a - way, we'll haul a - way, Joe.
tu - tion,

REFRAIN

'Way haul a - way, we'll haul a - way for bet - ter weath - er,

'Way haul a - way, we'll haul a - way, Joe.

Dancing in DUPLE METER

"*Gakavik*" is a folk song from the Republic of Armenia, a country that became independent after being part of the Soviet Union for seventy years.

This song is based on a strong and weak beat pattern known as **duple meter.** Clap the steady beat while you **sing** or **listen** to "*Gakavik.*"

> **Duple meter** is a basic pattern in which a measure has one strong and one weak beat.

Gakavik
(The Partridge)

1-12

English Words by Mary Shamrock

Armenian Folk Song

Ա - րեվ բաց - վեց թուխ __ ամ պե - րեն,
A - rev pats - vedz tugh __ am be - ren,
Threat-'ning clouds hide the sky, Soon the sun breaks the gloom;

կա - քավ թռ - ավ կա - նաչ ___ սա - րեն.
ga - kav te - rav ga - nach ___ sa - ren.
Moun-tains high, moun-tains green, Ev - 'ry - where bright flow - ers bloom.

կա - նաչ ___ սա - րեն՛ սա - րի ___ ծե - րեն,
ga - nach ___ sa - ren sa - ri ___ dze - ren,
Pret - ty par - tridge through the air, Feath-ers shin - ing in the sun;

թա — րեվ __ թէ — րավ ծա — ղիկ — նե __ րեն:
pa — rev ___ pe — rav dza — ghik — ne — ren:
Moun-tains green and flow-ers bright send their joy to ev - 'ry - one.

Սի — րու — նիկ, _____ սի — րու — նիկ,
Si — rov — nig, _____ si — rov — nig,
Soar __ and _____ sail, she's fly - ing far __ and free.

սի — րու - նիկ, ___ նախ — շուն կա — քա — վիկ.
si — rov — nig, ___ nakh — shoun ga — ka — vik.
Pret - ty par - tridge, love - ly bird, greet - ing you and me.

Duple Meter in Movement

Follow these steps to **create** a dance for "*Gakavik.*"

- Step right, together, step right, easy kick
- Step left, together, step left, easy kick

Listening for Form

Follow the listening map as you **listen** to "Galop" from *Masquerade Suite*. Make up a story that involves a masquerade and fits with the music.

1-16
Galop

**from *Masquerade Suite*
by Aram Khachaturian**

"Galop" is one section of music intended to be played at different points during a play titled *Masquerade*.

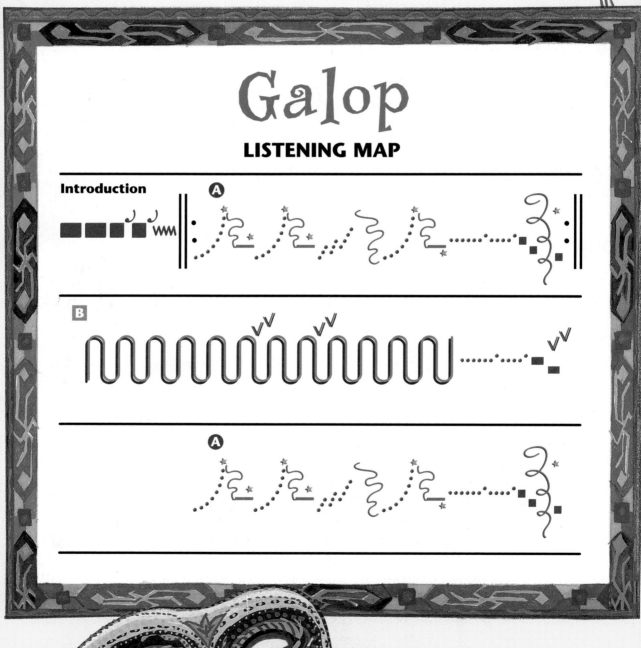

Aram Khachaturian

Aram Khachaturian (1903–1978) Though counted as one of the outstanding composers of the Soviet Union, Aram Khachaturian's music demonstrates his Armenian roots and background. Although he had great musical talent as a child, he did not begin formal training in music until he was nineteen years old. He drew upon the folk music of Armenia, as well as other countries in what was then the Soviet Union, to create a rich, colorful musical style.

Show What You Know!

1. Which of these rhythm patterns is the beginning of *"Gakavik"*? Which is the beginning of "Soldier, Soldier"?

A.

B.

2. Create a rhythm pattern in duple meter that is eight beats long using these note durations.

I Sing, You Sing

Some songs have parts for a solo and parts for a group to sing. This is known as **call and response,** and it is very similar to a conversation. The solo parts need to be completed by a response from the group.

> **Call and response** is a musical device in which a portion of a melody (call) is followed by an answering portion (response).

Sing "Limbo Like Me" and take turns being the soloist.

1-17

Limbo Like Me

Words and Music Adapted by Massie Patterson and Sammy Heyward

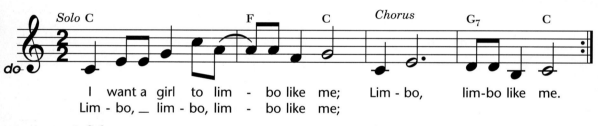

I want a girl to lim - bo like me; Lim - bo, lim-bo like me.
Lim - bo, __ lim - bo, lim - bo like me;

Ev - 'ry - bod - y lim - bo like me; Lim - bo, lim-bo like me.
My lit - tle goat can lim - bo like me;

Mon - key try to lim - bo like me; Lim - bo, lim-bo like me.
Mon - key no can lim - bo like me;

One an' all come lim - bo like me; Lim - bo, lim-bo like me.

Lim - bo, lim-bo like me; Lim - bo, lim - bo like me.

Do the Limbo

This song and movement game come from the Caribbean Calypso tradition. To play the game, two people hold a stick. The other players take turns bending backwards to go under the stick. The stick is lowered until the last player able to pass under the stick wins.

Move as you **listen** to Samaroo Jets perform *Brasidad del Zulia.*

1-18

Brasidad del Zulia

as performed by Samaroo Jets

This performance features steel drums made from oil barrels.

MAKING A MELODY

Some songs express hope. "Gonna Ride Up in the Chariot" originated with African Americans during slavery when life was very harsh. It is a song of hope for freedom. **Sing** the song and **listen** to the words.

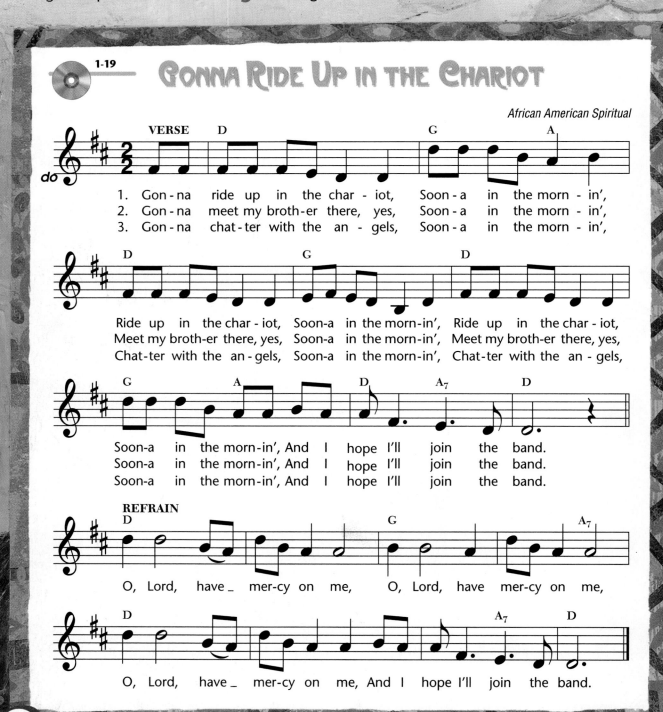

1-19

GONNA RIDE UP IN THE CHARIOT

African American Spiritual

VERSE

1. Gon - na ride up in the char - iot, Soon - a in the morn - in',
2. Gon - na meet my broth-er there, yes, Soon - a in the morn - in',
3. Gon - na chat - ter with the an - gels, Soon - a in the morn - in',

Ride up in the char - iot, Soon-a in the morn-in', Ride up in the char - iot,
Meet my broth-er there, yes, Soon-a in the morn-in', Meet my broth-er there, yes,
Chat-ter with the an - gels, Soon-a in the morn-in', Chat-ter with the an - gels,

Soon-a in the morn-in', And I hope I'll join the band.
Soon-a in the morn-in', And I hope I'll join the band.
Soon-a in the morn-in', And I hope I'll join the band.

REFRAIN

O, Lord, have _ mer-cy on me, O, Lord, have mer-cy on me,

O, Lord, have _ mer-cy on me, And I hope I'll join the band.

Interval Practice

The melody of this song is composed of notes that either repeat, move by step, or move by skip. **Sing** "Gonna Ride Up in the Chariot" again and look for the **intervals** below in the melody.

An **interval** is the distance between two pitches.

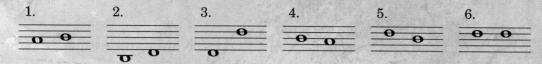

What are the intervals shown above? To determine the interval, count the bottom tone as 1. Then count all lines and spaces up to the next pitch.

Sing "Gonna Ride Up in the Chariot" and **listen** for the steps, repeats, and skips.

Compose Using Intervals

Compose an introduction for "Gonna Ride Up in the Chariot" to play on a melody instrument. Choose the notes from these pitches. Make sure you use a step, a skip, and a repeated tone in the melody.

Tune In

Africans who were brought to America created spirituals. The subject of spirituals was often freedom.

Pentatonic Patterns

Here is a Japanese melody made up of three melodic patterns.
Follow its contour or shape as you **listen** to *"Tsuki."*

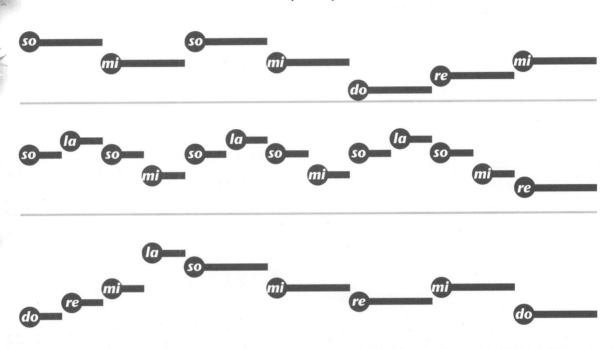

Reading Pentatonic Scales

A song's notes make up its scale. **Read** the **pentatonic scale** on the syllable ladder. Find the steps and skips in the scale. Use hand signs as you **sing** the scale up and down.

> A **pentatonic scale** is a scale of five notes.

Read the pentatonic scale from the staff. The *do* symbol at the beginning of the staff will help you find your way around.

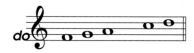

Now you are ready to **read** *"Tsuki"* from the staff.

Tsuki
(The Moon)

1-20

English Words by Kazuo Akiyama   *School Song from Japan*

で　　た　　　で　　た　　　つ　　き　　が
1. De - ta,   de - ta,   tsu - ki   ga
1. Now the moon is com - ing out!

ま＿＿　る　い　ま＿＿　る　い　ま　ん　ま　る　い
Ma - ru - i   ma - ru - i   ma - n   ma - ru - i,
Big and round, so big and round, as round＿ as a tray.

ぼ　ん　の　よ　う　な　つ　き　が
Bo＿＿ n - no   yo - na   tsu - ki   ga.
Moon is big and round, just like a tray.

2. *Kaku reta kumoni,*
   Kuroi, kuroi makuroi,
   Sumino yona kumoni.

2. Now the moon is hiding.
   Gone away, O gone away, O gone away so far.
   Up behind the clouds as black as tar.

♫rts Connection

◀ *Moonlight on Sebu River* (c. 19th century Japan) by Hiroshige

Tonal Center

Name the first and last note of this song. Count how many times this pitch occurs. Where does it occur most often? The pitch G is the **tonal center** of this song.

Now **listen** to the song's melody while humming G. Sometimes G fits with the melody, and sometimes it does not. Like a magnet, the melody always pulls back to G.

> A **tonal center** is a pitch that acts as a resting place or "home" for all of the other pitches that happen around it.

1-24

Waitin' for the Light to Shine
from *Big River*

Words and Music by Roger Miller
Arranged by Linda Twine

VERSE

1. I have lived an un - di - rect - ed life, a cloud - y
2. Far be - yond hor - i - zons I have seen, be - yond the

way I know, the on - ly way I knew. So the
things I've done, be - yond the dreams I've dreamed. Are the

things I've done, in fact, each and ev - 'ry one, are the
things I've done, in fact, each and ev - 'ry one, are the

way that I was taught to run.
way that I was taught to run.

A Song of Revelation

In "Waitin' for the Light to Shine," the singer shares his feelings. Explain what he means by *darkness* and *light*.

A Light on Broadway

The American Broadway musical has been going strong for more than seventy years. The name *Broadway* comes from the famous New York City street where most of the musical theaters are located. Musicals are plays with speaking, singing, and dancing. The music is usually played by an orchestra in a pit in front of the stage. *West Side Story, The Sound of Music,* and *Les Misérables* are famous Broadway musicals. Can you name others?

"Waitin' for the Light to Shine" is from the Broadway musical *Big River*. This show is based on Mark Twain's book, *The Adventures of Huckleberry Finn*. In this book, set in the mid-1800s, the main characters, Huck and Jim, travel together on a raft down the mighty Mississippi River.

of HUCKLEBERRY FINN.
(Tom Sawyer's Comrade.)
BY MARK TWAIN.
ILLUSTRATED.

Tune In

Rene Auberjonois (Odo in *Deep Space 9*) and Brent Spiner (Data in *Star Trek— The Next Generation*) have both played the character Duke in *Big River* on Broadway.

ROGER MILLER AND LINDA TWINE

Roger Miller (1936–1992) wrote the music for *Big River*. He was famous as a country music singer and songwriter. *Big River* was his first attempt at writing a show for the stage, and the show was a big success. It had more than 1,000 performances in New York from 1985 to 1988, and it won seven Tony Awards. Roger Miller was made a member of the Country Music Hall of Fame in 1995.

Linda Twine began her career on Broadway as musical director of *Big River*. After she graduated from the University of Oklahoma, she began teaching music in New York City public elementary schools. Roger Miller met her and discovered that she understood the style of music he wanted for *Big River*, so he asked her to be musical director for the Broadway show.

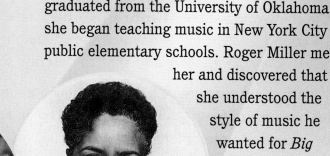

Show What You Know!

Read the following melodies using pitch syllables.

Look at the phrases above. How would you identify the tonal center of these phrases if the beginning were not marked with *do?*

MANY Voices

There are as many different "colors" in the sounds we hear as in the world we see. **Timbre** [TAM-ber] means "the color of a sound." Musicians use words such as *bright, dull, dark, mellow, clear, light, open,* and *shrill* to describe sound colors.

> **Timbre** is the unique difference or tone color of sounds.

Every musical instrument has its own timbre, and each instrument can produce different shades of its own color. For example, just as you are able to see differences in shades of yellow or blue, musicians are able to hear differences in sounds.

An instrument with many timbre possibilities is the human voice. Every voice has a slightly different sound. The singing voice can take on many different timbres. Singing needs to have a sound that is appropriate for the musical style of a song. This requires singers to learn how to make that particular sound, or timbre. Let's listen to a few examples from different parts of the world.

Voices Around the World

These groups of people are trained to sing in different manners.
Listen to the timbre of the voices of these singers.

▲ 1-26
Ghel moma

by S. Moutaftshiev
as performed by Le Mystère des Voix Bulgares

One quality of Bulgarian vocal music is harmony created by singing notes very close together, producing a special ringing sound.

◀ 1-27
Sigit "Alash"

Tuvinian Singers and Musicians

This man from Tuva is singing *choomej* (singing technique). He changes the inside shape of his mouth to make the higher and lower pitched sounds.

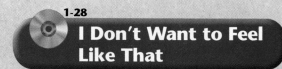

1-28
I Don't Want to Feel Like That ▶

by Teresa Radigan and Donald Schlitz, Jr.
as performed by Patty Loveless

Loveless, a native of Kentucky, is known in country music for her soulful singing.

▲
Patty Loveless

1-29
Round Dance

Powwow song of the Plains Indians

This music is a social dance performed at powwows. Notice the quality of the performers' voices.

1-30
Nahandove

**from *Chansons Madecasses*
by Maurice Ravel**

This selection is performed by Jessye Norman, a well-known soprano who has performed all over the world.

1-31
Rain, Rain, Beautiful Rain

**song in Mbube [MM-boo-beh] style
as performed by Ladysmith Black Mambazo**

This group sings in simple harmony with open and natural voices. They are able to slide from pitch to pitch together perfectly.

Your Voice—Your Song

Children's voices have a wonderful sound of their own—clear and somewhat light. As you grow into your teenage years, you will develop the power and flexibility needed for adult singing. Here's a song about singing. Mix your own special vocal timbre with all the other timbres of your classmates to make a vocal rainbow.

1-32

I'm Gonna Sing

African American Spiritual

1. I'm gon - na sing when the spir - it says "Sing," _____
2. I'm gon - na shout when the spir - it says "Shout," _____
3. I'm gon - na pray when the spir - it says "Pray," _____
4. I'm gon - na sing when the spir - it says "Sing," _____

I'm gon - na sing when the spir - it says "Sing," _____
I'm gon - na shout when the spir - it says "Shout," _____
I'm gon - na pray when the spir - it says "Pray," _____
I'm gon - na sing when the spir - it says "Sing," _____

I'm gon - na sing when the spir - it says "Sing," _____
I'm gon - na shout when the spir - it says "Shout," _____
I'm gon - na pray when the spir - it says "Pray," _____
I'm gon - na sing when the spir - it says "Sing," _____

And o - bey the spir - it of the Lord. _____

LAYERED SOUNDS... CHA' CHA' CHA'

Music has **texture.** Like a piece of cloth, it can be thick or thin depending on the number of layers. The first two measures of *"Sonando"* are rhythmic ostinatos you can **play** while you **sing** the song. Practice clapping each ostinato, then **perform** *"Sonando."*

> **Texture** is the layering of sounds to create a thick or thin quality in music.

1-33

SONANDO

English Words by Alice D. Firgau

Words and Music by Peter Terrace
Arranged by Ted Solis, Adapted and Arranged by Kay Edwards

So - nan - do (clap)   pa - ra bai - lar,
They're play - ing   a cha - cha - cha.

Go - za (clap)   mi cha - cha - cha.
Come on,   let's have some fun.

Play 4 times (all instruments)

Sing 4 times

G   F   G

Lle - ga - ré Ma - rí - a, lle - ga - ré.
Here I am, Ma - ri - a, dance with me.

Play 2 times (all instruments)

G   F

So - nan - do (clap)   pa - ra bai - lar,
They're play - ing   a cha - cha - cha.

G   F

Go - za (clap)   mi cha - cha - cha.
Come on,   let's have some fun.

More Layered Sounds

Listen for layered instruments in Poncho Sanchez's recording of *Night in Tunisia.* How many instrument parts can you identify?

2-1
Night in Tunisia

**by F. Paparelli and Dizzy Gillespie
as performed by Poncho Sanchez**

This version of *Night in Tunisia* has a tenor saxophone and timbales. These instruments are part of the Latin/jazz fusion style.

How's the Texture?

When is a country a continent? When it's Australia. Australians have their own names for things found only in their country. Here is an Australian song that plays with names.

Perform these ostinatos. Then **play** them as a layered accompaniment while you **sing** "Tie Me Kangaroo Down, Sport."

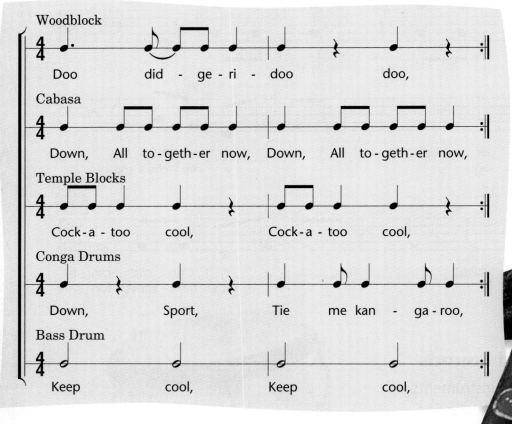

Listen to *Brolga One* and notice the sound of the *didgeridoo* [DID-jeh-ree-doo]. The *didgeridoo* was invented and played by the aboriginal people of Australia. Now, everyone wants to play the *didgeridoo!* Wouldn't you?

2-2
Brolga One

created and performed by aboriginal musicians with didgeridoo

This recording includes singing along with the *didgeridoo*.

Tie Me Kangaroo Down, Sport

Words and Music by Rolf and Bruce Harris

VERSE

1. Watch me wal - la - bys feed, mate.
2. Keep me cock - a - too cool, Curl.
3. Take me ko - a - la back, Jack.
4. Mind me plat - y - pus duck, Bill.

Refrain Tie me kan - ga - roo down, sport.

Watch me wal - la - bys feed.
Keep me cock - a - too cool.
Take me ko - a - la back. He
Mind me plat - y - pus duck. Don't
Tie me kan - ga - roo down.

They're a dan - ger - ous breed, mate. So
Don't go act - ing the fool, Curl. Just
lives some - where _ on the track, Mac. So
let him go run - ning a - mok, Bill. So
Tie me kan - ga - roo down, sport.

watch me wal - la - bys feed. All to - geth - er now! *(to Refrain)*
keep me cock - a - too cool.
take me ko - a - la back.
mind me plat - y - pus duck.
Tie me kan - ga - roo down. *(to Verses)*

5. Play your didgeridoo, Blue.
   Play your didgeridoo.
   Keep playing 'til I shoot thro', Blue.
   Play your didgeridoo.
   All together now! *Refrain*

6. Tan me hide when I'm dead, Fred.
   Tan me hide when I'm dead.
   So we tanned his hide when he died, Clyde.
   And that's it hanging on the shed.
   All together now! *Refrain*

Power in Numbers
Layers of SOUND

"Pay Me My Money Down" is a work song originally sung by stevedores. The workers are singing about getting paid for their labor.

A solo voice sings the call. Many voices answer in the response and sing on the refrain to create a powerful sound. **Listen** for the layering of voices in the recording of "Pay Me My Money Down."

2-5

Pay Me My Money Down

Work Song from the Georgia Sea Islands
Collected and Adapted by Lydia A. Parrish

1. I thought I heard ___ the cap - tain say,
2. As soon as the boat was clear of the bar,

"Pay me my mon-ey down," _ To - mor - row is our
He knocked me down with the

sail - ing day, ___ "Pay me my mon-ey down." _
end of a spar,

Singing a Work Song

African Americans along the southeastern coast sang this song. **Listen** as the Georgia Sea Island Singers perform this song. **Create** work movements while you **sing** along.

2-7
Pay Me My Money Down

Work Song Collected and Adapted by Lydia A. Parrish

Notice the "work sounds" the performers are making while singing.

REFRAIN

"Pay me, _ oh, pay me, _ Pay me my mon-ey down. _

Pay me or go to jail, _ Pay me my mon-ey down." _

3. Well, I wish I was Mr. Steven's son,
"Pay me my money down,"
Sit on the bank and watch the work done,
"Pay me my money down." *Refrain*

The Power of Layers of Percussion

Caribbean music is filled with layers of instruments. In particular, the music of steel drums is made by layering many parts to create an exciting sound. About sixty years ago, musicians in Trinidad discovered how to make drums out of 55-gallon oil storage barrels. Steel drums can be tuned to specific pitches.

Many steel drum bands have fifty players or more! No matter what the size, every band has an "engine room" of instruments such as congas, drum sets, maracas, and claves. The engine room supplies a rhythmic background for the music.

Here is how steel drums are made.

▲ **1.** One end of the barrel is removed. The "skirt" of the barrel is cut to make a high-, medium-, or low-sounding drum.

◀ **2.** The top is hammered into a bowl shape with flat areas that produce definite pitches.

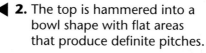

3. The entire drum is heated red-hot in a fire to cure the steel. ▶

Video Library Watch *Percussion Instruments: Tuned* to learn more about steel drum bands.

Classical Music with a Caribbean Flavor

Although steel drum bands are known for playing calypso music, they also play many other styles. **Listen** to the calypso rhythms and layers in this version of *Eine Kleine Nachtmusik (A Little Night Music)*.

2-8
Eine Kleine Nachtmusik (A Little Night Music)

by Wolfgang Amadeus Mozart

Often steel drum bands will play European classical orchestral works.

M·U·S·I·C M·A·K·E·R·S
AMOCO RENEGADES

The **Amoco Renegades** are one of Trinidad's oldest steel drum bands. Jit Samaroo, director of the band, commented that the name of their group goes back to when "panmen" were considered ruffians more than musicians. The group had over 100 members when it was named champion in 1989 at the steel band competition called "Panorama." The Amoco Renegades performed *Somebody*.

Listen for layers of sound in this recording of *Somebody*.

2-9
Somebody

by Winsford deVine
as performed by the Amoco Renegades

This recording was made three days before the Amoco Renegades were named champions.

Putting It

What Do You Know?

1. Look at the notation for *"Tsuki"* on page 23. Then answer these questions.

   a. Where is *do* located in the music?

   b. Point to all the notes named *so.* How many did you find?

   c. Do the same activity for the notes named *mi, re, la,* and *do.*

2. Name each dynamic symbol and point to the correct definition.

   a. *mf*   loud

   b. *p*   gradually louder

   c. *mp*   medium loud

   d. ⟩   soft

   e. *f*   medium soft

   f. ⟨   gradually softer

2-10

What Do You Hear? 1

Listen to these examples of vocal timbre. Briefly describe the timbre of each example using at least three adjectives in each description.

1. *Rain, Rain Beautiful Rain*

2. *I Don't Want to Feel Like That*

3. *Nahandove*

4. *Sigit "Alash"*

All Together

Create Dynamics

Create a dynamics roadmap to follow while you sing "Waitin' for the Light to Shine" on page 24. Remember that dynamics should express the feelings and mood of the song.

Move to the Beat

Use movement to show strong and weak beats while you sing "*Gakavik*" on page 14. With a partner, create work movements to perform as you sing "Haul Away, Joe" on page 13.

Read a Melody

Read the notation for "Tsuki" on page 23, using pitch syllables and hand signs. Then perform the song again with the words.

Create Textures

Divide into two groups and perform "Pay Me My Money Down" on page 36, in call-and-response form. Sing the song again with only a few students singing the call and the rest of the class singing the response. Create additional verses to the song and perform them as a solo caller while the rest of the class sings the responses.

Sing and Swing

In the late 1950s and early 1960s, songs with nonsense words were called doo-wop.

Sing "We Go Together," a song with lots of nonsense words.

We Go Together

2-14

Lyrics and Music by Warren Casey and Jim Jacobs

1. We go to - geth - er, ___ like ra - ma la - ma la - ma ka
2. We're one of a kind _____ like dip da dip da dip

ding - a da ding ___ a - dong, Re - mem - bered for -
doo - wop ___ da doo - bee doo. Our names ___ are

ev - er _____ as shoo - bop sha wad - da wad - da
signed _____ boog-e - dy boog-e - dy boog-e - dy boog-e - dy

yip - pi - ty boom - de boom. Chang chang
shoo - by - doo - wop ___ she - bop Chang chang

EXPLORING MUSIC

chang-it-ty chang shoo-bop, that's the way it ___ should
chang-it-ty chang shoo-bop, we'll al-ways be _____ like

be. _____ wha-oooh, yeah! one, _____

wa wa ___ wa waah. _____ When we go

out at night, _ and stars are shin-in' bright _

up in the skies a-bove, _____ or at the

high school dance, _ where you can find ro-mance, _

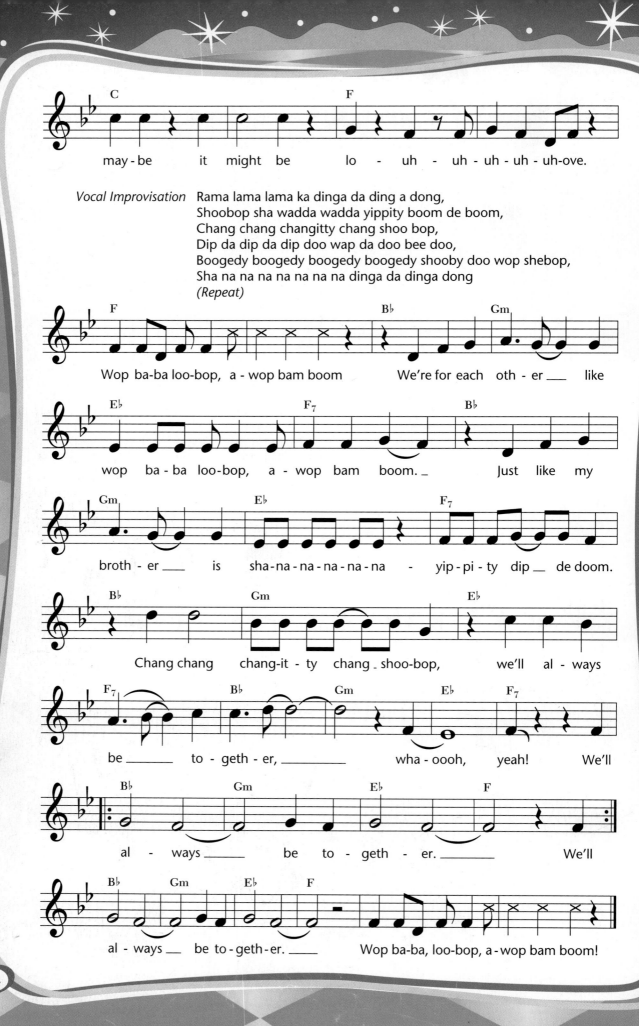

may - be it might be lo - uh - uh - uh - uh - uh-ove.

Vocal Improvisation Rama lama lama ka dinga da ding a dong,
Shoobop sha wadda wadda yippity boom de boom,
Chang chang changitty chang shoo bop,
Dip da dip da dip doo wap da doo bee doo,
Boogedy boogedy boogedy boogedy shooby doo wop shebop,
Sha na na na na na na na dinga da dinga dong
(Repeat)

Wop ba-ba loo-bop, a - wop bam boom We're for each oth - er ___ like

wop ba - ba loo-bop, a - wop bam boom. _ Just like my

broth - er ___ is sha-na - na - na - na - na - yip - pi - ty dip __ de doom.

Chang chang chang-it - ty chang _ shoo-bop, we'll al - ways

be ___ to - geth - er, _____ wha - oooh, yeah! We'll

al - ways ____ be to - geth - er. _____ We'll

al - ways __ be to - geth-er. ____ Wop ba-ba, loo-bop, a-wop bam boom!

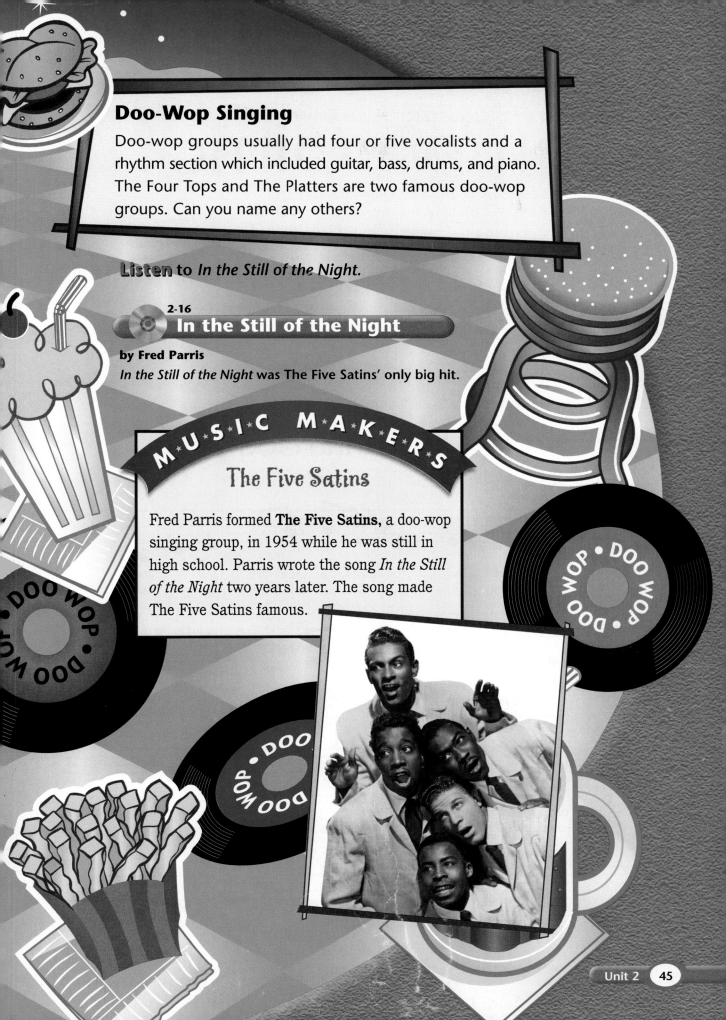

Doo-Wop Singing

Doo-wop groups usually had four or five vocalists and a rhythm section which included guitar, bass, drums, and piano. The Four Tops and The Platters are two famous doo-wop groups. Can you name any others?

Listen to *In the Still of the Night.*

2-16
In the Still of the Night

by Fred Parris
In the Still of the Night was The Five Satins' only big hit.

M·U·S·I·C M·A·K·E·R·S

The Five Satins

Fred Parris formed **The Five Satins,** a doo-wop singing group, in 1954 while he was still in high school. Parris wrote the song *In the Still of the Night* two years later. The song made The Five Satins famous.

Tempo Time

"Walk! Don't run!" When someone says that to you, what do you do? You change the speed of your movement. In music, **tempo** can help communicate the feeling of a song.

Tempo is the speed of the beat.

Read the words of "Oh, Danny Boy." Before you **sing** the song, decide what tempo would be best.

2-17

Oh, Danny Boy

Words by Thomas Moore   *Folk Song from Ireland*

1. Oh, Dan-ny Boy, the pipes, the pipes are cal - ling,
2. But when you come and all the flow'rs are dy - ing,

From glen to glen, and down the moun - tain side;
If I am dead, as dead I well may be;

The sum-mer's gone, and all the ros - es fal - ling,
You'll come and find the place where I am ly - ing,

'Tis you, 'tis you must go, and I must bide.
And kneel and say an A - ve there for me.

What's the Best Tempo?

"Oh, Danny Boy" is based upon a famous Irish melody. Composers and musicians from many different cultures have created their own arrangements of this tune. **Listen** to this version by Percy Grainger. Here are some words you can use to describe the tempo.

adagio—slow   *andante*—walking speed   *presto*—very fast

moderato—moderate *allegro*—fast

2-19

Irish Tune from County Derry

**Irish Folk Melody
arranged by Percy Grainger**

This version of the "Oh, Danny Boy" melody is performed by a wind ensemble.

Listening for Tempo

Listen to *Hungarian Dance No. 6*, a composition for orchestra. There are many tempo changes in this music. As you **listen**, point to the tempo meter below.

2-20
Hungarian Dance No. 6

by Johannes Brahms

The Hungarian Dances were inspired by folk melodies of Eastern Europe.

Hungarian
Dance No.6

LISTENING MAP

108   120

Moderato

Andante   Allegro

76   168

speed
indicator

Adagio   Presto

bpm

Tempo Meter

Do the Chicken Dance!

Listen to *The Chicken Dance* and **move** with the music. Do your movements match the tempo of the music?

The Chicken Dance

by Werner Thomas

The Chicken Dance is a favorite activity at celebrations and dances.

▲ **1.** Chirp with your hands.

▲ **2.** Flap your wings.

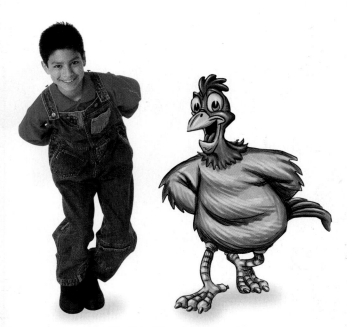

▲ **3.** Waddle downward.

▲ **4.** Clap four times.

The Score is Tied

Rhythm is created by patterns arranged in many ways. What makes rhythm interesting is the way long and short sounds are arranged over the steady beat.

Listen to the rhythms in "Somebody's Knockin' at Your Door."

Using rhythm syllables, **read** the following rhythms. Then clap the rhythms as you **sing** the song. Are these rhythms the same as the rhythms in the song?

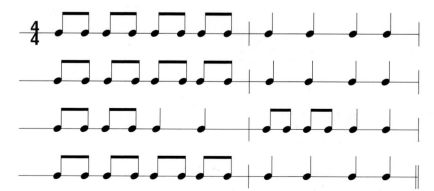

Somebody's Knockin' at Your Door

2-23

African American Spiritual

do

D   G   D
Some - bod - y's knock - in' at your door,

D   A₇
Some - bod - y's knock - in' at your door.

D   G
Oh, _____ sin - ner, why don't you ans - wer?

D   G   D
Some - bod - y's knock - in' at your door.

Tie It All Together

We can notate the rhythm of the words using the **tie.**

> A **tie** connects two notes of the same pitch.

Some-bod - y's knock-in' at your   door, _____

Did you know tied notes can be written another way? For instance, these two rhythms sound the same: ♪ ♪♪♪ ♪ = ♪ ♪ ♩ ♪

For practice, let's add ties to the rhythm on page 50 to transform it into the rhythm of the words. Be careful, the third phrase is tricky!

Rhythms of the Railroad

Rhythm has a powerful effect on people. Some rhythms make work easier and smoother. "Rock Island Line" is a railroad work song that uses rhythm to help everyone work together. ♪ ♩ ♪ is one important rhythm in the song. **Sing** "Rock Island Line" and **identify** this rhythm. How many times does it occur?

 2-24

Rock Island Line

Edited with New Additional Material by Alan Lomax

Railroad Song
New Words and New Arrangement by Huddie Ledbetter

REFRAIN

I say the Rock Is - land Line is a might-y good road,

I say the Rock Is - land Line is the road to ride.

I say the Rock Is - land Line is a might-y good road,

If you want ____ to ride it, got to ride it like you find it,

Get your tick - et at the sta - tion for the Rock Is - land line.

VERSE

1. May be right and I may be wrong, —
2. A, B, C, dou - ble X, Y, Z, ____

Know you're gon - na miss me _____ when I'm gone.
Cats ____ in the cup - board, but they don't see me.

D.C. al Fine

> **Syncopation** is an arrangement of rhythm in which important tones begin on weak beats or weak parts of beats, giving an off-balance movement to the music.

All Aboard for Rhythm!

♪ ♩ ♪ is called **syncopation.**

Play these syncopated ostinatos on percussion instruments.

Form two groups. As everyone **sings** the song, group one **performs** the first ostinato, and group two performs the second.

Time for the Blues

If you say, "I feel blue," it usually means you feel sad about something. If you sing the blues, you are singing about your feelings.

A **time signature** is found at the beginning of most written music. Find the time signature in "Joe Turner Blues."

Perform this four-beat pattern while you **sing** "Joe Turner Blues."

1	2	3	4
pat	*clap*	*snap*	*clap*

> The **time signature** tells how many beats are in each measure (top number) and the kind of note that gets one beat (bottom number).

Joe Turner Blues

Blues Song from the United States

C   C₇

1. They tell me __ Joe Turn-er's __ come and gone, __
2. He came here __ with for-ty __ links of chain, __
3. Joe Turn-er, __ he took my __ man a-way, __

F₇   C

They tell me __ Joe Turn-er's __ come and gone. __
He came here __ with for-ty __ links of chain. __
Joe Turn-er, __ he took my __ man a-way, __

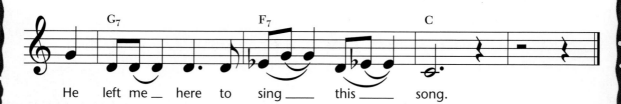

G₇   F₇   C

He left me __ here to sing ___ this ___ song.

54

Singing the Blues

The first blues songs were recorded in the 1920s. **Listen** to another example of the blues. **Move** to the beat in $\frac{4}{4}$ meter. What is the performer of the *St. Louis Blues* singing about?

2-28
St. Louis Blues

by W.C. Handy

St. Louis Blues is one of many famous blues melodies. It was released in 1914.

▲ In 1926, W.C. (William Christopher) Handy published a book of blues songs composed by himself and others. He is called the "Father of the Blues."

1. Clap and **perform** these rhythms with rhythm syllables. **Identify** the song.

2. Write your own rhythms in $\frac{4}{4}$ meter. Use one example of syncopation and one rest.

One Song—Two Sections

Think of a river in your town or state. **Listen** to the song "River," then **sing** along.

  2-29

River

Words and Music by Bill Staines

1. I was born in the path of the win-ter wind, And was
2. I've ___ been to the cit-y and back a-gain, I've been
3. Some-day when the flow-ers are bloom-ing still, Some -

raised where the moun-tains are old. _____ The
moved by some things _ that I've learned. _____ Met a
day when the grass _ is still green, _____ My

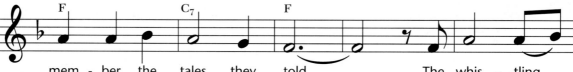

spring-time _____ wa-ters came danc-ing down, I re-
lot of ___ good peo-ple and I've called them my friends, Felt the
roll-ing _____ riv-er will round the bend And flow

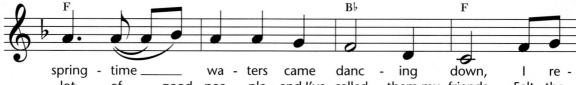

mem-ber the tales they told. _____ The whis-tling __
change when the sea-sons turned. _____ I've heard all the
in-to the o-pen sea. _____ So here's to the

ways of my young-er days Too quick-ly have
songs that the chil-dren sing And lis-tened to
rain-bow that's followed me here, And here's to the

Different Ways to Move

Move to show the different sections of "River." **Improvise** one motion for the Ⓐ section **(verse)** and one for the Ⓑ section **(refrain)**. Move as you **listen** to the song.

> A **verse** is a section of a song where the melody stays the same when it repeats, but the words change.
> A **refrain** is a section of a song that is sung the same way every time it repeats.

fad - ed on by. _____ But all of the mem - o - ries
love's _ mel - o - dies, _____ I've felt my own mus - ic with -
friends _ that I know, _____ And here's to the song that's with -

lin - ger still, Like the light in a fad - ing sky. _____
in me rise Like the wind in the au - tumn trees. _____
in me now; I will sing it where' - er I go. _____

REFRAIN

Riv - er, take me a - long, In your sun - shine sing me your

song. Ev - er mov - ing and wind - ing and _ free, You

roll - ing old riv - er, you chang - ing old riv - er, Let's

you and me, riv - er, Run down to the sea. _____

Sing It with Signing

Practice the signs below, then **sing** and sign the refrain
of "River."

▲ *river*   ▲ *sunshine*   ▲ *rolling*

Flowing Along

Listen to *The Boatman's Dance*. This song has a verse and a refrain, as well as an introduction, **interludes,** and a *coda*. **Move** to show the different sections of the music. Here are some clues to help you.

Movement Clues

An **interlude** is a short musical connection between sections of a piece of music.

- The music for the introduction, interludes, and *coda* is slow.

- The music for the verse, section **A**, is fast.

- The music for the refrain, section **B**, has the word *boat* in it.

2-30

The Boatman's Dance

from *Old American Songs*
by Aaron Copland

This piece was written for solo baritone voice, orchestra, and choir.

Read the poem "River" to yourself. Think about how a river moves. Read this poem aloud, then **move** while a friend reads the poem.

River

by Lawrence Locke

The river moans.
The river sings.

Listen to the Fox, the Menominee,
The Susquehanna, Colorado, Platte,
The Ottowa, Snake, Bear,
And the Delaware.

Listen to the river.
The river moans.
The river sings.

The river is always going home.

Melody Goes 'Round

"*Hashewie*" comes from Eritrea in North Africa. It is a pentatonic song. **Sing** the pentatonic scale as indicated in the color box. Remember to use hand signs.

so₁ la₁ do re mi so la

The notes outside the color box are low *la* and low *so*. When *do* is written in a space on the staff, low *la* is in the space below. In the scale above, *do* is in the bottom space. Low *la* must be written in a space below the staff and low *so* is written on a **ledger line.**

Ledger lines are extra lines for pitches above and below the staff.

Sing these pentatonic patterns. Which ones can you find in "*Hashewie*"?

mi
re
do   do

so
mi
re
do

        do
    la   la
so   so

        mi
do   do   re
    la

Reading low *la* and low *so*

Read "*Hashewie*" using pitch syllables and hand signs. Then **sing** the leader's part while your friends sing the response *shewie*.

3-1

Hashewie
(Going 'Round)

Words by Hidaat Ephrem

Folk Song from Eritrea, Africa

Call

Ha - shew - i - e_____ Shew - i - e Ha - shew - i - e_____
I will go 'round, _ Shew - i - e You will go 'round, _

Response *Call* *Response* *Fine*

_____ Shew - i - e Ha - shew - i - e_____ Shew - i - e
_____ Shew - i - e We all go 'round, _ Shew - i - e

Call (Tigrinya) *Response* *D. C. al Fine*

Bi - ha - de ha - bir - na Shew - i - e.
Ha-shew - ie e - na - bel - na
A - lem kit - fel - to
Ku - lu - me - nin - et - na
Ha-shew - i - e ni - bel
Nef' - lit - a - di - na
Bi - ha - de ha - bir - na

Call (English) *Response* *D.C. al Fine*

All to - geth - er 'round, Shew - i - e.
Say - ing 'round and 'round,
So the world would know,
Who ____ we ____ are,
Let's ____ say ____ 'round,
All to - geth - er 'round,
Go - ing 'round and 'round,

Scale the Mountain

Have you ever climbed a mountain or been to the top of a tall building? You probably saw things from the top that you could never see from the bottom. Let's climb the pentatonic mountain below and discover what's at the top.

You already know some notes below *do.* Now **identify** the mystery note at the top of the pentatonic scale.

Sing the notes up and down the pentatonic scale. Then try skipping around from *do* to all the other notes.

Read this melody using pitch syllables and hand signs.

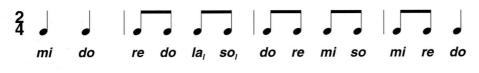

mi   do   re do la, so,   do re mi so   mi re do

so   so   la do' la mi   so so so la   mi re do

Sourwood Mountain

Folk Song from the Appalachian Mountains

1. Chic-ken crow-in' on Sour-wood Moun-tain, Hey, de-ing dang did-dle al-ly day.

So ma-ny pret-ty girls I can't count 'em, Hey, de-ing dang did-dle al-ly day.

My true love, she lives in Letch-er, Hey, de-ing dang did-dle al-ly day.

She won't come and I won't fetch her, Hey, de-ing dang did-dle al-ly day.

2. My true love's
   a blue-eyed daisy, Hey, . . .
   If I don't get her
   I'll go crazy, Hey, . . .
   Big dogs bark
   and little ones bite you, Hey, . . .
   Big girls court
   and little ones slight you, Hey, . . .

3. My true love
   lives by the river, Hey, . . .
   A few more jumps
   and I'll be with her, Hey, . . .
   My true love
   lives up in the hollow, Hey, . . .
   She won't come
   and I won't follow, Hey, . . .

Mountain Music

Create a pentatonic ostinato to accompany "Sourwood Mountain." Take turns playing the ostinato or singing the song.

Tune In

"Sourwood Mountain" is from the Southern Appalachian Mountains and is often played on the fiddle. American pioneer fiddlers kept alive the traditional tunes of their ancestors from England, Ireland, and Scotland.

Melody Rhymes in Time

Humor can happen in any language. **Listen** for the humorous Spanish rhymes in this song.

🔘 **3-7**

Riquirrán

Translated by J. Olcutt Sanders

Folk Song from Latin America

1. A - se - rrín, a - se - rrán. Los ma - de - ros de San Juan co - men
1. A - se - rrín, a - se - rrán. All the woods-men of San Juan eat their

que - so, co - men pan. Los de Ri - que, al - fe - ñi - que; los de
cheese and eat their *pan.* Those from Ri - que, *al - fe - ñi - que;* Those from

Ro - que, al - fon - do - que, Ri - qui, ri - que, ri - qui - rrán. 2. A - se -
Ro - que, al - fon - do - que, Ri - qui, ri - que, ri - qui - rrán. 2. A - se -

rrín, a - se - rrán. Las a - be - jas vie - nen, van; Miel la -
rrín, a - se - rrán. Los chi - qui - llos ¿dón - de es - tán? To - dos
rrín, a - se - rrán. All the bees fly hith - er, yon; Gath - er
rrín, a - se - rrán. Where have all the chil - dren gone? They have

bo - ran pa - ra el pan. Li - ban flor - es las de Ri - que cual al -
a dor - mir se van. So - ña - rán con al - fe - ñi - que co - mo
nec - tar for their *pan.* Sip - ping from the flowers of Ri - que nec - tar
put their night-gowns on. They will dream of *al - fe - ñi - que* as the

mi - bar de al - fe - ñi - que, Y el pa - nal de los de Ro - que se pa -
sue - ñan los de Ri - que, Y ma - ña - na un al - fon - do - que co - me -
sweet as al - fe - ñi - que, Just as hon - ey combs of Ro - que look like
chil - dren dream in Ri - que, And to - mor-row al - fon - do - que they will

re - ce a un al - fon - do - que. Ri - qui, ri - que, ri - qui - rrán. 3. A - se -
rán con los de Ro - que. Ri - qui, ri - que, ri - qui - rrán.
loaves of al - fon - do - que. Ri - qui, ri - que, ri - qui - rrán. 3. A - se -
eat with those from Ro - que. Ri - qui, ri - que, ri - qui - rrán.

Name It and Play It

Name the notes in this melody for recorder. **Play** the melody
with the first four measures of each verse of *"Riquirrán."*

Name the notes below and find these measures in *"Riquirrán."*

Show What You Know!

1. **Sing** this melody on pitch syllables.

2. Now find the letter names for the pitches above. **Play** the melody
   on a xylophone or keyboard.

3. **Sing** this melody using pitch syllables. Then sing the notes by
   letter and **play** the melody on recorder.

Each instrument has its own special sound or timbre. To make a sound on most wind instruments, the player blows air into the instrument, causing the air to vibrate. The string instrument's sound is made by vibrating strings. **Sing** this Italian song about six instruments.

3-11

Eh, cumpari! (Hey, Buddy!)

Words and Music by Julius La Rosa and Archie Bleyer

Eh, cum - pa - ri!   Ci vo' su - na - ri.
Hey, good bud - dy!   It's time to play! _____

Chi si so - na

1. 'U fris - ca - let - tu?
2. 'U sax - o - fo - na?
3. 'U man - du - li - nu?

Who will play on

1. the pic - co - lo? _____
2. the sax - o - phone? __
3. the man - do - lin? _____

E co - mu si so - na

'u fris - ca - let - tu?
'u sax - o - fo - na?
'u man - du - li - nu?

And how do you play on

the pic - co - lo? _____
the sax - o - phone? __
the man - do - lin? _____

CD-ROM Using *Making Music* software, compose a piece of music with two different timbres. Think about how you can use timbre to organize your composition.

A - fu - mm'a - fu - mm'a la   trom - bon', pa - pa   pa - pa   a   la   trum -
A-foom - a - foom on the trom-bone, pa - pa - pa - pa   on the trum -

be - tt', a-zing - a - zing 'u vi - u - lin,   a-pling - a - pling 'u man - du -
pet,   a - dzing - a - dzing the vi - o - lin,   a-pling - a - pling the man - do -

lin,   tu - tu   tu - tu   'u sax - o - fon,   'u fris - ca -
lin,   too-too - too - too the sax - o - phone, *(whistle)* _____ the pic - co -

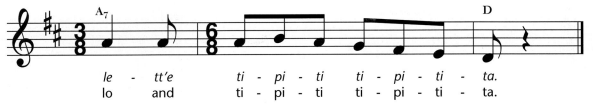

le - tt'e   ti - pi - ti   ti - pi - ti - ta.
lo   and   ti - pi - ti   ti - pi - ti - ta.

4. . . . 'U viulinu? . . .   4. . . . the violin? . . .
5. . . . A la trumbetta? . . .   5. . . . the brassy trumpet? . . .
6. . . . A la trombona? . . .   6. . . . the slide trombone? . . .

One-Minute Woodwind Mysteries

Listen to the solo instrument in each piece of music. Find the picture of the woodwind instrument you hear playing the solo. You have one minute (or less) for each selection!

3-15

One–Minute Woodwind Mysteries

B.B.'s Blues
by Branford Marsalis

"Serenata"
from *Pulcinella Suite*
by Igor Stravinsky

The Bee ("L'Abeille")
by Franz Schubert

"Vivace"
from *Sonata in F*
by Georg Philipp Telemann

"Aviary"
from *Carnival of the Animals*
by Camille Saint-Saens

Woodwind Quartet

Listen to *Allegro molto,* and **identify** the four instruments playing.

3-20

Allegro molto

from *Quartet*
by Jean Françaix
as performed by Aulos Woodwind Quintet

This composition is for four woodwind instruments.

One-Minute Brass Mysteries

Listen to the solo instrument in each piece of music. Find the picture of the brass instrument playing the solo.

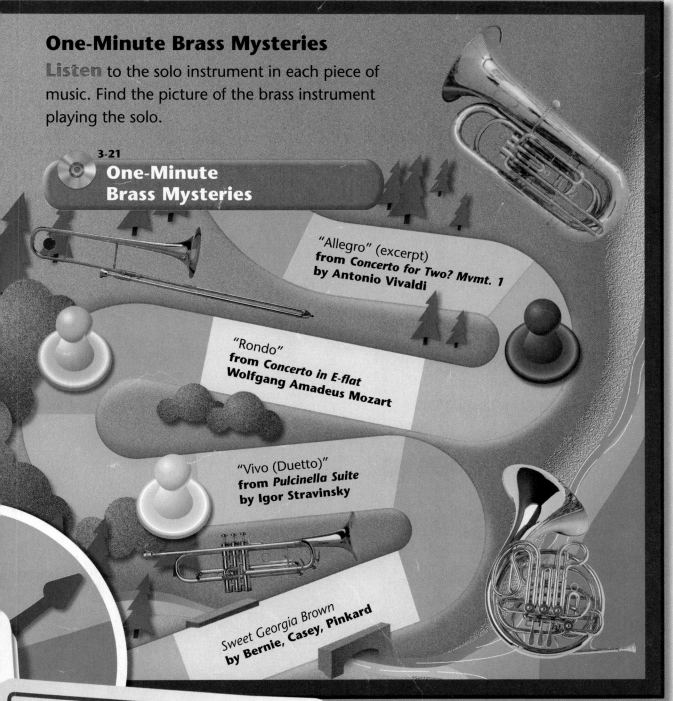

3-21

One-Minute Brass Mysteries

"Allegro" (excerpt)
**from *Concerto for Two? Mvmt. 1*
by Antonio Vivaldi**

"Rondo"
**from *Concerto in E-flat*
Wolfgang Amadeus Mozart**

"Vivo (Duetto)"
**from *Pulcinella Suite*
by Igor Stravinsky**

Sweet Georgia Brown
by Bernie, Casey, Pinkard

Brass Quartet

Listen to *Fanfare*. A fanfare is a musical announcement, usually played by brass instruments. How would you describe this music?

3-25

Fanfare

from *La Peri*
by Paul Dukas

Paul Dukas also composed *The Sorcerer's Apprentice*, which is featured in the Disney movie, *Fantasia*.

Listening to Wind Instruments

Orchestras contain string, woodwind, brass, and percussion instruments. Look at this picture of an orchestra. How many woodwind and brass instruments can you **identify**?

Listen to this music for orchestra. After an introduction played by a snare drum, you will hear woodwind and brass instruments accompanied by string instruments. **Identify** the woodwind and brass instruments in the order you hear them played.

3-26

Presentation of Pairs

from *Concerto for Orchestra* by Béla Bartók

Concerto for Orchestra was Béla Bartók's last complete work for orchestra.

Béla Bartók

Béla Bartók (1881–1945) was a composer, folk song collector, and pianist. He traveled through Hungary, Romania, Slovakia, Turkey, and North Africa recording on a phonograph and collecting thousands of songs. In his own compositions, Bartók often used the folk music he had collected.

Winds in the Band

Almost all of the instruments in a band are members of the wind and percussion families. Look at the picture on this page of a band and **identify** the various woodwind and brass instruments.

Now **listen** to this performance. Which instruments play first—woodwinds or brass?

3-27
Lord Melbourne

from *Lincolnshire Posy*
by Percy Grainger

The selections in *Lincolnshire Posy* are based on folk melodies collected by Percy Grainger.

M·U·S·I·C M·A·K·E·R·S

Marsalis Family

Ellis Marsalis ▶

◀ Wynton Marsalis

Branford, Wynton, Delfeayo, and Ellis Marsalis are members of a very musical family. Branford plays saxophone, Wynton plays trumpet, Delfeayo plays trombone, and Ellis (the father of the three brothers) plays the piano. When playing together, they make a jazz combo. As solo performers, Branford and Wynton have won several awards. They have performed on television shows such as Jay Leno's *Tonight Show*. Wynton also serves as the artistic director of "Jazz at Lincoln Center."

3-28
Knozz-Moe-King

by Wynton Marsalis

Wynton Marsalis is best-known as a jazz musician. In *Knozz-Moe-King*, he is playing a trumpet in a quartet.

◀ Branford Marsalis

▲ Delfeayo Marsalis

3-29
Little Birdie

by Vince Guaraldi

Little Birdie is a reference to Woodstock, the bird character in the "Peanuts" cartoon strip. This recording is performed by the Marsalis family.

3-30
Allegro

by Antonio Vivaldi

Wynton Marsalis also performs classical music. In *Allegro*, he is playing with an orchestra.

Paddle Along, Singing a Song

Have you ever paddled a canoe? To go forward, you pull the paddle through the water. You repeat this motion to keep the canoe moving. In "Canoe Song," repeated patterns help the song to move along.
Listen to "Canoe Song." Find the repeated patterns.

3-31

Canoe Song

Words and Music by Margaret E. McGhee

1. My pad - dle's keen and bright, Flash - ing with sil - ver,
2. Dip, dip and swing her back, Flash - ing with sil - ver,

Fol - low the wild goose flight, Dip, dip and swing.
Fol - low the wild goose track, Dip, dip and swing.

Sing this **ostinato** to accompany "Canoe Song."

Melodic ostinato

Dip, dip and swing.

> An **ostinato** is a repeated rhythmic or melodic pattern played throughout a piece or a section of a piece.

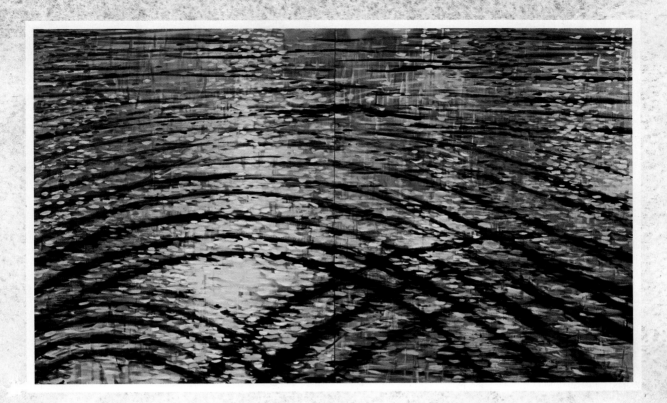

Arts Connection

▲ *Watercolor Ripple* (1995)
by Gerrit Greve. What repeated
patterns do you see in this
painting?

Play an Ostinato

Adding melodic ostinatos to a song changes the
musical texture. As more ostinatos are added, the
texture and harmony become thicker.

Practice these ostinatos for "Canoe Song." Then
perform them with the song to make the
texture thicker.

OSTINATOS EVERYWHERE

Look at the art around the edge of this page. How many repeated patterns can you find? Repeated patterns occur in music, too.

This repeated pattern is an ostinato. **Play** it on a melody instrument with "*Hey, m'tswala.*"

Hey, m'tswala

Folk Song from Africa

3-33

Hey, m'tswa - la, ne - ye ti - pa sa - me tswa - la. _____

Create a Texture

To **create** a thicker texture, **play** these ostinatos as you **sing** *"Hey, m'tswala."*

Circlesong Ostinatos

Listen to *Circlesong 7*. The melody and ostinatos are by Bobby McFerrin and other musicians.

3-36
Circlesong 7

by Bobby McFerrin

Bobby McFerrin says, "I've always felt that singing a song without words makes one song a thousand songs, because the people who hear it can bring their own stories to it."

MUSIC MAKERS

BOBBY McFERRIN

Bobby McFerrin (born 1950) began piano and music theory lessons as a child. He turned to singing in his twenties and soon became a leading vocal recording artist. Many of his recordings are *a cappella*—singing with no accompaniment. McFerrin performs in many styles, such as jazz, classical, and free improvisation. He has won many Grammy awards and is often a guest conductor of symphony orchestras.

Layers of Movement

How good are you at doing several movements at once?
Create a movement ostinato while you **listen** to
Circlesong 7. Be ready to **improvise** a movement solo
while your classmates **move** to the ostinato.

▲ Half the class improvises a movement.　　　　　▲ Half the class performs the ostinato.

The Night

Poem of the Fipa, Africa

The night is over
before one has finished counting the
stars.

Enjoy the Earth

Poem of the Yoruba, Africa

Enjoy the earth gently
Enjoy the earth gently
For if the earth is spoiled
It cannot be repaired
Enjoy the earth gently

What Do You Know?

1. Look at the notation for "Joe Turner Blues" on page 54. Point to the time signature. How many beats are in each measure?

2. Name the title of a song in unit 2 that has:

    a. Three beats in each measure

    b. Two beats in each measure

3. Reorder these musical terms for tempo from slowest to fastest.

    andante   *presto*   *adagio*   *allegro*   *moderato*

3-37

What Do You Hear? 2

Listen to these instrumental excerpts. Identify the instrument or instruments you hear.

1. brass   strings   woodwinds

2. brass   percussion   woodwinds

3. flute   oboe   clarinet

4. french horn   trumpet   trombone

5. clarinet   saxophone   bassoon

6. trumpet   trombone   tuba

All Together

Move with Rhythm

Sing "Somebody's Knockin' at Your Door" on page 50, and perform a four-beat body percussion ostinato as you sing.

Sing *"Riquirrán"* on page 64, while performing small steady beat movements during the verse.

Play the Notes

Play this recorder part with the recording of *"Riquirrán"* on page 64. Play once through silently in chin position and then play aloud.

Move to Show Form

Listen to "River" on page 56 and create a movement for the **A** section and a different movement for the **B** section. Then perform the movements as you sing the song.

Song of Home

People often sing about places that are dear to them. In the United States, we sing our national anthem, or we sing a state song to express pride and love for our home.

"My Home's Across the Blue Ridge Mountains" is about fond memories of home. **Sing** the song and think of a place that is special to you.

3-43

MY HOME'S ACROSS THE BLUE RIDGE MOUNTAINS

Collected by Louis Land Bascom

Folk Song from the Southern United States

REFRAIN

My home's __ a-cross __ the Blue Ridge Moun - tains.

My home's __ a-cross __ the Blue Ridge Moun - tains.

My home's __ a-cross __ the Blue Ridge Moun - tains.

And I may nev-er see you an-y - more.

VERSE

1. I'm go-in' back to North Caro - li - na.
2. I'm gon-na leave here Mon - day morn - in'.
3. One __ more kiss be - fore I leave __ you.

Learning the Language of Music

I'm go - in' back to North Caro - li - - na.
I'm gon - na leave here Mon - day morn - - in'.
One _____ more kiss be - fore I leave _____ you.

D

I'm go - in' back to North Caro - li - - na.
I'm gon - na leave here Mon - day morn - - in'.
One _____ more kiss be - fore I leave _____ you.

D. C. al Fine

I may nev - er see you an - y - more.

Music from the Ozarks

Listen to the Oak Ridge Boys sing about their home in *Ozark Mountain Jubilee.*

3-45
Ozark Mountain Jubilee

by Roger Murrah and Scott Anders
This song is in the mountain style of the Ozarks.

MUSIC MAKERS

THE OAK RIDGE BOYS

This country music group consists of four main members: Joe Bonsall–tenor, Duane Allen–lead, Steve Sanders–baritone, and Richard Sterban–bass. Their music reflects the area where most of them were raised, the southern United States.

WALKING ALONG, SINGING A SONG

When people walk in groups, they sometimes like to sing walking songs. "The Happy Wanderer" is a walking song. **Sing** the two phrases in the verse of the song *legato*. In the refrain, **sing** the *ha-ha-ha's* **staccato**.

The term *legato* describes music performed in a smooth and connected style. The term *staccato* describes music performed in a short and detached style.

Move with Expression

To help you sing the phrases smoothly, draw an arc in the air with your hand.

Hear the Difference

Listen to a *legato* theme with **slurs.**

A **slur** is a curved line connecting two or more notes of different pitch that tells the performer to play or sing the notes *legato*.

Joseph Haydn

 4-3

Serenade, Opus 3 No. 5

by Joseph Haydn

Serenade is written for string quartet.

In this piece the violins always play *legato*. Sometimes they play two-note slurs, which connect the notes. Slurs above or below the note heads look like this.

Now **listen** to the viola and cello. They are playing ***pizzicato.***

The term ***pizzicato*** refers to plucking the strings instead of bowing.

Listen to the entire *Serenade.* **Move** in your space by floating your arms in the air for the *legato* theme. Move to show light, bouncy movements for *pizzicato.*

M·U·S·I·C M·A·K·E·R·S

Franz Joseph Haydn

Joseph Haydn (1732–1809) was born in a small town in Austria, near the Hungarian border. He had a beautiful singing voice. At the age of eight, he was asked to go to Vienna and join the choir of St. Stephen's Cathedral. As an adult, he supported his family by serving as a royal court musician for a noble family named Esterházy. In this job, he wrote music to please the royal family. He had his own maid and footman, as well as a good salary. Haydn wrote more symphonies than any other composer, well over 100. He lived a long life and died a world-famous figure.

Rhythm and Dance

Listen to "Paw-Paw Patch," a popular game song. This version comes from the Ozark Mountains in Missouri, Arkansas, and Oklahoma. A paw-paw is a wild fruit that grows throughout the South.

Sing the words of "Paw-Paw Patch" as you tap a steady beat. Then **sing** it again as you clap the rhythm. How many sounds did you clap on the beats in color boxes?

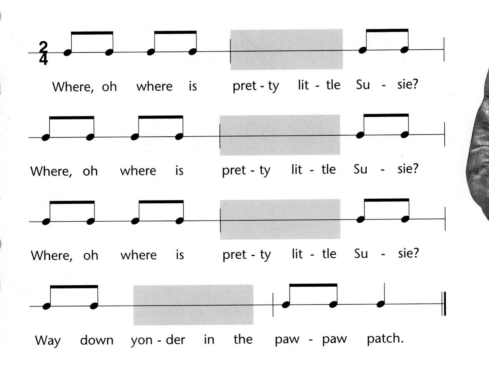

Where, oh where is pret - ty lit - tle Su - sie?

Where, oh where is pret - ty lit - tle Su - sie?

Where, oh where is pret - ty lit - tle Su - sie?

Way down yon - der in the paw - paw patch.

Arts Connection

Wooden folk art carving from the Ozark Mountain region of a fiddle player ▶

Paw-Paw Patterns

When there are four even sounds on a beat, you can **notate** them like this.

Read the song again using rhythm syllables. **Perform** it with body percussion.

♩ stamp   ♫ clap   pat

4-4

Paw-Paw Patch

Play–Party Song from the United States

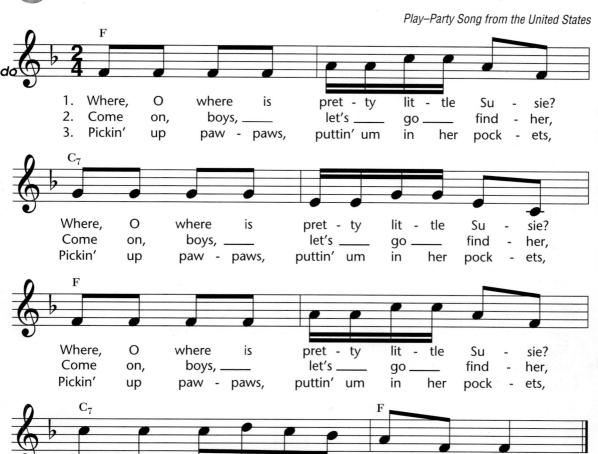

1. Where, O where is pret - ty lit - tle Su - sie?
2. Come on, boys, _____ let's _____ go _____ find - her,
3. Pickin' up paw - paws, puttin' um in her pock - ets,

Where, O where is pret - ty lit - tle Su - sie?
Come on, boys, _____ let's _____ go _____ find - her,
Pickin' up paw - paws, puttin' um in her pock - ets,

Where, O where is pret - ty lit - tle Su - sie?
Come on, boys, _____ let's _____ go _____ find - her,
Pickin' up paw - paws, puttin' um in her pock - ets,

Way down yon - der in the paw - paw patch.

Party Time

In the frontier days, before television and stereos were in most homes, the "play-party" was a popular singing and dancing game. Young people made up motions to familiar songs and accompanied their plays with singing. The fiddle and banjo were often used in play-parties.

Sing and **move** to "Paw-Paw Patch," and you'll see why it was one of the favorites.

▲ Lead girl walks around the lines.

▲ Lead girl walks around the lines and boys follow.

▲ Partners join hands and walk the same pathway.

▲ Partners join hands and form an arch while others pass under.

Listen to *College Hornpipe* and follow the  pattern throughout the music.

4-8

College Hornpipe

Traditional

College Hornpipe features Yo-Yo Ma, cello; Edgar Meyer, bass; and Mark O' Connor, fiddle.

COLLEGE HORNPIPE
LISTENING MAP

Rhythm in the Wind

The song *"Ōsamu kosamu"* is about children facing the bitter cold wind.

Look at the music for *"Ōsamu kosamu."* How many groups of  can you find?

Listen for the pattern in the song *"Ōsamu kosamu."*

4-9

Ōsamu kosamu (Biting Wind)

English Words by Gloria J. Kiester

Folk Song from Japan

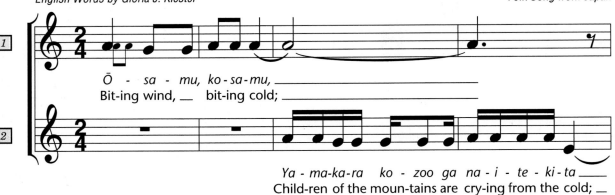

Ō - sa - mu, ko - sa - mu, _____
Bit-ing wind, __ bit-ing cold; _____

Ya - ma-ka-ra   ko - zoo ga na - i - te - ki - ta _____
Child-ren of the moun-tains are cry-ing from the cold; __

na - n   to   it - te   na - i - te - ki - ta? _____
Why are they cry-ing, cry-ing from the cold? _____

"Sa-mu-i to   it - te   na - i - te - ki - ta!"
"We are in the wind; it's bit-ter, bit-ter cold!"

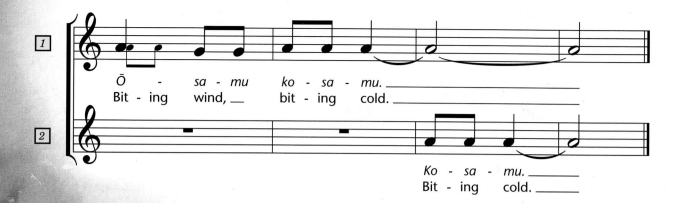

Ō - sa - mu ko - sa - mu. _____
Bit - ing wind, __ bit - ing cold. _____

Ko - sa - mu. _____
Bit - ing cold. _____

Practicing Rhythms

Play this accompaniment with mallets while you **sing** "Ōsamu kosamu" in two parts.

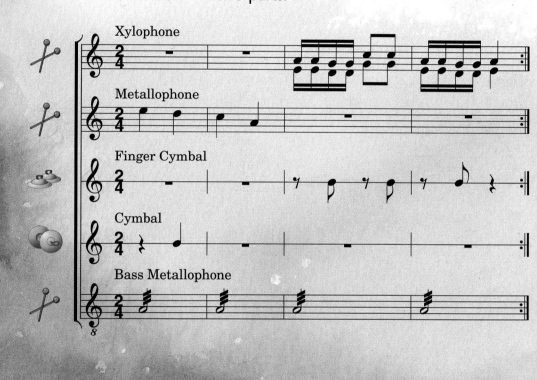

Xylophone

Metallophone

Finger Cymbal

Cymbal

Bass Metallophone

Tune In

The *koto* is the national instrument of Japan. It generally has 13 strings and is a member of the zither family. The sound is produced by plucking the silk strings.

SHINING WITH METER

The song "Rise and Shine" can make you want to **sing** and dance. The time signature is $\frac{4}{4}$. This tells you there are 4 beats in every measure. **Bar lines** divide the song into measures. Look at the rhythms below. Notice where the bar lines are placed.

A **bar line** is the vertical line drawn through a staff to separate measures.

bar line

Clap the rhythm above. **Create** new measures in $\frac{4}{4}$ time by saying first names of classmates in rhythm.

Sing "Rise and Shine."

 4-14

RISE AND SHINE

Folk Song from the United States

1. Rise ___ and shine ___ and give God the glo - ry, glo - ry.
2. God said to No - ah, "There's gonna be a flood - y, flood - y."
3. No - ah, he built him, he built him an ark - y, ark - y.
4. Ani - mals, they came on, they came on by two - sies, two - sies.

Rise ___ and shine ___ and give God the glo - ry, glo - ry.
God said to No - ah, "There's gonna be a flood - y, flood - y."
No - ah, he built him, he built him an ark - y, ark - y.
Ani - mals, they came on, they came on by two - sies, two - sies.

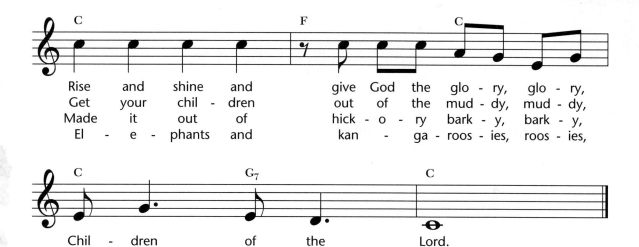

Rise and shine and give God the glo - ry, glo - ry,
Get your chil - dren out of the mud - dy, mud - dy,
Made it out of hick - o - ry bark - y, bark - y,
El - e - phants and kan - ga - roos - ies, roos - ies,

Chil - dren of the Lord.

5. Rained and rained
   for forty daysies, daysies.
   Rained and rained
   for forty daysies, daysies.
   Nearly drove those animals crazy, crazy, . . .

6. Noah, he sent out,
   he sent out a dovey, dovey.
   Noah, he sent out,
   he sent out a dovey, dovey.
   Sent him to the heavens abovey, bovey, . . .

7. Sun came out
   and dried off the landy, landy.
   Sun came out
   and dried off the landy, landy.
   Ev'rything was fine and dandy, dandy, . . .

8. This is the end,
   the end of my story, story.
   This is the end,
   the end of my story, story.
   Ev'rything is hunky-dory, dory, . . .

Show What You Know!

Move to show meter in four. With a partner, perform this body percussion ostinato as you **sing** "Rise and Shine."

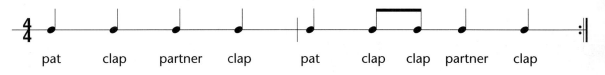

pat   clap   partner   clap   pat   clap   clap   partner   clap

BACK to the Beginning

The song, "Walk in Jerusalem," is an African American spiritual. Look at the song. Notice that the **A** section is repeated after the **B** section. **Sing** "Walk in Jerusalem."

4-16

WALK IN JERUSALEM

African American Spiritual

REFRAIN **A**

I want _____ to be read - y,

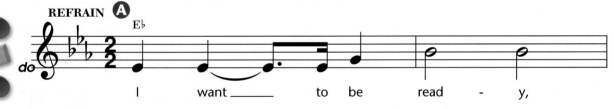

I want _____ to be read - y, _____

I want _____ to be read - y to

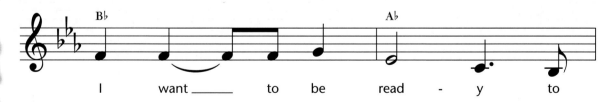

walk in Je - ru - sa - lem just like John.

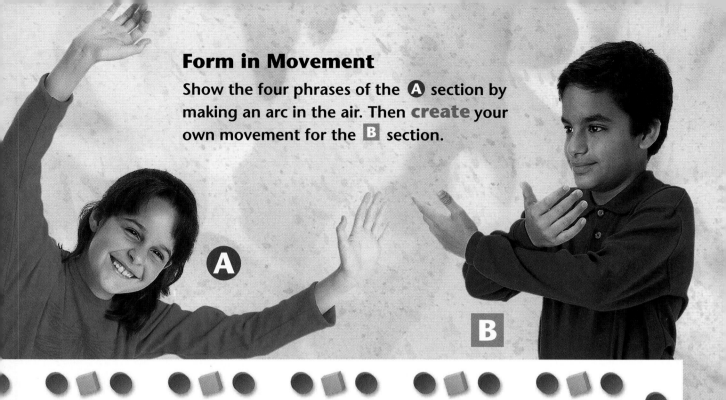

Form in Movement

Show the four phrases of the **A** section by making an arc in the air. Then **create** your own movement for the **B** section.

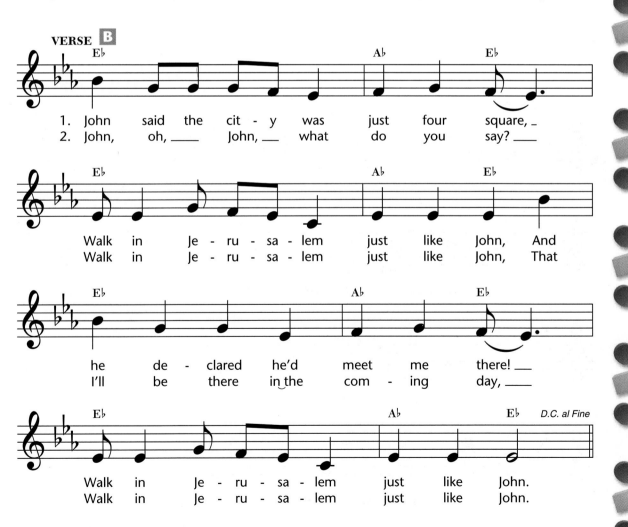

VERSE **B**

Eb / Ab Eb

1. John said the cit - y was just four square, _
2. John, oh, _____ John, ___ what do you say? ___

Eb / Ab Eb

Walk in Je - ru - sa - lem just like John, And
Walk in Je - ru - sa - lem just like John, That

Eb / Ab Eb

he de - clared he'd meet me there! ___
I'll be there in the com - ing day, ___

Eb / Ab Eb *D.C. al Fine*

Walk in Je - ru - sa - lem just like John.
Walk in Je - ru - sa - lem just like John.

A Multiplication Melody

la
so

mi
re
do

la₁
so₁

This American play-party song is based on an old song from Scotland. "Charlie" is really Bonnie Prince Charles Stuart. Many songs have been written about his valiant, but unsuccessful, attempts to restore his family to the Scottish throne in the 1700s.

Do you recognize the scale shown on this pitch ladder? What kind of scale is it?

First, notice where *do* is placed on the staff. In this song, *do* is written on line two. **Identify** the other notes of the scale from the lines and spaces on the staff. **Read** the scale using pitch syllables and hand signs.

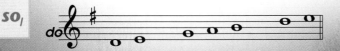

Twistification Hand Game

Sing "Weevily Wheat." The multiplication game mentioned in the last two lines of "Weevily Wheat" is known as "Twistification." **Create** your own verses using other multiplication tables.

4-18

Weevily Wheat

Traditional

Don't want your wee-vi-ly wheat, Don't want your bar-ley.

Take some flour in half an hour and bake a cake for Char-lie.

Five times five is twen-ty-five, Five times six is thir-ty.

Five times sev'n is thir-ty-five, Five times eight is for-ty.

Twistification Hand Game ▼

A New Home Tone

mi
re
do

Even though "See the Children Playin'" uses the same notes as "Weevily Wheat" in its scale, it sounds very different. Can you figure out why?

"See the Children Playin'" uses the notes of the pentatonic scale, and its **tonic** note is low *la*. Its scale is called the *la*-pentatonic scale.

The **tonic** is the key, or home, tone in a scale.

la₁
so₁

do   so₁ la₁   do re mi

𝒜rts Connection

▼ *Children Dancing* (1948) is by Robert Gwathmey. He is famous for painting African American life.

◀ Woman weaving basket at Charleston's Old City Market

Read the song using pitch syllables and hand signs. Use *do* to find your starting pitch.

4-19

See the Children Playin'

Words by Reginald Royal

Folk Melody from Mississippi

1. See ___ the chil-dren play-in', two - by - two play-in',
2. Ma - ma calls the chil-dren, "Do ___ your chores now, chil-dren."

In ___ the fields play-in', and the work ain't done play-in'.
In ___ the fields chil-dren, dad-dy's com-in' home chil-dren.

Ma - ma she's watch-in', chil - dren play-in' watch-in',
See ___ the chil-dren play-in', with ___ their dad-dy play-in',

And it's get-tin' late watch-in' still the work ain't done watch-in'.
And their ma-ma too play-in', 'cause the work's all done play-in'.

Follow that Melody!

"*Son macaron*" is believed to be a nonsense song. **Listen** to the song and follow the graph of the melody on the right.

Look at the song notation and use *do* to find your way around the staff. What is the starting pitch?

You may notice a note on the staff that you do not yet know. **Read** the song with pitch syllables and hum the mystery note. How many times does it occur in this song?

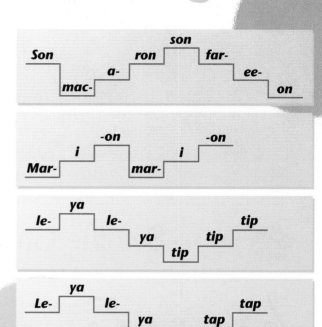

One beat, two beats, three beats. Catch!

Stay in the Game

Sing "*Son macaron.*" After you learn the song, play the game.

4-21

Son macaron

Traditional

Son   ma - ca - ron,   son   far - ee - on.

Mar - i - on,   mar - i - on,   le - ya   le - ya   tip   tip   tip.

Le - ya   le - ya   tap tap tap.   One   beat,   two   beats,   three beats,   catch!

Show What You Know!

Identify whether these melodies are *do-* or *la*-pentatonic.

1.

2.

3.

4.

Compose a melody using the G-pentatonic scale. Choose either *do* or *la* as your tonic.

Strings and Things

Almost every culture has instruments that produce sound through the vibration of strings. Here are some examples of instruments from various cultures. **Listen** to *String Instrument Montage* to hear how these instruments sound.

4-23
String Instrument Montage

▲ The *koto* [KOH-toh] is a Japanese zither with 7-17 strings. The body is a long rectangular box.

◀ The **lute** [loot] was an important instrument of the Renaissance period (1450–1600).

The *sitar* [SIH-tahr] is a string instrument of north India. There are seven strings, which are plucked. Nine to thirteen additional strings vibrate to give a special sound to the instrument. ▶

The *rebab* [REH-bahb] dates from the eighth century and is thought to be the ancestor of the violin. ▶

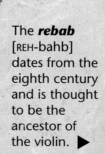

106

M·U·S·I·C M·A·K·E·R·S

Wolfgang Amadeus Mozart

Wolfgang Amadeus Mozart [MOHT-zahrt] (1756–1791) was a child prodigy who grew up in Salzburg, Austria. Many people consider him to be one of the greatest composers. His father, Leopold, was a musician who taught Wolfgang and his sister piano, violin, and music theory. When they were very young, Leopold took them all over Europe, where they played concerts. Wolfgang composed his first symphony at age eight, his first oratorio at age eleven, and his first opera at age twelve.

Strings of the Symphony Orchestra

Listen to Mozart's *Eine Kleine Nachtmusik.* You will hear the traditional string instruments of the symphony orchestra—violin, viola, cello, and bass viol.

 4-24
Eine Kleine Nachtmusik

by Wolfgang Amadeus Mozart

This piece is a minuet and trio. Minuets originally were courtly dances, and they are always in meter in 3.

Tune In

"I am never happier than when I have something to compose, for that, after all, is my sole delight and passion."

Wolfgang A. Mozart

Moving to the Music

Hum the melody of *Eine Kleine Nachtmusik*.
Choose a partner and walk gracefully
toward each other for two measures and
away for two measures.

Arts Connection

▲ *Danse dans un Pavillion*
by Jean Antoine Watteau
(1684–1721). The dancers in
this painting are performing
a courtly dance, similar to the
minuet.

W.A. Mozart

Tune In

When Mozart was a child, he enjoyed stunts such as playing piano with his hands hidden under a cloth so that he couldn't see the keys.

Classical Music—Here and Now

Many great classical composers are so widely respected that musicians today continue to perform their works. **Listen** to Bach's *Gigue* as performed by Vanessa-Mae.

4-25
Gigue

from *Partita in E Major*
by Johann Sebastian Bach
This composition features solo violin.

MUSIC MAKERS

Vanessa-Mae

Vanessa-Mae (born 1978) was a child prodigy. She gave her first performance at age nine and completed three classical recordings by the time she was thirteen. In 1996 she was nominated for "Best Female Artist" at the BRIT Awards in the United Kingdom. In 1997 she was invited to perform at the "Hong Kong to China" reunification ceremony. To Vanessa, the violin is like a voice, and she plays it with the grace of a fine singer.

Partners in Song

Calypso is a lively style of music from the Caribbean. This style has African roots, but it was developed in Trinidad. "Turn the World Around" is a Calypso song with three melodies that are sung at the same time. Melodies that fit together in this way are known as **partner songs.**

Sing "Turn the World Around."

> **Partner songs** are two or more different songs that can be sung at the same time to create a thicker texture.

 4-26

Turn the World Around

Words by Harry Belafonte   *Music by Robert Freedman*

1. We come from __ the fire, ____ liv-ing in ____ the fire, ____
2. We come from __ the wa-ter, liv-ing in ____ the wa-ter,
3. We come from __ the moun-tain, liv-ing on ____ the moun-tain,

Go back to ____ the fire, ____ turn the world _ a-round.
Go back to ____ the wa-ter, turn the world _ a-round.
Go back to ____ the moun-tain, turn the world _ a-round.

4. Water make the river,
   river wash the mountain,
   Fire make the sunlight,
   turn the world around.

5. Heart is of the river,
   body is the mountain,
   Spirit is the sunlight,
   turn the world around.

6. We are of the spirit,
   truly can the spirit,
   Only can the spirit,
   turn the world around.

More Songs—More Texture

Sing "So Is Life" alone and then with "Turn the
World Around."

So Is Life

Words by Harry Belafonte

Music by Robert Freedman

Wo - ho! so is ___ life. Ah - ha! so is ___ life.

Wo - ho! so is ___ life. Ah - ha! so is ___ life.

Listen to the recording of "Turn the World Around."
You will hear a third melody being sung to create a
thicker texture. **Sing** "Do You Know Who I Am?" alone
and then with "Turn the World Around" and "So Is Life."

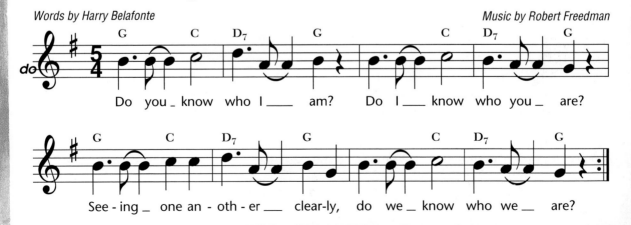

Do You Know Who I Am?

Words by Harry Belafonte

Music by Robert Freedman

Do you _ know who I ___ am? Do I ___ know who you _ are?

See - ing _ one an - oth - er ___ clear-ly, do we _ know who we _ are?

Playing Partners

Now that you can sing the partner songs, let's add some instruments. Practice each percussion part by clapping the rhythm. Now **play** an instrument.

Perform a different movement for each partner song.

2. Touch your chest, reach up, and look side to side. ▼

▲ **1.** Move backward, then forward, and turn.

The Man and His Music

Harry Belafonte is known for his performances of Calypso music.

Listen to him perform *Jump in the Line*.

4-28
Jump in the Line

by Harry Belafonte, Ralph DeLeon, Gabriel Oller, Steve Samuel

In this selection, Belafonte refers to getting up and dancing.

▲ **3.** Step out, raise your hands, and then step back.

Echo a Sentiment

"Over My Head" is a song strongly tied to the American civil rights movement.

Sing the song and make an arc in the air with one arm to help hold the long notes for four counts. During the long note held in each phrase, a second group of singers repeats the phrase. This is known as echo singing. Next, **sing** the song with a friend echoing the melody.

4-29

Over My Head

African American Spiritual

1. O - ver my head, (O - ver my head,) I hear mu - sic in the
2. O - ver my head, (O - ver my head,) I hear sing - ing in the

air. (I hear mu - sic in the air.) Yes, o - ver my head, (Yes, o - ver my
air. (I hear sing - ing in the air.) Yes, o - ver my head, (Yes, o - ver my

head,) I hear mu - sic in the air. (I hear mu - sic in the air.) O - ver my
head,) I hear sing - ing in the air. (I hear sing - ing in the air.) O - ver my

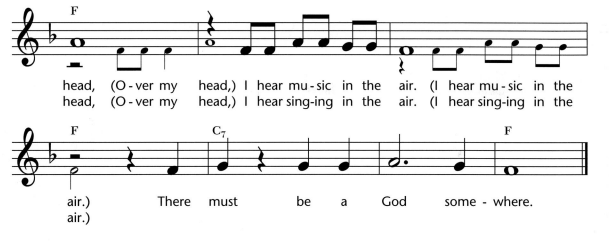

head, (O-ver my head,) I hear mu-sic in the air. (I hear mu-sic in the
head, (O-ver my head,) I hear sing-ing in the air. (I hear sing-ing in the

air.) There must be a God some-where.
air.)

3. Over my head,
   I hear freedom in the air . . .
   There must be a God somewhere.

4. Over my head,
   I hear victory in the air . . .
   There must be a God somewhere.

Echo Moving

Sing "Over My Head" and **create** a movement your partner can echo.

▲ **1.** Create a movement.

▲ **2.** Echo the movement of your partner.

Play F and C₇ Piano Chords

Follow the song notation and play these chords as you **sing.**

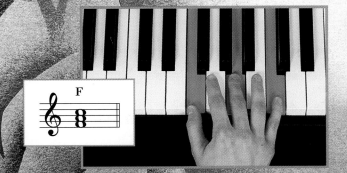

MUSIC, MUSIC... EVERYWHERE

Music can be found in almost any place. Think about the sounds you hear at a construction site. The machinery creates sounds. These sounds can have a steady beat, or other rhythmic pattern, and even pitch. When layered together, they create a unique texture that has a musical character. Many musicians are fascinated with these types of sounds and use them in their own compositions.

Listen to the recording of "Bundle-Buggy Boogie Woogie." Notice the layering of sounds to create texture.

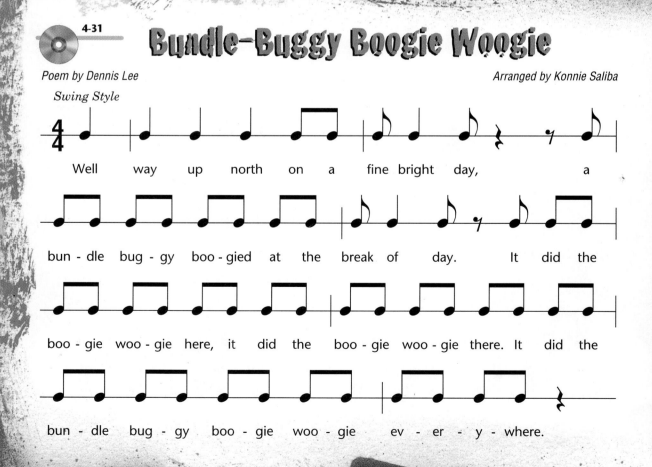

4-31

Bundle-Buggy Boogie Woogie

Poem by Dennis Lee

Arranged by Konnie Saliba

Swing Style

Well way up north on a fine bright day, a

bun – dle bug – gy boo – gied at the break of day. It did the

boo – gie woo – gie here, it did the boo – gie woo – gie there. It did the

bun – dle bug – gy boo – gie woo – gie ev – er – y – where.

Layering with a Speech Piece

Voices can be used to create texture.
Perform "Bundle-Buggy Boogie Woogie."

TEXTURE

SOUNDS

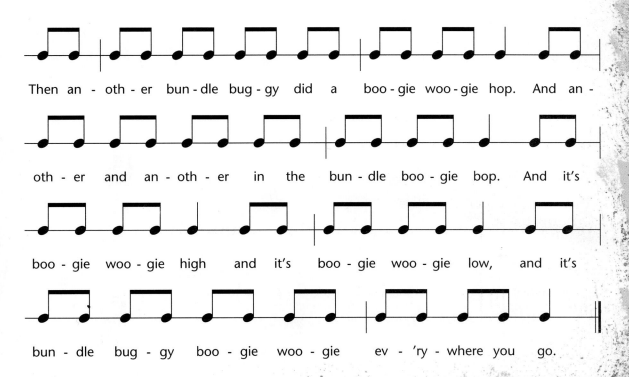

Then an - oth - er bun - dle bug - gy did a boo - gie woo - gie hop. And an -

oth - er and an - oth - er in the bun - dle boo - gie bop. And it's

boo - gie woo - gie high and it's boo - gie woo - gie low, and it's

bun - dle bug - gy boo - gie woo - gie ev - 'ry - where you go.

Playing the Part

Create a thicker texture by adding these percussion parts to "Bundle-Buggy Boogie Woogie."

Listen for layers of sound and texture in this recording.

4-33

Kitchen Stomp

from *Stomp Out Loud*

Stomp Out Loud was a major Off-Broadway hit. It uses sounds found on the streets of New York in creative ways.

Your Turn to Stomp

As the creators of *Stomp* know, sounds can be organized, and music can be made without traditional instruments. Let's create an indoor storm by performing these actions in sequence.

Action One: Rub your palms together.

Action Two: Snap your fingers.

Action Three: Pat your legs lightly, getting faster.

Action Four: Stand and stamp your feet.

The storm can fade away if you reverse the order and end with rubbing your palms together.

Create another kind of composition using things found in the room. Organize your composition with a beginning, a middle, and an end.

Perform your composition for your class.

M·U·S·I·C M·A·K·E·R·S

LUKE CRESSWELL and STEVE McNICHOLAS

In 1991, Luke Cresswell and Steve McNicholas created the percussion dance troupe known as *Stomp*. What is it that makes attending *Stomp* so special for people of any age? It is probably because the performers create their music from everyday items such as brooms, hubcaps, lids, and signs. They even make percussion instruments out of aluminum sinks tied around their shoulders! Both Cresswell and McNicholas believe that anyone can make music with common household items.

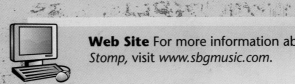

Web Site For more information about *Stomp*, visit *www.sbgmusic.com*.

Putting It

What Do You Know?

1. Look at the notation for "Weevily Wheat" on page 101 and answer these questions.

   a. Where is *do* located in the music?

   b. What are the letter names for *do, re, mi, so,* and *la* in this song?

   c. Point to all the notes that are named *so* and *la* . How many did you identify?

2. Perform these examples using rhythm syllables and patting.

5-1

What Do You Hear? 3

Identify which string instrument is being played in each example.

1. *koto*   cello

2. violin   banjo

3. viola   *sitar*

All Together

What You Can Do

Read Melody

Read the notation for "See the Children Playin'" on page 103, and identify whether the song is *do* or *la* pentatonic. Sing the song using pitch syllables and hand signs. Sing the song again using the words.

Play Rhythms

Sing *"Ōsamu kosamu"* on page 94. Perform the ostinato accompaniment on page 95 by patting the rhythms on your thighs. Then sing the song and play the accompaniment on the percussion instruments.

Find Sounds

Perform the speech piece "Bundle-Buggy Boogie Woogie" on page 116. Practice the rhythm ostinatos on page 118, and then perform them with the speech piece. Look around your classroom and home for materials that produce musical sounds when struck by a mallet. Create other ostinatos in $\frac{4}{4}$ time and play them using those sounds. Be sure to use the ♩♩♩♩ pattern. Perform these patterns with "Bundle-Buggy Boogie Woogie."

Swing It!

Listen for swing style in the The Singers Unlimited version of *On Green Dolphin Street*.

5-4
On Green Dolphin Street

by Ned Washington and Bronislaw Kaper
as performed by The Singers Unlimited
Many musicians perform *On Green Dolphin Street* because it is a jazz standard.

M·U·S·I·C M·A·K·E·R·S

The Singers Unlimited

The members of **The Singers Unlimited** are Gene Puerling (founding member), Don Shelton, Len Dresslar, and Bonnie Herman. The group gained popularity by singing jingles in the 1970s. Len Dresslar was the distinctive voice of the "green giant." Each member of the group is an accomplished vocalist. Using multiple track recording technology, The Singers Unlimited has produced amazing recordings in which they sound like sixteen or more people.

Building Our Musical Skills

Swinging Music

Although swing **style** has its roots in 1930s-1940s jazz, today it is still a favorite style of music for performing, listening, and dancing.

Style is the special sound that is created when music elements such as rhythm and timbre are combined.

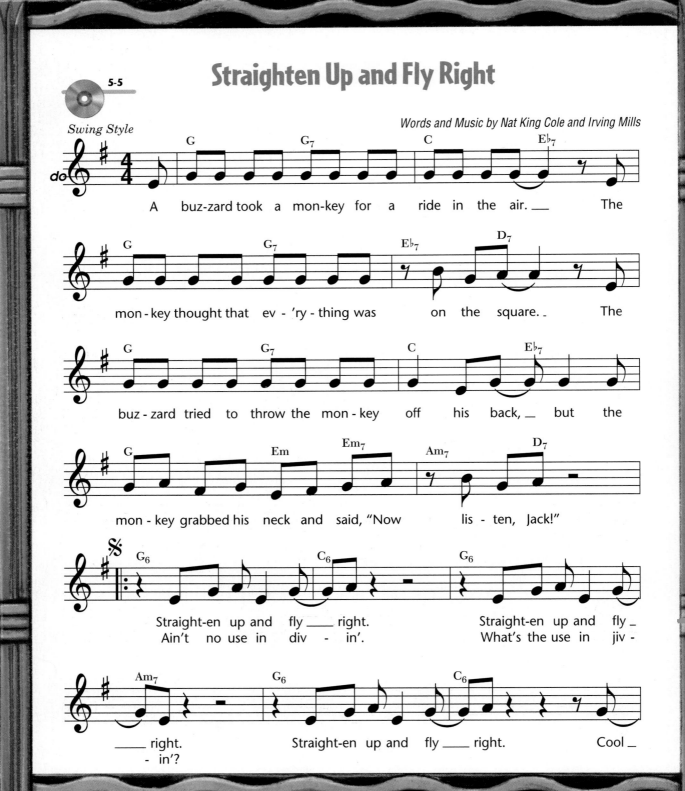

Straighten Up and Fly Right

5-5

Swing Style

Words and Music by Nat King Cole and Irving Mills

A buz-zard took a mon-key for a ride in the air. ___ The mon-key thought that ev-'ry-thing was on the square. _ The buz-zard tried to throw the mon-key off his back, ___ but the mon-key grabbed his neck and said, "Now lis-ten, Jack!"

Straight-en up and fly ___ right. Straight-en up and fly _
Ain't no use in div - in'. What's the use in jiv -

___ right. Straight-en up and fly ___ right. Cool _
- in'?

A DYNAMIC SONG

Listen for the changes in *dynamics* as you **sing** "The Lion Sleeps Tonight." When you have learned this song, **create** your own dynamic plan. Decide where the music should be softer or louder.

Playing Dynamics

Pick a percussion instrument to play. Practice playing your part. Then **perform** your part with the other players. Plan different dynamics to make the piece more interesting. Now use it as an accompaniment to "The Lion Sleeps Tonight."

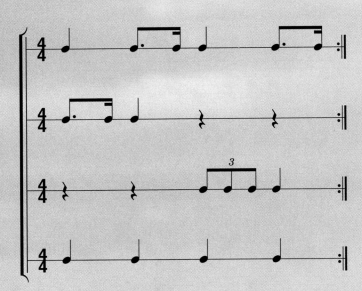

126

THE LION SLEEPS TONIGHT
(Wimoweh) (Mbube)

Words and Revised Music by George David Weiss,
Hugo Peretti, and Luigi Creatore

REFRAIN

Wim - o-weh, o-wim - o-weh, o - wim - o-weh, o-wim - o-weh, o -

wim - o-weh, o-wim - o-weh, o - wim - o-weh, o-wim - o-weh,

VERSE

1. In the jun - gle, the might - y jun - gle, the
2. Near the vil - lage, the peace - ful vil - lage, the
3. Hush, my dar - ling, don't fear, my dar - ling, the

li - on sleeps to - night. _____
li - on sleeps to - night. _____
li - on sleeps to - night. _____

In the jun - gle, the qui - et jun - gle, the
Near the vil - lage, the qui - et vil - lage, the
Hush, my dar - ling, don't fear, my dar - ling, the

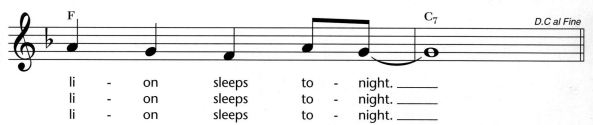

li - on sleeps to - night. _____
li - on sleeps to - night. _____
li - on sleeps to - night. _____

Lebo M.

Lebo M. (Lebo Morake, born 1966) is from South Africa. When he was fifteen, Morake left his home to pursue a music career in the United States. After studying at the Duke Ellington School of Music, he worked with the band Earth, Wind & Fire. One of his most famous projects was providing the authentic African instruments and singing for *The Lion King* Broadway production. He is a well-known musician in South Africa and the United States.

5-9
The Lion Sleeps Tonight

Listen for dynamic contrast as Lebo M. performs his version of *The Lion Sleeps Tonight*.

by George David Weiss, Hugo Peretti, and Luigi Creatore as performed by Lebo M.

This song is based on the South African style of *a cappella* singing called *mbube*.

Another Dynamic Song

This lullaby from South Africa is in the Bantu language. Will you sing it loudly or softly? Why?

5-10
T'HOLA, T'HOLA
(Softly, Softly)

Folk Song from South Africa

T'ho - la, t'ho - la ngoa-na - me; T'ho - la, t'ho - la ngoa-na - me,
Soft - ly, soft - ly, my ba - by; Soft - ly, soft - ly, my ba - by.

Li pe - re se - ra peng. _____ Ra - peng sa - ma ha - pu.
Hush, it is just the wind _____ Blow - ing through the branch - es.

Creating Dynamics

You can make many different dynamic sounds with your voice. Look at these shapes on the right. First experiment with a vocal sound that the picture seems to suggest. Then see how softly or loudly you can perform the sound. Plan a piece by putting the symbols in an order that you like. Decide what dynamics will make your performance expressive and interesting.

Use a neutral syllable such as "ah." Repeat any symbol as many times as you like.

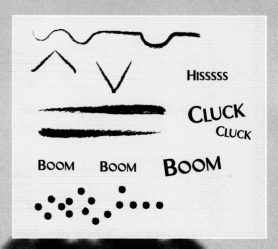

FEELING UPBEAT

This song is about the *ochimbo* bird, which is found in Kenya and other central African countries. What is the message the singers are sending to the bird?

Sing "*Ochimbo*" and tap the strong, or first, beat of each measure.

5-14

OCHIMBO

English Words by Margaret Marks

Folk Song from Kenya
As Sung by Ruth Nthreketha

Leader

O take your fair share, _ good fish-ing / good hunt-ing O - chim-bo bird.

Chorus

O take your fair share, _ good fish-ing / good hunt-ing O - chim-bo bird.

Leader

Take fish from the stream, _ good fish-ing / Take game from the plain, _ good hunt-ing O - chim-bo bird.

Chorus

Take fish from the stream, _ good fish-ing / Take game from the plain, _ good hunt-ing O - chim-bo bird.

Find the Upbeat

Look at the first phrase of "*Ochimbo.*" Does the phrase begin on the strong beat? When a phrase begins before a bar line, an **upbeat** occurs.

An **upbeat** is one or more notes that occur before the first bar line of a phrase.

Play these ostinatos on drums or other percussion instruments to accompany "*Ochimbo.*" Find the upbeat in each ostinato.

Create your own ostinato to accompany "*Ochimbo.*"

This drummer belongs to the Kikuyu tribe, a farming group in Kenya. He is performing at a lodge in a game reserve. ▶

Discover a New Rhythm

Read the words of "*Ala Da′lona.*" What feelings are expressed? Will this affect how you **sing** this song?

5-17

Ala Da′lona

English Words by Alice Firgau   *Arabic Folk Song*

A - la   Da' - lo - na,   A - la   Da' - lo - na,

Hi - war   shi - ma - li   gha - yar   ih   lo   na
Through the   night   the   des - ert ___ winds   are   sigh - ing.   *Fine*

Ma - ba - di   i - mi   ma - ba - di   ba - yi;
Tell   me   where she's   gone,   My ___ fair   Da' - lo - na,
Dark   and   love - ly   braids,

Ba - di   ha - bi - bi   as - mar   ih - ho - na.   *D.C. al Fine*
She   is   sweet and   kind   and ___ brings such   glad - ness.
Has   she   gone for - ev - er? ___ Oh, what   sad - ness.

Find the New Rhythm

Find the ♩ ♫ pattern in the song. **Read** this pattern with rhythm syllables.

Instruments of the Middle East

The recording of "Ala Da´lona" features an instrument called the *oud* [ood]. How does this instrument produce sound?

Listen for the *oud* and drums in the introduction of the recording of "Ala Da´lona." The drums are the *tabl* [TAH-buhl] and the *darabukah* [dah-rah-BOO-kuh].

◄ The *oud* has been used in Middle Eastern music for more than 1,000 years.

Play these ostinatos on percussion instruments to accompany "Ala Da´lona." Which ostinatos contain the new rhythm pattern you learned?

These players from Hammamet, Tunisia are playing a frame drum, a *zurna*, and a *darabukah*. ▼

Finding New Rhythm Patterns

The Cumberland Gap is a passage through the mountains of Virginia, Kentucky, and Tennessee.

Look at the music for "Cumberland Gap" and find the rhythm pattern. Now **listen** carefully to hear this pattern and the ♫ pattern.

5-21

Cumberland Gap

Play-Party Song from Kentucky
Adapted by Jill Trinka

1. Lay down, boys,   take a lit-tle nap,   lay down, boys,   take a lit-tle nap,

Lay down, boys,   take a lit-tle nap,   for-ty-one miles to   Cum-ber-land Gap.

Cum-ber-land Gap,   Cum-ber-land   Gap, _____   Ooo, _____

Hoo, _____   Way low down in   Cum-ber-land   Gap. _____

2. Cumberland Gap is a mighty fine place, . . .
    (3 times)
    Three kinds of water to wash your face.
    Refrain

3. Cumberland Gap with its cliffs and rocks, . . .
    (3 times)
    Home of the panther, bear, and fox.
    Refrain

4. Me and my wife and my wife's grandpap, . . .
    (3 times)
    We raise Cain at Cumberland Gap.
    Refrain

Cumberland Patterns

Find the word *Cumberland* in the song. Ask yourself these questions.

• How many beats are used for the word *Cumberland*?

• How many sounds are on the beat?

• Does *Cumberland* have the same sound as ?

• What rhythm pattern fits with *Cumberland*?

Now **read** "Cumberland Gap" using rhythm syllables.

Show What You Know!

Show what you know and **read** the following patterns.

1. (4/4 rhythm pattern)

2. (4/4 rhythm pattern)

3. (4/4 rhythm pattern)

4. (4/4 rhythm pattern)

Create four rhythm patterns of your own using (rhythm symbols).

Notate your patterns. Then have a partner clap them.

Finding the Form

Have you ever had a day when nothing seemed to go right? In *The Wizard of Oz,* Dorothy is unhappy on her family's farm in Kansas. She sings of hope and looks for happiness "somewhere over the rainbow."

Sing Dorothy's song after listening to the recording.

5-22

Over the Rainbow

Words by E. Y. Harburg

Music by Harold Arlen

Some - where   o - ver the rain - bow,   way   up   high,

There's   a   land that I heard of   once   in a lull - a - by.

Some - where   o - ver the rain - bow   skies   are   blue,

And   the   dreams that you dare to   dream real-ly do come true.   Some -

Find the Phrases

Find the phrases of "Over the Rainbow" that are the same. Look for a melody that repeats, even though the words are different. How many **A** phrases can you find? How many **B** phrases? What is the order of the **A** and **B** phrases in this song?

The Wizard of Oz was just the first of many adventures for Dorothy. L. Frank Baum wrote 14 books about the "Wonderful World of Oz."

Move Over the Rainbow

As you **listen** to the recording, of "Over the Rainbow" **move** to show the Ⓐ and Ⓑ phrases of the song.

Ⓐ Make large, slow, circular motions by moving your arms through the air.

Ⓑ Make small, quick, zigzag motions by moving your hand through the air in front of you.

Create your own motions to show the Ⓐ and Ⓑ phrases of the song. Then **move** as you **listen** to the recording again.

M·U·S·I·C M·A·K·E·R·S

Judy Garland

Judy Garland (1922–1969) born Frances Gumm, was one of the most famous movie stars of the 1930s and 1940s. Her career as an actress began when she was just two years old. It lasted for more than 40 years.

She was fourteen when she recorded her first album and just sixteen when the movie *The Wizard of Oz* was filmed. Her role as Dorothy made her a superstar, and her performance of *Over the Rainbow* made the song a hit. The song became her lifelong theme song.

Listen Over the Rainbow

Listen to Patti LaBelle's version of "Over the Rainbow." Tell a partner how it is the same as Judy Garland's version, and how it is different.

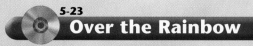

5-23
Over the Rainbow

by E.Y. Harburg and Harold Arlen
as sung by Judy Garland from *The Wizard of Oz*

This song, which was almost cut from the movie, went on to earn an Oscar in 1939 for "Best Song."

5-24
Over the Rainbow

by E.Y. Harburg and Harold Arlen
as sung by Patti LaBelle

LaBelle said, " 'Over the Rainbow' was one of those songs I always loved from the time I heard Judy Garland sing it in *The Wizard of Oz*. It has such a beautiful melody, and that line, 'if birds can fly, why can't I?' That's always been my line because I have often thought of myself that way—as a bird who could fly. . . "

M·U·S·I·C M·A·K·E·R·S

Patti LaBelle

Patti LaBelle (born 1944) born Patricia Holt, is one of the most famous rhythm and blues singers of today. The song "Over the Rainbow" has been a source of inspiration for her since she first heard Judy Garland sing it in *The Wizard of Oz*. She made recordings both as a member of her group, The Blue Belles, and as a solo performer. Many of her recordings reached number one on the charts and won awards. LaBelle has performed in concerts, on Broadway, and in movie productions.

IN SEARCH OF A New Note

This song comes from Latin America. The Cunas are Native Americans who live on the northern shore of Panama and the San Blas Islands.

5-25

Canción de cuna
(Cradle Song)

Folk Song from Latin America

Duer-me pron - to, ni - ño mí - o, Duer-me pron-to y sin llo - rar.
Go to sleep now, go to sleep now, go to sleep now, lit - tle child.

Que es - tás en los bra - zos de tu ma - dre, que te va a can - tar.
You are in your moth-er's arms. __ She will sing a lull - a - by.

A New Note

Read the five notes on the staff below. A new note goes in the color box below.

la
so
fa
mi
re
do

The name of the new note is *fa*. Notice that *fa* is the note between *so* and *mi*. The step between *mi* and *fa* is called a half-step because it is only half the size of the whole-steps between other notes. Can you hear the difference?

Using the letter ladder, **sing** up and down the notes from *do* to *la*. Now try skipping around.

▲ Mola textile pattern of the Cuna people

Cuna woman making a mola ▶

Focus on *Fa*

Find *fa* in the examples below. The *do* finder will help you find your way around the staff.

Here is another song with *fa*. The words of this song from Latin America send a silly message. **Listen** to *"Cantando mentiras."* What makes this song funny?

5-29

Cantando mentiras
(Singing Tall Tales)

English Words by Alice Firgau

Folk Song from Latin America

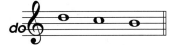

1. A ho - ra que es - ta - mos des - pa - cio,
2. Los pe - rru - cos po - nen hue - vos,
1. Let's make up fan - tas - tic sto - ries,
2. Hound dogs lay eggs, we can tell you,

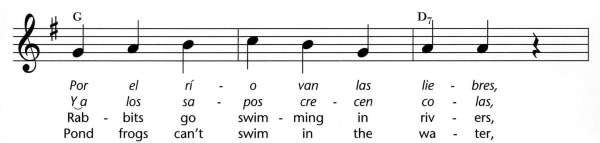

Va - mos a can - tar men - ti - ras.
Las ga - lli - nas a la - drar, _____
Let's sing of tales that are tall; _____
Chick - ens can bark, it is true; _____

Por el rí - o van las lie - bres,
Y a los sa - pos cre - cen co - las,
Rab - bits go swim - ming in riv - ers,
Pond frogs can't swim in the wa - ter,

Por el mon - te las an - gui - las.
Por - que no sa - ben na - dar. _____
Eels through the un - der - brush crawl. ____
So they grow tails that are new. _____

▲ *Mariachi* ensemble

Practice *fa*

Now that you know *fa*, find the patterns below in the song. **Sing** the patterns as you **read** them from the staff.

so fa mi fa   *re mi fa so*   *do re mi fa mi*

One of the lines in the song contains a note you do not yet know. Point to the mystery note. You will learn about this note later.

From Panama to Colombia

Guitar is a popular instrument throughout Latin America. **Listen** for the guitar in *Ojo al toro*.

▶ Latin guitarist

5-33

Ojo al toro

Contemporary *Bambuco* from Colombia as performed by Aires Colombianos

Bambuco is a style that combines elements of both Spanish and Native American music.

MOVING A New Note

Let's see what happens to *fa* when a different note becomes *do*. Look at the half-steps and whole-steps on the keyboard below.

Fa is always a half-step above *mi*. When *do* is C, *mi* is E and *fa* is F. What happens when *do* is F? Find *fa* on the keyboard. Remember that *fa* is a half-step above *mi*.

To show this note on the staff, we mark it with a flat sign (♭) and call it B-flat.

do   re   me   fa   so

The flat sign at the beginning of a song is called a **key signature.** It means that all the Bs in this song are really B-flats.

do   re   mi   fa   so

key signature

A **key signature** tells which notes are to be performed with a flat or sharp throughout a piece of music.

whole-step

half-step   half-step   whole-step

D♭   E♭   G♭   A♭   B♭   D♭   E♭

C   D   E   F   G   A   B   C   D   E   F

What's for Sale?

Before the days of commercials, the street cry was a singing advertisement. You may have heard a similar cry from a vendor at a ball game. **Listen** to the song. What is being advertised?

Look at the key signature of this song. Can you find *fa?* **Sing** "Chairs to Mend" using pitch syllables. Then you can sing this song as a round.

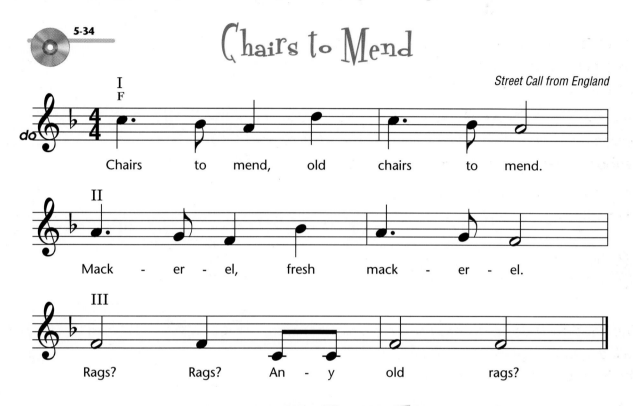

5-34

Chairs to Mend

Street Call from England

Chairs to mend, old chairs to mend.

Mack - er - el, fresh mack - er - el.

Rags? Rags? An - y old rags?

Show What You Know!

These melodies contain all of the notes you have learned. **Sing** each melody. Do any sound familiar?

so so so   so fa mi   fa fa

so   mi fa   so   mi fa   so so fa mi   fa re

mi fa so mi   mi fa so mi   mi fa so mi   so fa mi

UNITED by Melody

At the opening ceremonies of the 1998 Winter Olympics, Seiji Ozawa [SAY-jee oh-ZAH-wah] conducted seven performing groups at the same time. But this was no ordinary performance. The groups were on five different continents! Satellite technology allowed the musicians from all over the world to perform the fourth movement of Beethoven's *Symphony No. 9* together. Through this unique new way of performing, they delivered a powerful message of unity to the world.

New York

Berlin

Sydney

Capetown

Beijing

Nagano

◀ Seiji Ozawa

146

Follow that Melody!

Listen to "Ode to Joy" from Beethoven's *Symphony No. 9, Movement 4.* Follow the listening map below, and trace the contour of the melody with your finger.

Contour is the "shape" of a melody made by the way it moves upward and downward in steps, leaps, and repeated tones.

5-36

Ode to Joy

**from *Symphony No. 9, Movement 4*
by Ludwig van Beethoven**

Beethoven [BAY-toh-vehn] had lost his hearing by the time he composed *Symphony No. 9.* This symphony was performed at the 1998 Winter Olympics in Nagano, Japan. Millions of people throughout the world heard the music that Beethoven himself heard only in his mind.

A Message of Joy

Friedrich Schiller wrote the German words for this song. **Sing** the message of "Ode to Joy" in English or in German.

Letter Names for Notes

Beethoven's melody has only six notes. These notes are identified on the flags below. Find these notes in "Ode to Joy."

Review how to play the notes above on the recorder. Then **play** "Ode to Joy" along with the recording.

MUSIC MAKERS

Ludwig van Beethoven

Ludwig van Beethoven (1770–1827) is one of the most famous composers of all time. During his lifetime, Beethoven composed a variety of music including works for solo piano, small ensembles, and orchestra. He was born in Germany and began studying piano when he was very young. His first composition was published when he was only twelve years old. In his twenties, Beethoven gradually began to lose his hearing. Even after becoming completely deaf, he continued to write music.

Percussion on Parade

How do you think the first instruments were created? Long ago, people discovered that they could make sounds on objects they found around them. These objects developed into percussion instruments that we play today. You can also make sounds on objects you find around you.

Crash! Boom! Clang!

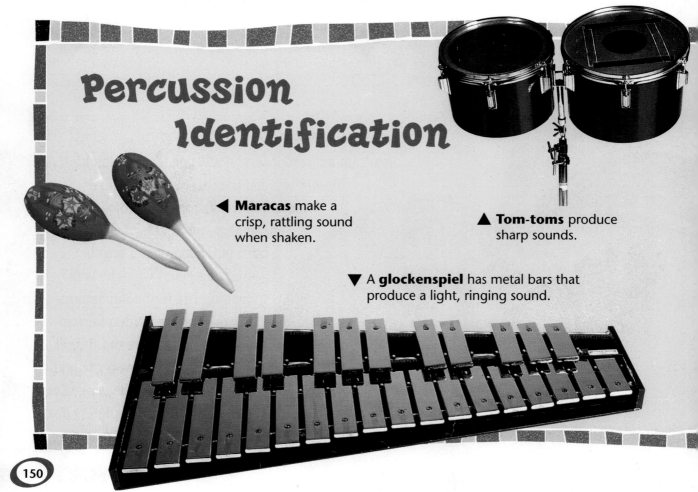

Percussion Identification

◄ **Maracas** make a crisp, rattling sound when shaken.

▲ **Tom-toms** produce sharp sounds.

▼ A **glockenspiel** has metal bars that produce a light, ringing sound.

Listen to *Toccata for Percussion.*
Identify the percussion
instruments as you hear them.

6-5

Toccata for Percussion, Movement 3

by Carlos Chávez

Carlos Chávez [CHAH-vehs] traveled all over Mexico learning about Mexican-Indian music. Much of the music he composed was influenced by the rhythms of these cultures.

◀ A **snare drum** can make a long, raspy roll or a sharp, short sound.

◀ **Claves** produce a bright, hollow sound when struck together.

A **bass drum** produces a deep boom or a soft "thudding" sound. ▶

▲ **Timpani,** also called kettledrums, can sound like a roll of thunder or a quiet "thump."

These instruments are featured in the Sound Bank on page 438.

Percussion in China

Percussion instruments play an important role in many types of music, including marching bands. Where have you heard a marching band perform? At a parade? At a football game? Children in Chinese communities hear *luogu* [loo-OH-goo] percussion ensembles at parades, festivals, and concerts. The sound of the *luogu* ensemble is as familiar in China as the sound of a marching band is in the United States.

▲ A *luogu* ensemble includes gongs, drums, cymbals, bells, and woodblocks.

As you **listen** to *Wu long*, follow the notation on the next page.

6-7

Wu long (Dragon Dance)

Traditional Dance from China

Wu long is played for the Dragon Dance, a traditional dance often performed in parades for Chinese New Year. It is performed by a *luogu* ensemble using Chinese instruments.

In the *Dragon Dance*, many people carry a fabric dragon on sticks. As they move in a spiraling pattern, the dragon's body appears to slither down the street. ▶

Your Turn to Play

You can play *Wu long* with your class. Practice each part below using rhythm syllables. Then **play** the parts on percussion instruments. The ♩ in the drum part indicates that you play on the rim of the drum.

Listen to another *luogu* piece. How is it different from *Wu long?* How is it the same?

6-8
Lian xi qu (étude)

Traditional Arrangement from China

This *étude*, or practice exercise, is from the south central area of China. It features two pairs of cymbals that sound quickly, one after the other.

America in Two Parts ~ Melody and

Katharine Lee Bates was feeling pride for her country when she wrote the words to "America, the Beautiful" in 1893. She found her inspiration for the song as she stood on the top of Pike's Peak in Colorado.

America, the Beautiful

6-12

Words by Katharine Lee Bates

Music by Samuel A. Ward
Countermelody by Buryl Red

1. O beau - ti - ful for spa - cious skies, For am - ber waves of grain,
2. O beau - ti - ful for Pil - grim feet, Whose stern im - pas-sioned stress
3. O beau - ti - ful for pa - triot dream That sees be-yond the years

For pur - ple moun-tain maj - es - ties A - bove the fruit - ed plain!
A thor-ough-fare for free - dom beat A - cross the wil - der - ness!
Thine al - a - bas - ter cit - ies gleam, Un - dimmed by hu - man tears!

A - mer - i - ca! A - mer - i - ca! God shed His grace on thee
A - mer - i - ca! A - mer - i - ca! God mend thine ev - 'ry flaw,
A - mer - i - ca! A - mer - i - ca! God shed His grace on thee

And crown thy good with broth - er-hood From sea to shin - ing sea!
Con - firm thy soul in self con-trol, Thy lib - er - ty in law!
And crown thy good with broth - er-hood From sea to shin - ing sea!

Countermelody

Two Parts United

Sing the **countermelody** below. Singing the melody and a countermelody at the same time creates a thicker texture than either part sung alone.

A **countermelody** is a contrasting melody that is played or sung at the same time as the main melody.

Countermelody

O _____ beau-ti-ful,   O _____ beau-ti-ful,

O _____ beau-ti-ful,   O _____ beau-ti-ful,

A-mer-i - ca,   A-mer-i - ca,   A-mer-i - ca, the beau-ti-ful.

We sing   A - mer - i - ca.   We sing A - mer - i - ca.

Patriotic Countermelodies

Listen for two countermelodies in *The Stars and Stripes Forever.*

6-14

The Stars and Stripes Forever

by John Philip Sousa

Sousa [soo-zah] composed more than 100 marches in his lifetime. *The Stars and Stripes Forever* was his favorite. It is played today by high school, college, and community bands throughout the United States.

View from Pike's Peak, Colorado ▲

One Song, DIFFERENT TEXTURES

John Newton was a slave trader. When he realized slavery was wrong, he expressed his feelings through lyrics. Later, his lyrics were used with this early American hymn. **Listen** to the song and describe the texture.

6-9

Amazing Grace

Words by John Newton

Early American Melody

1. A - maz - ing __ grace, how sweet the sound, That
2. 'Twas grace that __ taught my heart to fear, And

saved a _____ wretch like me! _____ I
grace my ____ fears like re - lieved; _____ How

once ____ was __ lost, but now ____ am __ found, Was
pre - cious _ did that grace ____ ap - pear The

blind, but ____ now I see. _____
hour I _____ first be - lieved! _____

3. Through many dangers, toils, and snares,
   I have already come;
   'Tis grace has brought me safe thus far,
   And grace will lead me home.

156

Sing "Amazing Grace." Then sing this countermelody with a small group while the rest of the class sings "Amazing Grace." How does the texture change?

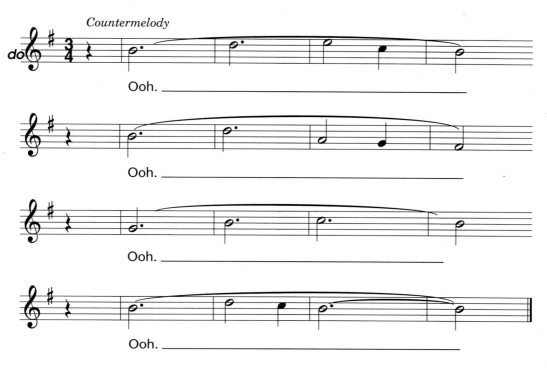

Countermelody

Ooh. _____

Ooh. _____

Ooh. _____

Ooh. _____

Comparing Textures

A thicker texture can be created by adding voices to the same melody line.

Listen to "Amazing Grace."
Compare the texture of the recording with the texture of the song.

6-11
Amazing Grace

as performed by Judy Collins
This recording by Judy Collins has two distinct textures—solo and chorus.

Painting by Michele Wood from
I See Rhythm by Toyomi Igus ▶

Reprinted with permission of the publisher, Children's Book Press, San Francisco, CA. Art copyright © 1998 by Michele Wood

HARMONY TONES

Listen to where the **harmony** changes in the song.

Harmony is two or more different tones sounding at the same time.

6-15

DRY BONES

African American Spiritual

A C ... G₇ ... C

E - ze-kiel cried, "Them dry _ bones!" E - ze-kiel cried, "Them dry _ bones!"

C ... G₇ ... C

E - ze-kiel cried, "Them dry _ bones!" Now hear the word of the Lord.

B C

The foot bone con-nect - ed to the leg ___ bone,

C♯

The leg bone con-nect - ed to the knee ___ bone,

D

The knee bone con-nect - ed to the thigh ___ bone,

D♯

The thigh bone con-nect - ed to the hip ___ bone,

E

The hip bone con-nect - ed to the back ___ bone,

Playing Harmony

Sing "Dry Bones." Then **play** C and G₇ **chords** in the A section of the song on the Autoharp or keyboard.

A **chord** is three or more notes arranged in intervals of a third, sounded at the same time.

What Do You Know?

1. Which symbol below is called *fortissimo*? What does it mean?

pp   *p*   *mp*   *mf*   *f*   *ff*

2. If you saw this symbol (*p*), how would you perform the music?

p

6-17

What Do You Hear? 4

Point to the line below that matches the rhythms performed on the recording.

1. a.   b.

2. a.   b.

3. a.   b.

All Together

What You Can Do

Move to Contour

Sing "Amazing Grace" on page 156 with eyes closed. Move your hand in an arc to show the contour of the melody.

Play Rhythms

Perform all four of the percussion lines of "*Wu long*" on page 153 using rhythm syllables. Perform the piece as a group using body percussion. Have different people play each part. Perform the piece again using percussion instruments.

Move to Form

Sing "Ode to Joy" on page 148. Perform small, steady beat movements during the **a** phrases and different movements during the **b** phrase.

Sing with Texture

Sing "America the Beautiful," on page 154. Create a thick texture by singing the melody and the countermelody together.

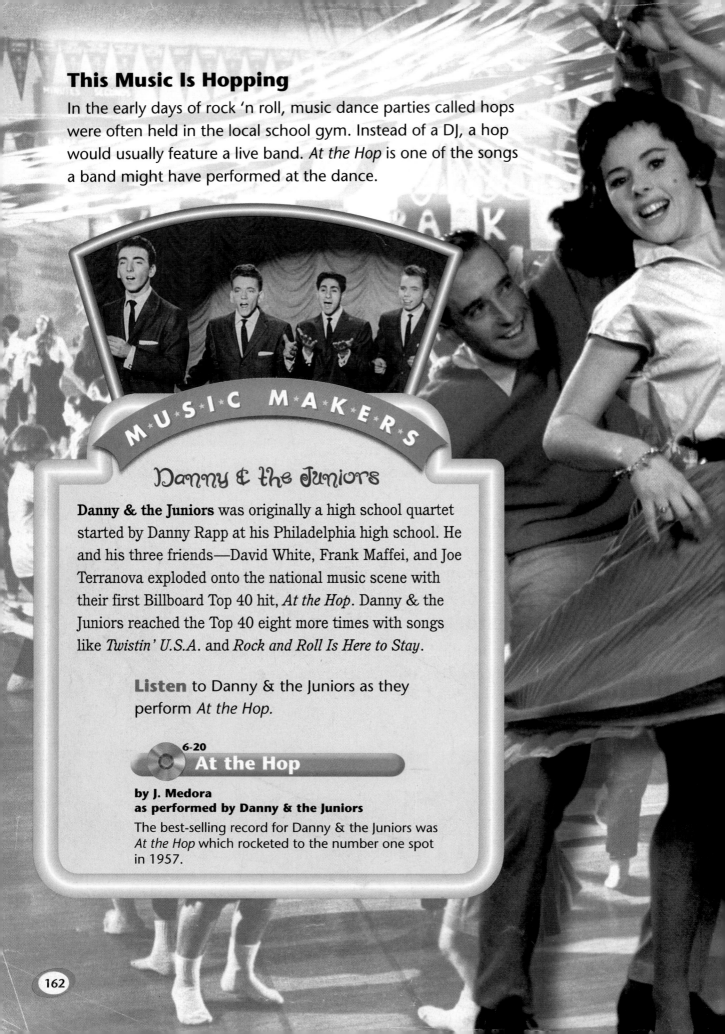

This Music Is Hopping

In the early days of rock 'n roll, music dance parties called hops were often held in the local school gym. Instead of a DJ, a hop would usually feature a live band. *At the Hop* is one of the songs a band might have performed at the dance.

M·U·S·I·C M·A·K·E·R·S

Danny & the Juniors

Danny & the Juniors was originally a high school quartet started by Danny Rapp at his Philadelphia high school. He and his three friends—David White, Frank Maffei, and Joe Terranova exploded onto the national music scene with their first Billboard Top 40 hit, *At the Hop*. Danny & the Juniors reached the Top 40 eight more times with songs like *Twistin' U.S.A.* and *Rock and Roll Is Here to Stay*.

Listen to Danny & the Juniors as they perform *At the Hop*.

6-20
At the Hop

by J. Medora
as performed by Danny & the Juniors
The best-selling record for Danny & the Juniors was *At the Hop* which rocketed to the number one spot in 1957.

Discovering
New Musical
Horizons

Moving and Singing

As you **sing** "At the Hop" add some dance movements.

At the Hop

Words and Music by A. Singer, J. Medora, and D. White

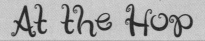

VERSE

1. Well, you can rock it, you can roll it, do the stomp and e-ven stroll it at the
swing it, you can groove it, you can real - ly start to move it at the

hop.
hop.
When the rec-ord starts a spin - nin', you ca -
Where the jump-in' is the smooth-est and the

lyp - so when you chick-en at the hop.
mu - sic is the cool-est at the hop.
Do the
All the

dance sen - sa - tion that is sweep-in' the na - tion at the hop.
cats and the chicks __ can __ get their __ kicks __ at the hop.

REFRAIN

Let's go to the hop! Let's go to the hop!

(Oh, ba - by!) Let's go to the hop! (Oh, ba - by!)

Let's go to the hop! Come on.

Let's go to the hop! 2. Well, you can Let's go to the hop!

Row with the TEMPO

The tempo, or speed of the beat, plays a big role in giving music mood or feeling. **Listen** to the following speech piece. Notice the tempo changes. Raise your hand when you hear the tempo change.

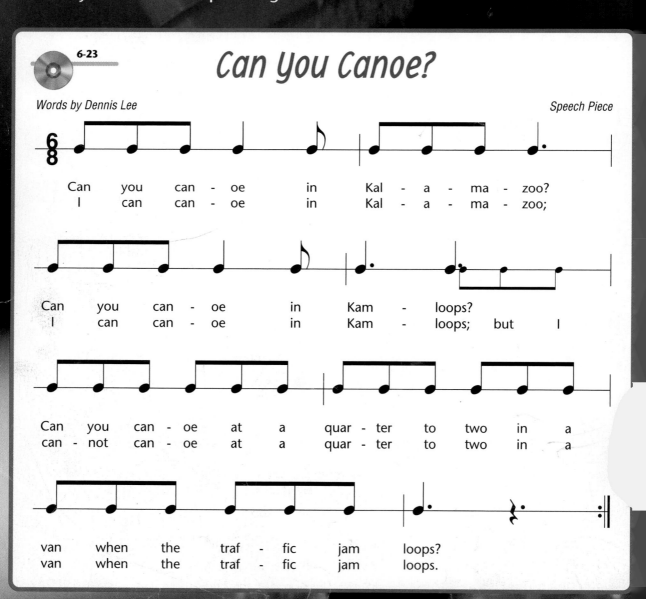

6-23

Can You Canoe?

Words by Dennis Lee

Speech Piece

Can you can-oe in Kal-a-ma-zoo?
I can can-oe in Kal-a-ma-zoo;

Can you can-oe in Kam-loops?
I can can-oe in Kam-loops; but I

Can you can-oe at a quar-ter to two in a
can-not can-oe at a quar-ter to two in a

van when the traf-fic jam loops?
van when the traf-fic jam loops.

Continue Canoeing

Use the speech piece for your own experiments with tempo.
Perform "Can You Canoe?" at an easy flowing tempo, called
andante. Next **perform** the piece in a medium tempo, *moderato.*
Now, repeat the speech piece in a rapid, lively tempo, *allegro.*

Perform these rhythm patterns with "Can You Canoe?"

Listen to the following piece. Notice the tempo
changes and name these tempos.

6-25
Hungarian Dance No. 19

by Johannes Brahms

Brahms wrote the *Hungarian Dances* for piano four hands.
This orchestral setting of No. 19 was arranged by
Antonín Dvořák.

M·U·S·I·C M·A·K·E·R·S

Johannes Brahms

Johannes Brahms (1833–1897) was born in
Hamburg, Germany, to a musical family. He began
piano lessons at an early age and was admired as
a composer and pianist. He composed piano
works, four symphonies, four concertos, choral
works, and many songs.

Doin' Fine in Triple Time

The following song, *"Santa Clara"* is from the Philippine Islands in the South Pacific. The text of this song is written in a language of the Philippines called *Tagalog* [ta-GAH-log].

6-26

Santa Clara

English Words by Alice Firgau

Folk Song from the Philippines
As sung by Sonny Alforque

San - ta Cla - rang, _____ pi - nung pi - no
San - ta Cla - ra, _____ this I will do.

Ang pa - nga - ko ko ay ga - ni - to.
In my heart I vow and prom - ise you,

Pag - da - ting ko po _____ sa U - ban - do.
On the road I'll go _____ to U - ban - do;

Ay mag -
While I'm

Feeling Strong

Listen to the strong triple feeling in this song: ONE-two-three, ONE-two-three. As you listen, **move** to show meter in 3 by performing these repeated motions: PAT-clap-snap.

Create hand movements of your own to go with the song. Always use the same movement for the strong beat.

◀ Filipino classical dancers

sa - sa - yaw _____ ng pan - dang - go.   A - ru -
there   I'll   dance ___   the   fan - dan - go.   A - ru -

ray, a - ra - ru - ray, Ang pa - nga - ko'y tu - tu - pa - rin.   A - ru -
ray, a - ra - ru - ray, And may   my   prom - ise   be ful - filled.   A - ru -

ray, a - ra - ru - ray, Ang pa - nga - ko'y tu - tu - pa - rin. _____
ray, a - ra - ru - ray, And may   my   prom - ise   be ful - filled. _____

Make Mine $\frac{3}{4}$ Time

Listen to the Korean song "*Doraji*," another song in $\frac{3}{4}$. Unlike most other Asian cultures, Korea has folk songs in $\frac{3}{4}$ time. Is the tempo faster or slower than the tempo of "*Santa Clara*"?

6-29

Doraji (Bluebells)

English Words by Patricia Shehan Campbell

Folk Song from Korea

Do - ra - ji, do - ra - ji, pek do - ra - ji,
Blue - bells, blue - bells, Love - ly blue - bells,

Sim - sim san - chuh __ neh __ pek do - ra - ji.
Deep in the moun - tains __ my __ blue - bells grow.

Hahn du bu - ri - man keh - yuh - do _____
Gather - ing blue - bells in wide val - leys.

Teh kwang - chu - ri su - ri - sal __ sal __ num - nun - goo - na.
Bas - kets of __ blue - bells __ will __ o - ver - flow.

Folk Melody, Folk Instruments

Listen for meter in 3 in this version of *Doraji*.

6-33
Doraji

Folk Song from Korea

This version of *Doraji* is played on traditional Korean instruments and is sung in Korean folk style.

MUSIC MAKERS

Hi-za Yoo

As a child in Korea, **Hi-za Yoo** studied Korean traditional dance and became an outstanding performer. She also plays the *kayagum* [ki-AH-gum], a Korean stringed instrument. She has performed in the Los Angeles area.

Sounds of Spain

The music of Spain has been influenced by many different cultures. The Moors, an Arabic people, lived in southern Spain for nearly seven centuries. They brought with them the *vihuela* [vee-HWAY-la], an ancestor of the guitar.

Listen for the sound of the *vihuela* in "*La Tarara*."

▲ castanets

6-34

La Tarara

English Words by Alice D. Firgau   *Folk Song from Spain*

REFRAIN   Em   B₇

La Ta - ra - ra, sí, la Ta - ra - ra, no,
La Ta - ra - ra, yes, La Ta - ra - ra, no,

Em   B₇   Em   *Fine*

La Ta - ra - ra, ma - dre, que la bai - lo yo.
La Ta - ra - ra, ma - ma, is a dance I know.

VERSE   Em   B₇

1. Tie - ne la Ta - ra - ra un jar - dín de flo - res y me
2. Tie - ne la Ta - ra - ra un ces - to de fru - tas y me
1. If I want to wan - der in her gar - den bow - ers, La Ta -
2. If I want a bas - ket of the fruit she'll har - vest, La Ta -

Em   B₇   *D. C. al Fine*

da, si quie - ro, siem - pre las me - jor - es.
da, si quie - ro, siem - pre las ma - du - ras.
ra - ra al - ways gives me her best flow - ers.
ra - ra al - ways gives me just the rip - est.

172

◀ *Girl with a Guitar* by Jan Vermeer (1632–1675).

It's All the Same

Say the words to the refrain in rhythm and tap the beat with your foot. Now clap the rhythm pattern below while you say the words.

La Ta - ra - ra sí,

You can use the tie to show the sound that lasts for one and a half beats.

La Ta - ra - ra sí,

There is an easier way to write the same rhythm, using

La Ta - ra - ra sí,

vihuela ▶

Identify and **read** the new rhythm pattern in *"La Tarara."*

TEARING THROUGH RHYTHM

Have you ever tried singing a song to pass the time while you work? Songs have long been used to make work go faster. **Sing** the song "Old House, Tear It Down!" Notice how the rhythms give the song energy.

OLD HOUSE, TEAR IT DOWN!

7-1

Collected by John Work

African American Work Song

1. Old   house,   tear it   down!   Who's gon-na help   me   tear it   down?
2. New   house,   build it   up!   Who's gon-na help   me   build it   up?

Bring me   a ham-mer,   tear it   down!   Bring me   a   saw, __   tear it   down!
Bring me   a ham-mer,   build it   up!   Bring me   a   saw, __   build it   up!

Next thing you bring me,   tear it   down! Is   a   wreck-ing ma-chine,   tear it   down.
Next thing you bring me,   build it   up! Is   a   car - pen-ter man,   build it   up.

Rewriting Rhythms

Read the first line of the song. Then clap the rhythm pattern below while you say the words.

Old   house   tear it __ down

You can use the ♪ ♩. to write the same rhythm.

Old   house   tear it   down

Read the entire song using rhythm syllables.

Two Patterns Alike and Different

The two patterns below are alike because both patterns are made up of two sounds: one long and the other short.

1. 2.

How are they different?

Sing "All Night, All Day"

Conduct the song in a four beat pattern.
Identify the lines that contain the above rhythm patterns.

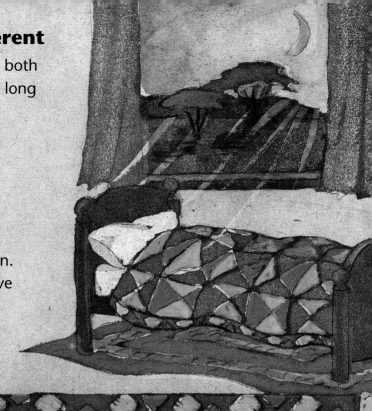

7-3

ALL NIGHT, ALL DAY

African American Spiritual

REFRAIN

All night, all ____ day, An-gels watch-ing o-ver me, my Lord. _

All night, all ____ day, An-gels watch-ing o-ver me.

Fine

VERSE *Call*

Response

1. Now I lay me down _ to sleep, An-gels watch-ing o-ver me, my Lord. _
2. If I die be - fore _ I wake,

Call

Response

D. C. al Fine

Pray the Lord my soul _ to keep, An-gels watch-ing o-ver me.
Pray the Lord my soul _ to take,

176

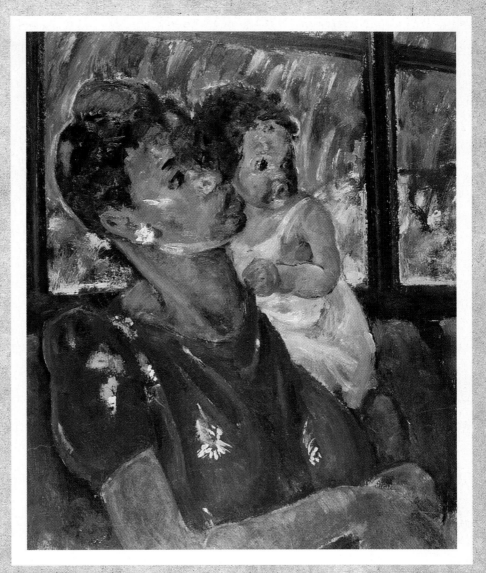

Arts Connection

▲ *Mother and Child* (1919) by Martha Walter

Show What You Know!

Perform these rhythms using rhythm syllables.

1.

2.

Using the rhythms above, **compose** your own rhythm pattern. Make it four measures long. Be sure there are four beats in each measure. Perform it for the rest of the class.

KNOW the RONDO

"Heave–Ho," "Going, Going, Gone," and "The Snow" are speech pieces. Each has different rhythm patterns. Keep a steady beat as you perform these speech pieces.

7-5

A Heave-Ho

Words by Dennis Lee   *Speech Piece*

Heave - Ho,   buck-ets of snow, the   gi - ant is comb-ing his beard.   The

snow is   as high as the   top of the sky, and the   world has dis - ap - peared.

B Going, Going, Gone

Words by Dennis Lee   *Speech Piece*

Go - ing, go - ing, gone,   your dad - dy won't be   long.

Where did he   go? To shov - el   the snow.   Go - ing, go - ing, gone.

 # The Snow

Words by Clifford Dyment

Speech Piece

In　no way that I　chose to go　could I　es-cape the　fal - ling snow. My

foot - steps made a　shal - low space and　then　the snow　filled　up　the place.

Accompaniment Rhythms

Learn these rhythms. Then **play** them on a percussion instrument. **Perform** the rhythms as an accompaniment for the three speech pieces.

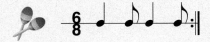

Now the Rondo

Now that you know three speech pieces, **perform** them in ABACA order. This order is a **rondo** form.

A **rondo** is a musical form in which the first section always returns. A common rondo form is ABACA.

A Mondo Rondo

Listen to *ABACA Dabble.* Remember the first melody—that's the
A section. Raise your hand each time you hear the **A** section.

7-7
ABACA Dabble

by Bryan Louiselle
This rondo is in a big band, swing style.

After each **A** section, you
hear a different section. The
new sections are labeled **B**
and **C**.

Now listen to *ABACA Dabble*
again and **move** to show
rondo form.

A
Create a
movement for the
A section that uses
your entire body.

B

Move your legs only for the **B** section.

C

Create a movement that uses your torso for the **C** section.

Element: MELODY | Skill: SINGING | Connection: SOCIAL STUDIES

Laugh and Sing

Do you know that the Kookaburra is a bird? It's called "the laughing bird" because its song sounds like a hilarious cackle! Of course, you know that a gum tree doesn't really grow bubble gum. It's actually a eucalyptus tree. And the bush in Australia isn't like the bush in your mother's rose garden—it's another name for the forest.

Sing this silly song from Australia.

7-8

Kookaburra

Words and Music by Marion Sinclair

Kookaburra Rhythm

Perform this pattern using rhythm syllables.

Kookaburra Pitch

Sing the melody below, using pitch syllables and hand signs. As you can see, there is a note missing! Hum the missing note. How does the new note sound compared to *la*? Compared to high *do*?

do ┐
     ?   do
   la   la
           so

WHERE'S THE NEW NOTE?

Have you ever lost something, only to find it right under your nose? Sometimes things seem to turn up where you least expect to find them.

Listen to the recording of "Missy-La, Massa-La." Learn the song, then play the game with your friends.

7-11 MISSY-LA, MASSA-LA

Game Song from the Caribbean

Mis - sy - la, ___ mas - sa - la, ___ Mis - sy lost ___ her gold ring, go 'way.

Mis - sy - la, ___ mas - sa - la, ___ Mis - sy lost ___ her gold ring. I got to

find 'em, find 'em, find 'em, find 'em, Find 'em, let me see ___ la, la, la, la

find 'em, find 'em, find 'em, find 'em, Find 'em, let me see.

184

Name the New Note

This guessing game about a lost gold ring is known all over the world. On the island of St. Lucia, the people sing "Missy-La, Massa-La" while they play the game. Speaking of things that are missing, we're still looking for that note between *la* and high *do!*

Can you find the new note in the song? **Sing** the first phrase of the song using pitch syllables and hand signs. Hum the new note. The new note is called *ti*. How does *ti* compare to *la* and high *do?*

Hear the New Note

As you **listen** to *A-Cling, A-Cling,* follow the map and **perform** the hand signs for *ti* and *do.*

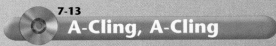

7-13
A-Cling, A-Cling

Traditional Melody from Nevis

This selection is from Nevis, an island in the West Indies.

Arts Connection

▲ Mural of musicians playing traditional Caribbean instruments (Anonymous)

Show What You Know!

1. **Identify** the note *ti* in these examples. Then **sing** each example using pitch syllables.

2. **Identify** the songs or listening selections that have these patterns. Find other songs in the book that use the new note *ti*.

Performing Together

Performing with others is a fun part of making music. Rock, pop, classical—just about any style of music can be performed by a group. Musicians use the French word **ensemble,** meaning "together," to talk about group performance. Everyone in an ensemble pays special attention to what every member of the group is doing. Everyone in an ensemble must listen to each other to perform well together.

In music, an **ensemble** is a group of musicians who perform together.

Listen to these examples of ensembles performing.

7-14
Scherzo

from *Piano Trio No. 2 in E-Flat Major, Opus 100* by Franz Schubert

In Western classical music, a piano trio is not three pianos. It is a piano, cello, and violin.

7-15
Rag puria kalyan

**Raga from North India
as performed by David Trasoff and Zakir Hussein**

This Indian classical music ensemble plays the *sarod*, a string instrument, and the *tabla* (drums).

Piano trio ▲

▼ Classical Indian musicians

Canadian Brass ▶

7-16
Canzoni prima a 5

from *Canzoni et Sonate*
by Giovanni Gabrieli
as performed by Canadian Brass

This brass piece is performed by two groups, one echoing the other. This is called antiphonal style.

7-17
That's the Way

by Greg Clark and Scott Leonard
as performed by Rockapella

This selection features close harmony and vocal percussion.

M·U·S·I·C M·A·K·E·R·S

Rockapella

Vocalists Scott Leonard (high tenor), Kevin Wright (tenor), Elliott Kerman (baritone), Barry Carl (bass), and Jeff Thacher (vocal percussion) are the group **Rockapella**. The group started out singing barbershop and doo-wop on the streetcorners of Manhattan, a borough of New York City. After some time, they began to sing contemporary music and recorded *Zombie Jamboree*. The group is best-known for recording the soundtrack to *Where in the World Is Carmen Sandiego?*

Playing Together

Here is an instrumental selection for your class to play.
Listen to all the parts and stay together.

Orfferondo

Music by Mary Shamrock

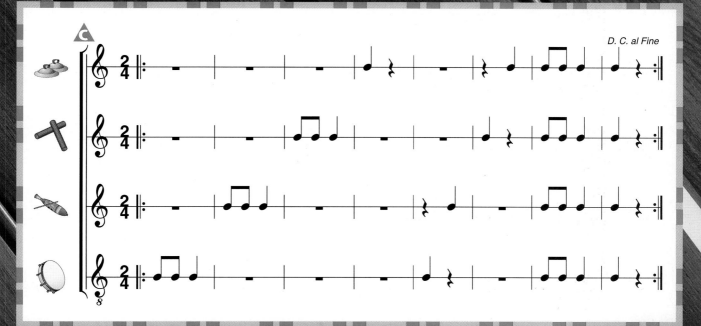

Sound of a Round

"Ah, Poor Bird" is a folk song from England. What do you think the lyrics mean?

Sing the song in unison.

A **round** is a follow-the-leader process in which all perform the same melody but start at different times.

 7-19

Ah, Poor Bird

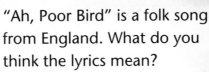

Traditional Round from England

Ah,   poor   bird,   take   your   flight.

Far   a - bove   the   sor - rows   of   this   sad   night!

Learning to Sing a Round

Let's add layers to the song. First, look at the music. **Sing** measure one as an ostinato. Do the same with measures two and three. Perform the ostinatos, together in groups.

Now that your ear is able to hear the harmony created by the ostinatos **perform** "Ah, Poor Bird" as a **round.** Each part must wait one measure before beginning.

Parts to Play

Add more layers to "Ah, Poor Bird." **Perform** this accompaniment as you **sing** the song.

Glockenspiel

Alto Xylophone

Bass Xylophone

Another Round

"*Liebe ist ein Ring*" is a round from Germany. **Sing** it in unison first. Then sing it as a round.

Love is like a ring, a ring has no ending...
Love is like a ring, a ring has no ending...
Love is like a ring, a ring has no ending...
Love is like a ring, a ring has no ending...

7-21

Liebe ist ein Ring
(Love Is Like a Ring)

Traditional Round from Germany

do

I   F   C₇   II F   C₇

Lie - be   ist   ein   Ring. _____   Ein
Love is   like   a   ring. _____   A

III F   C₇   IV F   C₇

Ring   hat _____   kein   En - - de.
ring   has _____   no   end - - ing.

ROUND AND A ROUND

Have you ever held down a key on a computer? The key keeps repeating until you move your finger. Rounds are like that, too. They don't end until a decision is made to stop.

Sing "The Computer" in unison. Then decide how many times you will **perform** it as a round.

Accompany "The Computer" on the keyboard using the chords C and G₇. **Play** the chords when they appear in the music.

THE COMPUTER

Words by Fitzhugh Dodson

Music by Mary Shamrock

A com-put-er is a think-ing ma-chine, the smart-est one you've

ev – er seen, but ev - 'ry com-put-er can on - ly do _____

what some per - son has told it to.

Describing Texture

Listen to "Orbital View" from *Mars Suite*. **Describe** the texture of this computer music.

Orbital View

from *Mars Suite*
by Michael McNabb

Mars Suite was composed for the NASA movie *Mars in 3-D*. Images from the film were sent by the Viking lander during its mission to Mars.

Computer music workstation ▼

CALLING ALL CHORDS

Believe it or not, frogs are a popular subject for song lyrics. **Sing** this song and **listen** to the accompaniment.

7-28

FROG MUSIC

Folk Song from Canada

There once was a frog who jumped in a bog, And played the bass

fid-dle in the mid-dle of a pud-dle, What a mud-dle!

"Bet-ter go 'round! Bet-ter go 'round!" _____

The Chord

Listen to the song again and raise your hand when you hear the chords change. Then point to the places in the music where the chords change.

Play these ostinatos with the song.

Glockenspiel

Alto Metallophone

Alto Xylophone

Bass Xylophone

His mu - sic was short, For soon he was caught, And now in the mid-dle

of a grid - dle he is fry - ing and is cry - ing:

"Rath - er be drown'd! Rath - er be drown'd!" _____

CHORDS IN A DIDDY

"Do Wah Diddy Diddy" has been a popular song for several decades. It has even been used in movie soundtracks. **Sing** the song and **listen** for the chord changes.

Play the Chords

Sing the lowest note of the A chord, then the D chord. Find these notes on a melody instrument. Now **play** them as an accompaniment to the song. Make sure you change notes at the right time.

Perform this accompaniment with the first eight measures of the song.

Resonator Bells

Glockenspiel

Alto Xylophone

Bass Xylophone

Putting It

What Do You Know?

1. Look at the notation for "The Computer" on page 195.

   a. What pitch is named *do* in this song?

   b. Point to all the pitches that are called *ti*. How many did you identify?

   c. Do the same activity for the pitches named *so, fa, mi, la, re,* and *do.*

2. Match each of these tempo words with the correct definition.

   a. *andante*   very fast

   b. *moderato*   slow

   c. *allegro*   moderate

   d. *adagio*   walking speed

   e. *presto*   fast

7-32

What Do You Hear? 5

Listen to these examples and point to the picture of the ensemble you hear.

▲ Classical music trio

▲ Pop group

▲ Brass quintet

Indian classical music ensemble ▶

All Together

Sing Rounds and Rhythms

Sing "*Liebe ist ein Ring*" on page 193 as a round. Create and perform steady-beat movement patterns that reflect the tempo and meter of the song.

Read and Sing *ti*

Sing "*Missy-La, Massa-La*" on page 184 from the notation using hand signs and pitch syllables. Then sing the song again using the words.

Play Chords

Practice the rhythm patterns for the accompaniment to "Do Wah Diddy Diddy" on page 198. Then sing the song and play the accompaniment on mallet instruments.

Move to Show Form

Perform a rondo speech piece by combining "Heave-Ho," "Going, Going, Gone," and "The Snow" on pages 178–179. Create a different steady-beat movement to accompany each section of the speech piece.

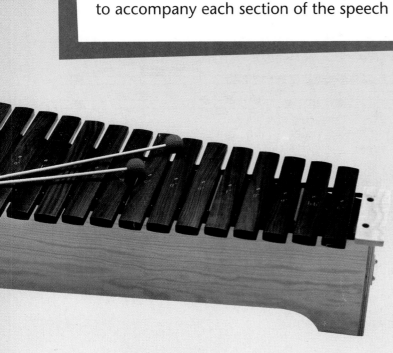

Singing Is Believing

"I Believe I Can Fly" is about believing in yourself.
As you **sing** the words, remember times when
you were able to accomplish something difficult
because you had faith in yourself.

7-36

I Believe I Can Fly

Words and Music by R. Kelly

1. I used to think that I could not go
   I was on the verge of break - ing

on, And life was noth - ing but an aw - ful
down. Some - times si - lence can seem so

song. But now I know the mean - ing of true
loud. There are mir - a - cles in life I must a -

Making Music Our Own

love. _____ I'm lean - ing on __ the ev - er - last - ing
chieve, _____ But first I know _ it starts _ in - side _ of

arms. _____ If I can see it, then I can
me. _____

do _____ it, if I just be - lieve it, _____ there's noth - ing

to it. _____ Oh, I be-lieve I can fly, I be-lieve I can

touch the sky. _ I think a-bout it ev-ery night and day, _ spread my wings and

fly a - way. _ I be-lieve I can soar, I see me run-ning through that

last time to Coda ⊕

o - pen door. _____ I be-lieve I can fly, I be-lieve I can

1.
fly, I be - lieve I can fly. _____

2.
2. See, fly, oh, I be - lieve I can

fly. _____ Hey, _____ 'cause I be - lieve _ in

R. Kelly, the composer, wasn't the only one who believed he could fly—Leonardo da Vinci did, too. In the 15th century he sketched a design for what he called a "flying machine." It resembled the helicopters of today. The first people to fly were Wilbur and Orville Wright. In 1903 their powered glider managed to stay in the air for 59 seconds.

Accent on Freedom

> An **accent** indicates to play or sing a note with more emphasis than the other notes.

A musical **accent** (>) gives special importance or stress to certain notes. Find the accents in the song "Freedom" and perform them as you sing the song.

7-38

Freedom
(from *Shenandoah*)

Words by Peter Udell

Music by Gary Geld

A VERSE

Solo F

1. Free - dom ain't a state like Maine or Vir - gin - ia,
2. Free - dom ain't a boat that's leav - in' with - out ya,
3. Free - dom is a no - tion sweep - in' the na - tion,

E♭   C

Free - dom ain't a - cross some coun - ty line.
Free - dom ain't a place ya float to find.
Free - dom is the right of all man - kind.

F

Free - dom is a flame that burns with - in ya,
Free - dom is the how ya think a - bout ya,
Free - dom is a bod - y's 'mag - i - na - tion,

E♭   >   C₇ >   F >

Free - dom's in the state of mind.

REFRAIN
Chorus

Free - dom, free - dom, Free - dom, free - dom.

1.,2.

Free - dom is a flame that burns with - in ya,
Free - dom is the how ya think a - bout ya,

Free-dom's in the state __ of mind.

3.

Free - dom is a no - tion sweep - in' the na - tion,

Free - dom is a bod - y's 'mag - i - na - tion,

Free - dom is a full - time oc - cu - pa - tion,

Free - dom's in the state __ of mind!

Arts Connection

▲ *Three Musicians* (1921) by Pablo Picasso. Many of Picasso's works feature musical subjects. *Three Musicians* is in the "cubist" style. Artists who painted in this style used geometric shapes such as circles, squares, and triangles in abstract forms.

Accents Everywhere

Accents can be found everywhere in music, poetry, art, and dance. Look at the painting by Picasso. Where do you see accents in the painting? **Identify** the instruments shown in *Three Musicians*.

Accents Make the Difference

Listen for accents in this instrumental piece. What instruments play the accents?

7-39
Thunder and Lightning Polka

by Johann Strauss

Johann Strauss lived in Austria where German is spoken. The words for thunder and lightning in German are *Donner und Blitz.*

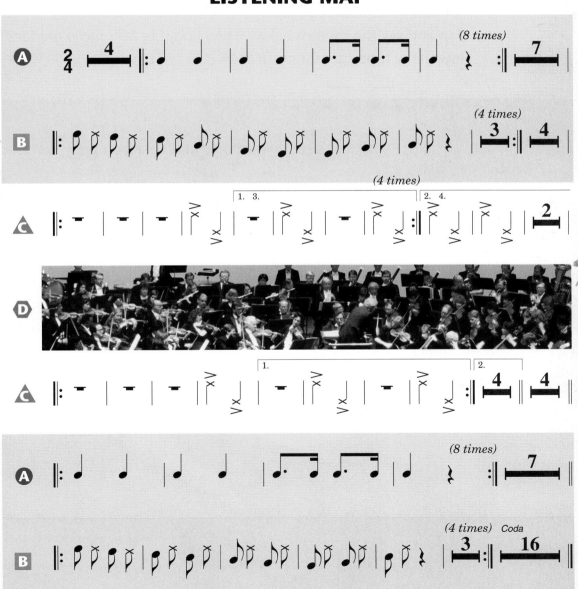

Thunder and Lightning Polka
LISTENING MAP

Rhythms on the Ranch

What is a ranch? Who lives there? What does a rancher do?
Sing "*El rancho grande*," a song about life on a ranch.

Working with Rhythm

Identify the time signature in "*El rancho grande*." How many beats are there in each measure of this song? **Move** to show the meter.

Clap and say the rhythm below. Then find it in "*El rancho grande*." How many times does it occur?

Play these rhythm ostinatos to accompany the song.

El rancho grande
(The Big Ranch)

English Words by Alice D. Firgau

Music by Silvano R. Ramos

VERSE

A - llá en el ran - cho gran - de, A - llá don - de vi -
Out yon - der on a prai - rie, The ranch where I was

ví - a, _____ Ha - bía u - na ran - che - ri - ta, Que a-
liv - ing, _____ I heard a pret - ty cow - girl, Who

le - gre me de - cí - a, Que a - le - gre me de - cí - a: _____
hap - pi - ly was sing - ing, Who hap - pi - ly was sing - ing: _____

REFRAIN

Te voy ha - cer tus cal - zo - nes,
A pair of chaps I will make you,

Co - mo los u - sa el ran - che - ro;
Just like the ones for a ranch - er;

Te los co - mien - zo de la - na,
With wool and leath - er I'll make them.

Te los a - ca - bo de cue - ro.
Oh, do please give me your an - swer.

Ringing Rhythm

"Oh, How Lovely Is the Evening" is a traditional German melody that can be sung as a round in three parts. Look at the song and **identify** where each part comes in. **Sing** the song as a round. Use a melody instrument to play the pitches of the last line as you sing.

8-2

Oh, How Lovely Is the Evening

Traditional German Melody

I
do

Oh, how love - ly is the eve - ning, is the eve - ning,

II

When the bells are sweet - ly ring - ing, sweet - ly ring - ing,

III

Ding, dong, ding, dong, ding, dong!

Rhythms in Time

- Look at the song again. **Identify** the rhythms you already know.

- Clap a steady beat and say the first two lines of "Oh, How Lovely Is the Evening" using rhythm syllables.

- How many notes are in the last line? How many measures? How many notes are in each measure?

- This song has three beats in each measure. How many beats is each note of the last line?

- Clap a steady beat and say the whole song using rhythm syllables.

Ringing and Singing

One group can **sing** the last line of the song as an ostinato, while others sing the entire song. Then sing the song as a three part round. **Create** your own instrumental accompaniment.

Skipping with Rhythms

Find the rhythms you know. Look at the first line of "Dry Bones Come Skipping." Tap and say the rhythm. **Compare** the first line to the rest of the song. What did you discover? Now **sing** "Dry Bones Come Skipping."

How many bones are in your body? Can you name any of them?

Dry Bones Come Skipping

Traditional Song from the United States

Dry bones come skip-ping up the val - ley.   Some of them bones are   mine. __

Dry bones come skip-ping up the val - ley.   Some of them bones are mine.

Some of them bones are   'Ze - kiel's   bones. _   Some of them bones are   mine. __

Some of them bones are   'Ze - kiel's   bones. _   Some of them bones are mine.

Create a *bones* composition. Use the same meter and **A** **B** **A** form as "Dry Bones Come Skipping."

A **Compose** four measures of rhythm in meter in 4. Use rhythms you know. Look at "Dry Bones Come Skipping" for ideas. Decide how you will perform your rhythm. Will you use an instrument or body percussion?

B Choose one of the poems below for the **B** section. Read the poem, then decide how you will **perform** it. Will you speak it or sing it? Will you use movements or instruments to accompany the poem? Will you perform the poem once or more than once?

A **Repeat** your **A** section rhythm!

Bones

by Jeff Moss

Bones are important,
They do a big job.
Without them, you'd be just
A big squooshy blob.

A Poem to Help You Figure Out What Bone the Patella Is

by Jeff Moss

A hairy young primate named Stella
Once yelled, "Ow, I hurt my patella!"
So her mom chimpanzee
Simply bandaged her knee
And made well a patella of Stella.

Old Bones

When plants or animals died, they sometimes were buried in layers of soil that eventually became stone. As the soil turned to stone, the plants or animal skeletons left fossils. Fossils are traces of plants' and animals' remains that have been preserved in the earth. **Listen** to *Fossils*.

8-6
Fossils

**from *Carnival of the Animals*
by Camille Saint-Saëns**

French composer Camille Saint-Saëns used xylophones to represent bones.

Say the rhythm below using rhythm syllables.
Listen for this rhythm in *Fossils*.

Snap
Clap
Pat
Stamp

MUSIC MAKERS
Camille Saint-Saëns

French composer **Camille Saint-Saëns** [san(n)-sa(hn)] (1835–1921) learned to play the piano and organ when he was young. Many of his compositions are for piano or organ with orchestra. In addition to performing and composing, Saint-Saëns was a writer. He wrote about music, history, and science.

Create a Fossil Rap

Fossils give us clues about plants and animals that lived many years ago. Much of what we know about dinosaurs comes from studying their fossilized bones.

Use "Gotta Find a Footprint" to **create** a rap in **A** **B** **A** **C** **A** **D** **A** form.

Gotta Find a Footprint

by Jeff Moss

A
Gotta find a footprint, a bone, or a tooth
To grab yourself a piece of dinosaur truth.
All the dino knowledge that we've ever known
Comes from a footprint, a tooth, or a bone.

B
A tooth can tell you what a dino would eat,
A sharp tooth tells you that he dined on meat.
A blunt tooth tells you that she dined on plants.
No teeth at all? Well, perhaps they slurped ants.

C
Footprints can tell you a dinosaur's size,
And how fast he ran when he raced with the guys.
Count all the footprints, you'll easily see
If he traveled alone or with a family.

D
Her bones will tell you if she stood up tall,
If she had a big tail or no tail at all.
Put the bones together and see how they'll look—
Pretty enough to get their picture took.

Show What You Know!

Speak "Gotta Find a Footprint" and pay attention to the rhythm of the words. Then **notate** the first two lines of the poem. Next perform the words using your notated rhythms.

Theme and Variations

A *balalaika* [bah-lah-LIE-kah] is a Russian folk instrument. Look at the pictures of the different *balalaikas*.

Listen to "*Minka*," a song from Ukraine about a soldier and the girl he left behind.

8-7

Minka

English Words by Margaret Marks

Folk Song from Ukraine

Ти ж ме - не під - ма - ну -ла,   Ти ж ме - не під - ве - ла —
1. Said the Cos-sack to the maid-en,   "Love, my heart is heav-y lad-en.
2. Off the Cos-sack went to bat - tle,   all a - lone poor Mink-a sat e -

Ти ж ме - не мо - ло - до - го,   Зу - ма ра - зу - ма зве - ла.
Du - ty calls so I'm a - fraid, en - chant - ress, we must part. _____
lev - en years and she grew fat, al - though her heart was   true. _____

218

Variety Is the Spice of Life

Sing *"Minka."* The melody of the song can be called a **theme.** Now think of a way to vary or change *"Minka."* How will you make the theme different? Will you change the dynamics, tempo, melody, rhythm, or timbre of the music? Practice your **variation,** then **perform** it for the class. Be ready to explain how you made your variation.

Theme is an important melody that occurs several times in a piece of music. **Variation** is music that is repeated, but changed in some important way.

Ти ж ме - не під - ма - ну - ла,   Ти ж ме - не під - ве - ла ___
I be-seech you fair - est Mink - a,   wait for me, I hate to think an -
When at last her Cos-sack lov - er,   came back home and looked her o - ver,

Ти ж ме - не мо - ло - до - го,   З у - ма ра - зу - ма зве - ла.
oth - er man might come and tink - er   with your faith - ful heart!" ___
he be - gan to court an - oth - er.   Broke her heart in two! ___

MIDI Use the *"Minka"* song file with sequencing software to create variations of the melody.

Matreshka dolls
(nesting dolls) ◀

Russian Variations

Tap the rhythm of Glière's theme as you **listen** to *Russian Sailors' Dance.*

8-12
Russian Sailors' Dance

from *The Red Poppy*
by Reinhold Glière

Russian composer Reinhold Glière wrote variations
on a theme in this piece.

Theme and variations is a musical form in which each section is a variation of the original theme.

Move to the rhythm of the theme using body percussion.

clap
pat
stamp

Now **listen** for the **theme and variations.**
How many variations do you hear?

Reinhold Glière

Reinhold Glière [glee-EHR]
(1875–1956) was a student and then a
composition professor at the Moscow
Conservatory. He wrote operas,
symphonies, music for ballets, and
piano music. Glière used Russian folk
melodies in his music. His operas and
ballets included stories and themes of
central Asia.

FIND THE SEQUENCE

Be a melody detective. Investigate the melody of *"Thula, thula, ngoana"* to find *fa* and *ti*. Here's a clue. The melody ends on *do*.

Listen to *"Thula, thula, ngoana,"* an African lullaby and work song. **Sing** the melody on pitch syllables. Then **sing** the words.

THULA, THULA, NGOANA
(Sleep, Sleep, Baby)

Folk Song from the Lesotho Region of South Africa

Thu - la, thu - la, ngoa - na, __ thu - la, thu - la, ngoa - na, __
Sleep my lit - tle ba - by, __ sleep my lit - tle ba - by, __

Thu - la, thu - la, ngoa - na, __ thu - la, thu - la, ngoa - na. __
Sleep my lit - tle ba - by, __ sleep my lit - tle ba - by. __

Sing and Sequence

Sing *"Thula, thula, ngoana"* again. Trace the shape of the melody as you sing. Notice the shape, or contour, of the first two measures. How many times does this contour occur in the melody?

Describe what happens to the starting note each time the pattern is repeated. The pattern you have found is a **melodic sequence.**

A **melodic sequence** is a melody pattern that begins on a different pitch each time it is repeated.

Create movements to show the melodic sequence of *"Thula, thula, ngoana."*

Show What You Know!

Here is another melodic sequence, but some of the notes are missing! The first pattern of the melodic sequence is shown. It has only three notes. The sequence continues four times. **Identify** the missing notes. Then **play** the sequence on a xylophone or keyboard instrument.

A Czech Melody

The people of the Czech Republic have a long history of folk songs and dances. Find a sequence in this melody. Look for lines that have a similar shape. Does the sequence move upward or downward? **Sing** "*Tancovačka*" and point to the sequences.

8-17

Tancovačka
(Dancing)

Folk Song from the Czech Republic

VERSE

F ... C₇

Tan - cuj, tan - cuj, vy - krú - caj, vy - krú - caj,
Come and dance, turn light - ly, turn light - ly A -

C₇ ... F

Len mi pie - cku ne - zrú - caj, ne - zrú - caj.
round the camp - fire burn - ing so bright - ly. The

F ... C₇

Do - brá pie - cka na zi - mu, na zi - mu,
snow falls fast and cold is the weath - er. Come

C₇ ... F

Keď ne - máme pe - ri - nu, pe - ri - nu.
dance, come dance, we'll all turn to - geth - er.

REFRAIN

Tra la la la, Tra la la la,

Tra la la la, Tra la la la la,

Tra la la la, Tra la la la,

Tra la la la, Tra la la la la la la la.

Practice *fa* and *ti*

Sing the first four lines of "Tancovačka" again. **Sing** the melody using pitch syllables.

Move to show the melodic contour of "Tancovačka." Use a repeated movement to go with the melodic sequence in the first four lines. Use different movements for the last four lines of the song.

KEYBOARD CLASSICS

The harpsichord is one of the oldest keyboard instruments. Harpsichords were popular in the 1600s and 1700s.

Although the harpsichord looks similar to a piano, it sounds much different. When you press a key on a harpsichord, the string inside is plucked by a quill. Originally, harpsichord quills were feathers. Today quills are made of leather or plastic.

Listen to the harpsichord in *Gigue* by Bach.

8-22
Gigue

**from *French Suite No. 5*
by Johann Sebastian Bach**

A "gigue" was a popular dance in the Baroque era (1600–1750).

Pipes Galore

Organ pipes can be small and thin, or long and thick. They are made of wood or metal. Pipe organs can have hundreds or even thousands of pipes. The different pipe shapes and sizes produce different sounds when air is blown through them.

Listen to this famous composition for organ. Notice how the timbre changes as the air moves through the different pipes of the organ.

8-23
Toccata in D Minor

by Johann Sebastian Bach

This organ selection was written in 1708. It is frequently performed today and is one of Bach's most famous works.

MUSIC MAKERS

Johann Sebastian Bach

Johann Sebastian Bach (1685–1750) was a German composer. Among the first instruments he learned to play were the violin and organ. During his lifetime, Bach became famous for his ability to improvise on the organ. He was employed by the nobility of several cities in Germany as an organist, choir director, and composer. Bach wrote church, orchestra, keyboard, vocal, and choral music.

Piano and Forte

The first pianos were called *pianoforte* because the performer could make both soft and loud sounds by touching the keys in different ways. When the player presses a piano key, a hammer inside the instrument strikes one or more strings. Striking harder makes a louder sound.

The first *pianofortes* were made around 1700. By 1825, the piano looked and sounded similar to the pianos we know today. **Listen** to these piano pieces.

8-24

Waltz in D Flat ("Minute" Waltz)

by Frederic Chopin

This waltz has the nickname "Minute" Waltz because it is played in a very fast tempo. However, it usually takes longer than one minute to play.

8-25

Prelude in A major

by Frederic Chopin
as performed by Vladimir Ashkenazy

Chopin is considered one of the greatest composers and pianists of his time.

MUSIC MAKERS

Vladimir Ashkenazy

Vladimir Ashkenazy [VLAH-dih-meer ahsh-keh-NAH-zee] (born 1937 in Gorky, Russia) is one of few musicians famous for both performing on the piano and conducting an orchestra. Ashkenazy burst onto the musical scene when he finished in second place at the Frederic Chopin International Piano Competition in Poland. From there, he went on to perform as a guest pianist with many famous orchestras. He has also been a guest conductor for the Los Angeles, Boston, San Francisco, and Cleveland symphony orchestras.

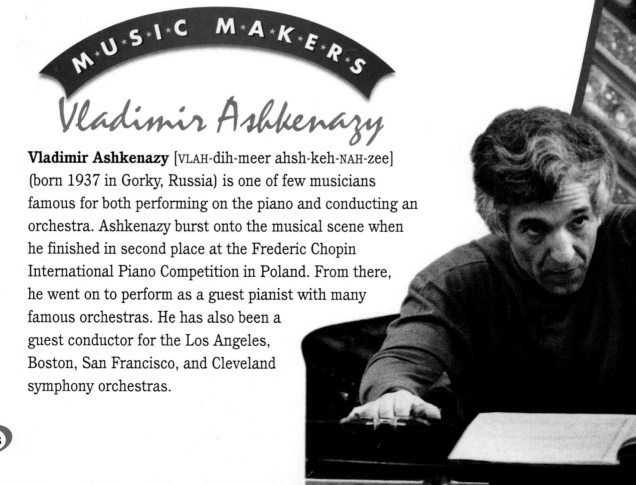

The Newest Keyboards

Electronic music was invented in the 20th century. The best-known electronic instrument is the synthesizer. It might look like a keyboard, but it can mimic the sounds of all types of instruments. **Listen** to this synthesizer version of *Close Encounters of the Third Kind*.

8-26
Close Encounters of the Third Kind

by John Williams

This music comes from the soundtrack of the movie *Close Encounters of the Third Kind*. The music features the pattern *re, mi, do,* low *do, and* low *so.*

Close Encounters of the Third Kind
LISTENING MAP

Round and Round

A melody performed alone has a thin musical texture. A melody performed with an accompaniment has a thicker musical texture.

When a melody is performed as a round, the musical texture changes from thin to thick.

Listen to "Frog Round." Point to the frog picture when the musical texture is thin or the flowers picture when it is thick. **Sing** "Frog Round."

8-27

Frog Round

Traditional Song from the United States

Hear the live - ly song of the frog in yon - der pond:

Crick!   Crick!   Crick-et - y crick!   Brrrr - ump!

Boundless Round

Here's another round! **Sing** this round in unison first. When you sing in unison, everyone is singing the same melody at the same time.

8-29

Los niños en España cantan
(In Spain the Children Sing)

English Words by S. T.

Folk Song from Mexico

I

F

Los   ni - ños   en   Es - pa - ña   can - tan,   can - tan   en   Ja - pón.
In   Spain, the   chil - dren   sing   all   day. Yes,   al - so   in   Ja - pan.

II

Los   pa - ja - ri - tos   can - tan, can - tan   to - dos   su   can - ción.
Oh,   ev - 'ry - where the   birds join   in   with   wom - an, child, and   man.

Now **sing** "*Los niños en España cantan*" as a round. Where does the second part begin?

When you sing in a round, you are singing in harmony. Which musical texture is thicker—unison or harmony?

Take the Texture Challenge!

Gather a group of friends. Choose one of the rounds—"Frog Round" or *"Los niños en España cantan."* **Sing** the song in unison.

Then sing it as a two-part round.

• Who will sing in each group?

• Which group will sing first?

• When will the second part start?

• How many times will you sing the song?

More Rounds

Silently read the words of "Let Music Surround You" as you **listen** to the song.

Sing "Let Music Surround You" in unison and in a round. Stand in a circle to let the music surround you as you sing.

Let Music Surround You

Words and Music by Fran Smartt Addicott

Let mus-ic sur-round you, let it warm your heart.

Those who sing in har-mo-ny, ne-ver __ grow a - part.

Create a motion for each phrase of the song. **Perform** the motions as you sing in unison and in a round.

A Symphony Goes Round

Now **listen** to an orchestra perform the melody below as part of a symphony.

Melody

8-35

Symphony No. 1, Movement 3

by Gustav Mahler

Mahler's music requires a very large orchestra.

Mahler changed the texture of this melody by presenting it as a round. He also added an ostinato and a countermelody. **Play** the ostinato below.

Ostinato

Listen to the countermelody. What instruments play the ostinato and countermelody?

Countermelody

Creating Textures

With a group of friends, **create** your own composition using patterns from the melodies above. Will you play in unison or a round? Will you start with ostinatos or the melody?

Harmony Moves Me

If the energy of this song doesn't get you moving, the message of the words will!

Listen to the Isley Brothers perform *Twist and Shout.* Do the "twist" as you **move** to the song.

8-36
Twist and Shout

**by Phil Medley and Bert Russell
as performed by the Isley Brothers**

This song has been recorded by many artists such as the Beatles and Ike and Tina Turner.

The Isley Brothers ▶

Play Your Own Harmony

Practice the ostinato pattern below on any melody instrument.

(8 times with verse)   *(4 times with interlude)*

Listen to *Twist and Shout* again. To add harmony, **play** the ostinato shown above. The notes of this ostinato are the lowest notes of the chords used in *Twist and Shout*.

M·U·S·I·C M·A·K·E·R·S
The Isley Brothers

The **Isley Brothers** began their career as a gospel singing group in the early 1960s. They crossed over to doo-wop and recorded hit songs like *Shout* and *Twist and Shout*. Due to frustration with record companies of the time, the Isley Brothers formed their own record label, T-Neck Records, and began recording a new sound with a young Jimi Hendrix. The Isley Brothers have since recorded with Motown and gone back to their own label. They are known for their originality and for laying the groundwork for rock, funk, and rap music.

▼ Teens dancing the twist in the 1960s

Chords Galore

Here's a hint to help you figure out what this song is all about. Just remember a keel is a kind of boat, and "weel" is a Scottish word for "well."

8-37

The Keel Row

Folk Song from Northumbria

VERSE   D(I)   G(IV)   D(I)

do

1. As I _____ came through Sand - gate, through Sand - gate, through
2. "He wears ___ a blue bon - net, blue bon - net, blue

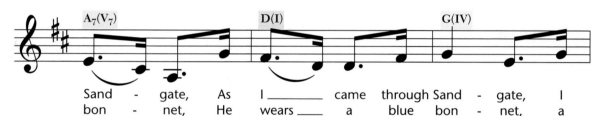

A₇(V₇)   D(I)   G(IV)

Sand - gate, As I _____ came through Sand - gate, I
bon - net, He wears ____ a blue bon - net, a

D(I)   A₇(V₇)   D(I)   REFRAIN   D(I)

heard a las - sie sing: "Oh, weel ___ may the
dim - ple in his chin."

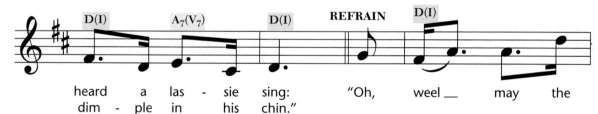

G(IV)   D(I)   A₇(V₇)

keel row, the keel row, the keel _____ row.

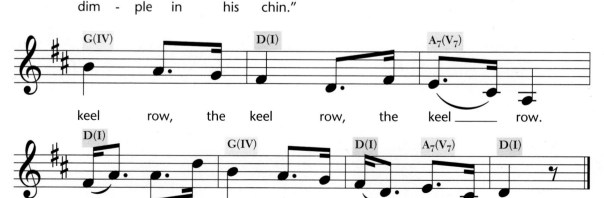

D(I)   G(IV)   D(I)   A₇(V₇)   D(I)

Weel _ may the keel row that my ___ lad - die's in."

236

> The **root** is the tone on which a chord is built.

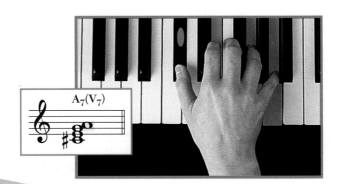

Playing Chords

Chords are created by playing three or more notes at a time. The highlighted notes in the chords are called the **root**. **Play** these chords on keyboard or Autoharp. **Sing** "The Keel Row." As you **sing,** notice the Roman numerals in the music.

Tune In

An average Scottish keel boat was about sixty feet long, ten feet wide, and four feet deep. The boats were propelled by long poles. Twelve to twenty men, including oarsmen and a pilot, were needed to push the boat up river.

SINGING IN PARTS

Gold was discovered in California in 1848. By 1849, thousands of Americans rushed to California to seek their fortunes. Some, like "Sweet Betsy from Pike," traveled in covered wagons to get there. The trip was long and hard. **Sing** "Sweet Betsy from Pike" and find out what happened on the way.

8-39

SWEET BETSY FROM PIKE

Folk Song from the United States
Adapted and Arranged by Lillian Wiedman

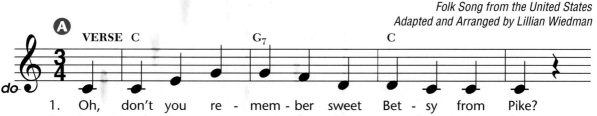

A VERSE C ... G₇ ... C

do

1. Oh, don't you re - mem - ber sweet Bet - sy from Pike?
2. One ev' - ning quite ear - ly they camped on the Platte,
3. They soon reached the de - sert where Bet - sy gave out.

C ... D₇ ... G

She crossed the wide prai - ries with her hus - band, Ike,
'Twas near by the road on a green shad - y flat.
And down on the sand she lay roll - ing a - bout.

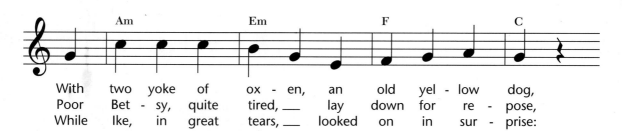

Am ... Em ... F ... C

With two yoke of ox - en, an old yel - low dog,
Poor Bet - sy, quite tired, ___ lay down for re - pose,
While Ike, in great tears, ___ looked on in sur - prise:

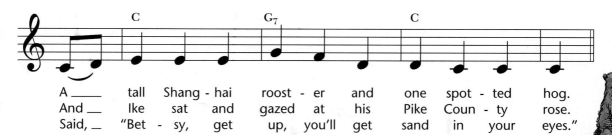

C ... G₇ ... C

A ___ tall Shang - hai roost - er and one spot - ted hog.
And ___ Ike sat and gazed at his Pike Coun - ty rose.
Said, ___ "Bet - sy, get up, you'll get sand in your eyes."

B Too - ra - lee, _____ too - ra - lay, _____

Too - ra - lee, too - ra - lay,

Sing-ing too - ra - lee, too - ra - lee, too - ra - lee ay.

4. The rooster ran off and the oxen all died,
   The last piece of bacon that morning was fried.
   Poor Ike got discouraged and Betsy got mad,
   The dog wagged his tail and looked awfully sad.   *Refrain*

5. The alkali desert was burning and hot,
   And Ike, he decided to leave on the spot:
   "My dear old Pike County, I'll go back to you."
   Said Betsy, "You'll go by yourself if you do."   *Refrain*

6. They swam the wide rivers, they crossed the tall peaks,
   They camped out on prairies for weeks and for weeks,
   Fought hunger and rattlers and big storms of dust,
   Determined to reach California or bust.   *Refrain*

Two-Part Harmony

Identify the refrain of "Sweet Betsy from Pike."
Sing the melody first, and then learn the harmony
part. **Perform** both parts together.

Putting It

What Do You Know?

Match the terms below with their definitions.

1. accent   a melody started at different times

2. theme and variations   a melody pattern repeated at a higher or lower pitch level

3. melodic sequence   stress on certain notes

4. round   a melody repeated with changes

8-41

What Do You Hear? 6

Listen to the following examples of keyboard music. Point to the name of the instrument you hear in each example.

1. piano   harpsichord   organ   synthesizer

2. piano   harpsichord   organ   synthesizer

3. piano   harpsichord   organ   synthesizer

4. piano   harpsichord   organ   synthesizer

Piano ▲   Harpsichord ▲   Organ ▲   Synthesizer ▲

All Together

Move to Variations

Listen to *Russian Sailors' Dance* on page 220 and perform the body percussion pattern. Create your own body percussion part for *Russian Sailors' Dance* and perform it for the class.

Perform with Accents

Sing "*El rancho grande*" on page 211. Decide where to add accents and perform them as you sing.

Create with Rhythms

Sing "Dry Bones Come Skipping" on page 214. Perform small steady-beat movements to accompany the **A** sections and different steady-beat movements with the **B** section. Using the rhythms in the song, create a rhythm ostinato. Perform the ostinato on nonpitched percussion as you sing the song.

Move with Sequences

Sing "*Tancovačka*" on page 224. Perform hand movements to show the contour of the melodic sequences in the verse.

Sing in Rounds

Sing "Frog Round," "*Los niños en España cantan*," and "Let Music Surround You" on pages 230–232 as rounds. Always sing with good vocal quality.

PATHS TO MAKING MUSIC

Song of the City

"Theme from New York, New York" was written for a movie *New York, New York*. Read the words to this song. Create a story about someone from a small town who really wants to live in the big city. What are some reasons a person might want to live in a big city?

9-1

Theme from New York, New York

Words by Fred Ebb

Music by John Kander

Start spread-in' the news, I'm leav-ing to-day, I wan-na be a part of it New York, New York.

NASHVILLE

GOING PLACES U.S.A.

Begin a musical trip around the United States. Start on the east coast with "Theme from New York, New York" and travel to the west coast with "California, Here I Come."

These vag-a-bond shoes are long-ing to stray,

And step a-round the heart of it New York, New York.

UNIT 7

NEW YORK CITY

I wan-na wake up in the ci-ty that does-n't sleep
to find I'm king of the hill, top of the heap.
My lit-tle town blues are melt-ing a - way.
I'll make a brand new start _ of it in old _ New York.
If I can make it there, I'd make it an - y - where,
It's up to you, New York, New York. And step a -
king of the hill, head of the list, cream of the crop at the
top of the heap, My lit - tle town

blues   are melt-ing a - way,   I'll make a

brand new start __ of it   in old __ New York.

If   I   can make   it   there   I'd make it

an - y-where   come on, come through New   York,   New   York.

Ride the Wave SING A SHANTY

We'll start our trip with whale watching in the Atlantic. Of course, on board you may have to work a little, and working on a ship can be really hard. Imagine being on board for weeks, or even years! How would you pass the time, raise your spirits, or lighten your work? You might sing a sea shanty. From about 1493 to 1928, this is what most sailors did.

Sing "Blow, Ye Winds." How do the tones in the color boxes move? Now sing "Rio Grande" on page 250 and **identify** steps, leaps, and repeated notes in the song.

Blow, Ye Winds

Folk Song from the United States

1. 'Tis ad-ver-tised in Bos-ton, New York, and Buf-fa-lo,
2. They send you to New Bed-ford, that fa-mous whal-ing port,
3. It's now we're out to sea, my boys, the wind be-gins to blow,
4. The skip-per's on the quar-ter-deck a-squint-ing at the sails,

Five hun-dred brave A-mer-i-cans, a-whal-ing for to go. ____
And give you to some land sharks ___ to board and fit you out. ____
One half the watch is sick on deck and the oth-er half be-low. ____
When up a-loft the look-out sights a school ___ of ____ whales. __

Sing-ing, "Blow, ye winds in the morn-ing, And blow, ye winds, high - O!

Clear a-way your run-ning gear, And blow, ye winds, high - O!"

5. "Now clear away the boats, my boys,
   and after him we'll trail,
   But if you get too near to him,
   he'll kick you with his tail!" *Refrain*

6. Now we've got him turned up,
   we tow him alongside;
   We over with our blubber hooks
   and rob him of his hide. *Refrain*

7. Next comes the stowing down, my boys;
   'twill take both night and day,
   And you'll all have fifty cents apiece
   when you collect your pay. *Refrain*

Rio Grande

Shanty from the United States

VERSE

Solo D ... A7 ... D

1. Oh say, were you ev - er in Ri - o Grande?
2. A jol - ly good ship and a jol - ly good crew,
3. The an - chor's a - weigh and the sails they are set,
4. Good - bye ___ to Sal - ly and Sar - ah and Sue,

Chorus D ... *Solo* G ... D

It's there that the riv - er runs
A jol - ly good mate and a
The gals that we're leav - ing we'll
To all who are list'-ning, it's

A - way ___ for Ri - o!

A7 ... D ... *Chorus* D ... A7 ... D

down gold - en sand,
jol - ly good crew, We are bound for Ri - o Grande! ___
nev - er for - get,
good - bye to you,

REFRAIN

Chorus D

And a - way ___ for Ri - o! A - way ___ for Ri - o!

Solo G ... D ... A7 ... D ... *Chorus* D ... A7 ... D

So fare ye well my bon-ny young girl, We are bound for Ri - o Grande!

Tune In

Hunting whales for oil was a main occupation of sailors. Voyages could last up to three years. Many sailors were injured or killed by a whale's tail.

Tales of the Sea

Sailors also told tales to pass the time. These tales were often about natural disasters they encountered. Many times they used their imagination to make their own tales more enjoyable. Listen to the recording of one such tale.

9-7

The Sea Wolf

by *Violet McDougal*

The fishermen say, when your catch is done
And you're sculling in with the tide,
You must take great care that the Sea Wolf's share
Is tossed to him overside.
They say that the Sea Wolf rides by day
Unseen on the crested waves,
And the sea mists rise from his cold green eyes
When he comes from his salt sea caves.
The fishermen say, when it storms at night
And the great seas bellow and roar,
That the Sea Wolf rides on the plunging tides,
And you hear his howl at the door.
And you must throw open your door at once,
And fling your catch to the waves,
Till he drags his share to his cold sea lair,
Straight down to his salt sea caves.
Then the storm will pass and the still stars shine,
In peace—so the fishermen say—
But the Sea Wolf waits by the cold Sea Gates
For the dawn of another day.

The Celtic Connection

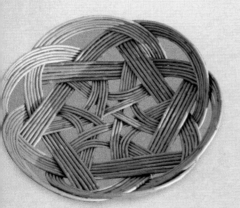

Celtic music comes from Ireland, Scotland, Wales, Brittany (France), and Galicia (Spain). When people from these areas came to the United States, they brought their music with them. "How Can I Keep from Singing?" is one of those songs.

Listen to the song. In this melody, there are two different repeated rhythmic patterns. Find these two patterns.

1.    2.

How many times do you hear pattern 1 in the first four measures? While listening to "How Can I Keep from Singing?" tap pattern 1 and snap pattern 2.

Play this accompaniment while you **sing** the song.

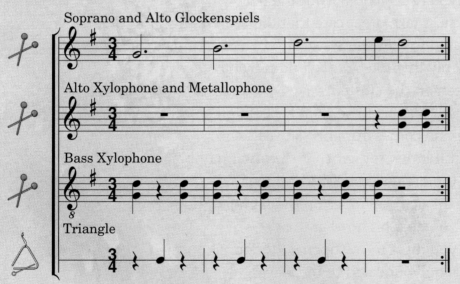

Soprano and Alto Glockenspiels

Alto Xylophone and Metallophone

Bass Xylophone

Triangle

Listen to this contemporary version of the song.

9-8
How Can I Keep from Singing?

Celtic Folk Song
as performed by Alfreda Gerald and the Taliesin Orchestra

This recording of "How Can I Keep from Singing?" features the uilleann pipes, a favorite instrument in Scotland and Ireland.

252

How Can I Keep From Singing?

Celtic Folk Song

1. My life flows on in end - less song, a - bove earth's lam - en -
2. What though the tem - pest 'round me roars, I know the truth, it
3. When ty - rants trem - ble, sick with fear, And hear their death knells

ta - tion. ___ I hear the real, though far - off song that
liv - eth. ___ What though the dark - ness 'round me close, songs
ring - ing. ___ When friends re - joice both far and near, how

hails a new cre - a - tion. ___ Through all the tu - mult
in the night it giv - eth. ___ No storm can shake my
can I keep from sing - ing? ___ In pris - on cell and

and the strife I hear that mu - sic ring - ing. ___ It
in - most calm while to that rock I'm cling - ing. ___ Since
dun - geon vile our thoughts to them are wing - ing. ___ When

sounds an ech - o ___ in my soul, how
love is lord of ___ heaven and earth, how
friends by shame are ___ un - de - filed, how

can I keep from sing - ing? ___
can I keep from sing - ing? ___
can I keep from sing - ing? ___

GET THAT PIONEER SPIRIT

The pioneer spirit has long been a source of pride for all Americans. Those who settled long ago and the most recent settlers to arrive on our shores are all pioneers. How do we keep our pioneer spirit alive? One really great way is to sing about it.

9-11

THE GLENDY BURKE

Words and Music by Stephen Foster

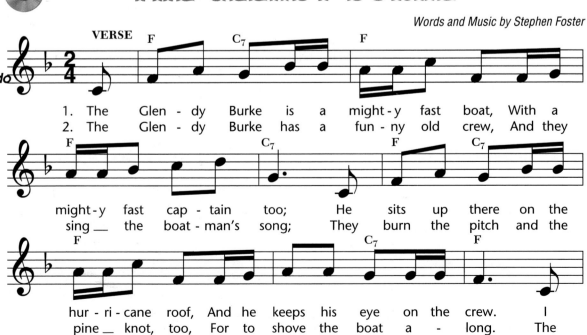

VERSE

1. The Glen-dy Burke is a might-y fast boat, With a
2. The Glen-dy Burke has a fun-ny old crew, And they

might-y fast cap-tain too; He sits up there on the
sing __ the boat-man's song; They burn the pitch and the

hur-ri-cane roof, And he keeps his eye on the crew. I
pine __ knot, too, For to shove the boat a - long. The

Preparing for Pioneer Singing

Read the following examples using rhythm syllables. Then clap the rhythm patterns.

Sing "The Glendy Burke."

can't stay here, for the work's too hard, I'm __ bound to leave this town; I'll
smoke goes up and the en - gine roars, And the wheel goes round and round; So

take my duds and tote 'em on my back, When the Glen - dy Burke comes down.
fare ye well, for I'll take a lit - tle ride, When the Glen - dy Burke comes down.

REFRAIN

Ho! for Lou' - si - an - a! I'm bound to leave this town, I'll

take my duds and tote 'em on my back, When the Glen - dy Burke comes down.

Reading Challenges

Count the *do-re-mi* and the *mi-re-do* patterns in "Oh, Susanna." Sing only the *do-re-mi* patterns and "think" the rest of the song.

Take this challenge. **Sing** all of "Oh, Susanna" with pitch syllables.

OH, SUSANNA

Words and Music by Stephen Foster

1. I ___ came from Al - a - ba - ma With my ban - jo on my knee,
2. I ___ had a dream the oth - er night, When ev - 'ry - thing was still,

I'm ___ going to Loui - si - an - a, My ___ true love for to see;
I ___ thought I saw Su - san - na A - com - ing down the hill.

It ___ rained all night the day I left, The weath - er it was dry;
The ___ buck-wheat cake was in her mouth, The tear was in her eye.

The ___ sun so hot I froze to death; Su - san - na, don't you cry.
Says ___ I, "I'm com - ing from the South, Su - san - na, don't you cry."

REFRAIN

Oh, Su - san - na, Oh, don't you cry for me, I've _ come from Al - a - ba - ma With my ban - jo on my knee.

Pioneer Dancing

Move to the song "Oh, Susanna" or "The Glendy Burke" by following these dance movements.

Verse

Refrain

▲ Girls take 8 steps in and 8 steps back while boys clap. Switch the movements.

▲ Partners link right arms and circle to the right. Link left arms and circle to the left.

Web Site To learn more about the life of Stephen Foster and his music, go to www.sbgmusic.com.

What's in a Song?

"Follow the Drinkin' Gourd" was a song with a secret message for African American slaves in the 1800s. The words *drinkin' gourd* were code for "The Big Dipper." Escaping slaves followed the stars in the constellation to find their way north to freedom. People who formed the "Underground Railroad" took big risks by providing secret hiding places along the way.

9-14

Follow the Drinkin' Gourd

Song of the Underground Railroad

REFRAIN

Fol - low _____ the drink - in' gourd. _ Fol - low _____ the

drink - in' gourd. _ For the old man is a - wait - ing for to

car - ry you to free-dom If you fol - low the drink - in' gourd.

Vocal Timbres

Listen to "Follow the Drinking Gourd."
Who is singing—men, women, children?
Do you hear a chorus or a solo voice? Is this song
accompanied? If you hear instruments, name them.
Musicians refer to differences in sound as timbre.

Choose an instrument and **play** this accompaniment
while you **sing** "Follow the Drinkin' Gourd."

Soprano and Alto Glockenspiels

Alto Xylophone

Bass Xylophone

VERSE

Em   Am

1. When the sun comes up and the first quail calls, ___ Fol - low ____ the
2. Now the river-bank will make a ____ mighty good road; ___ Dead trees ____ will

Em   G   D

drink - in' gourd. ___ For the old man is a - wait - ing for to
show you the way. ___ And the left ____ foot, peg - foot,

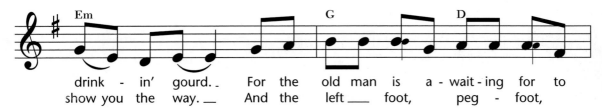

Em   Bm   Em   Bm   Em *D.C. al Fine*

car - ry you to free-dom If you fol - low the drink - in' gourd.
trav - el - in' on, ___ Just you fol - low the drink - in' gourd.

Wade in the Water

9-15

African American Spiritual

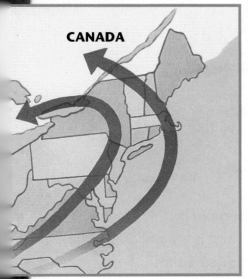

CANADA

▲ Routes of the Underground Railroad.

An Important Song— An Important Person

Harriet Tubman was born a slave around 1820 in Maryland. In 1849, she escaped to freedom in Philadelphia by way of the Underground Railroad. After experiencing freedom, she knew that she must free other slaves. Harriet Tubman made numerous trips south to lead about 300 people to freedom. It is said that she often sang "Wade in the Water" to send a message of hope to the people she helped.

9-17

Harriet Tubman

by Eloise Greenfield

Harriet Tubman didn't take no stuff
Wasn't scared of nothing neither
Didn't come in this world to be no slave
And wasn't going to stay one either.

"Farewell!" she said to her friends one night
She was mighty sad to leave 'em
But she ran away that dark, hot night
Ran looking for her freedom.

She ran to the woods and ran through the woods
With the slave catchers right behind her
And she kept on going till she got to the North
Where mean men couldn't find her.

Nineteen times she went back South
To get three hundred others
She ran for her freedom nineteen times
To save black sisters and brothers.

Harriet Tubman didn't take no stuff
Wasn't scared of nothing neither
Didn't come in this world to be no slave
And didn't stay one either.

And didn't stay one either.

Meter Matters

Here's a riddle: What has three to twelve instruments (violins, trumpets, guitars, harps), plays terrific music, and is really popular in Mexico and the southwestern part of the United States?

. . . A *mariachi* band!

Listen to *"Cielito lindo"* and "Streets of Laredo." Both songs are in meter in 3. **Identify** the tempo of each song.

9-18

Cielito lindo

English Words by Alice Firgau   *Folk Song from Mexico*

VERSE

1. De   la   sie - rra   mo - re - na,   Cie - li - to
1. From   the   dark, _____ dis - tant   moun-tain,   Cie - li - to

lin - do,   vie - nen   ba - jan - do, _____
lin - do,   I _____   see   de - scend - ing, _____

Un   par   de o - ji - tos   ne - gros,   Cie - li - to
Your   dark   eyes _____ flash - ing   bright - ly,   Cie - li - to

lin - do,   de _____   con - tra - ban - do. _____
lin - do,   love's _____ mes - sage   send - ing. _____

2. Ese lunar que tienes, *Cielito lindo,*
   Junto a la boca,
   No se lo des a nadie, Cielito lindo,
   que a mi me toca. Refrain

2. For your kisses, my lovely *Cielito lindo,*
   My heart is aching,
   And when I can't be near you, *Cielito lindo,*
   my heart is breaking. *Refrain*

Streets of Laredo

Cowboy Song from the United States

1. As I _____ walked out in the streets of La - re - do,
2. "I see by your out - fit that you are a cow - boy,"
3. "Now once in the sad - dle I used to ride hand - some,

As I walked out in La - re - do one day,
These words he said as I bold - ly walked by;
'A handsome young cow - boy' is what they would say,

I spied a young cow - boy wrapped up in white lin - en,
"Come lis - ten to me and I'll tell my sad sto - ry
I'd ride in - to town and go down to the card - house,

Wrapped up in white lin - en and cold as the clay."
I'm shot in the chest and I'm sure I will die."
But I'm shot in the chest and I'm dy - ing to - day."

4. "Go run to the spring for a cup of cold water,
To cool down my fever," the young cowboy said.
But when I returned, his poor soul had departed,
And I wept when I saw the young cowboy was dead.

5. We'll beat the drum slowly and play the fife lowly,
We'll play the dead march as we bear him along.
We'll go to the graveyard and lay the sod o'er him;
He was a young cowboy, but he had done wrong.

Creating Accompaniments for Cowboy Songs

Perform the following rhythms. Then **create** a four-measure ostinato for "Streets of Laredo" to play on temple blocks while you sing the song.

1. 2.

3. 4.

Listen to *El siquisirí*, a folk song from Mexico.
Identify the meter.

9-23
El siquisirí

**Traditional Music from Mexico
as performed by Xocoyotzin Herrera**

This recording uses the harp and various other string instruments.

MIDI Use sequencing software to open the song file for "Streets of Laredo." Play the file at fast and slow tempos.

Take a Road Trip

As we continue our journey, let's take a detour down Route 66. You may have heard of this famous highway that ran from Chicago to California. Many jazz artists have performed the song "Route 66" using their own vocal style.

HISTORIC
ROUTE
66

9-24

Route 66

Swing Style

Words and Music by Bobby Troup

If you ev - er plan to mo - tor west, ___

trav - el my ___ way, ___ take the high - way ___ that's the best. ___

Get your kicks on Route ___ Six - ty - six!

It winds from Chi - ca - go to L. A., ___

more than two thou - sand miles ___ all ___ the way. ___

Swing Rhythms

Listen to "Route 66." Are the rhythms performed exactly as they are notated?

Get your   kicks   on   Route ___   Six - ty - six! ___

Now you   go   thru Saint Loo - ey   and   Jop - lin, Mis-sour - i   and

O - kla - ho - ma   Cit - y   is   might   -   y   pret - ty;   You'll see ___

___   Am - a - ril - lo; ___   Gal-lup, New Mex - i - co; ___   Flag -

- staff, Ar - i - zo - na;   Don't ___ for - get Wi - no - na,   King-

- man,   Bar - stow,   San ___   Ber - nar - di - no. Won't you ___

Natalie and Nat "King" Cole

Known for his mellow voice, **Nat "King" Cole** (1919–1965) was also one of the most advanced jazz pianists of the 1940s. He recorded *Route 66* in 1946. It was a hit on both the rhythm and blues charts and the pop charts. His style was an important link between swing style and bebop. Nat "King" Cole grew up in Chicago and later moved to Santa Monica—the two ends of Route 66!

_____ get hip ___ to this time - ly tip, ___

When you make _ that Cal - i - for - nia trip, _

get your kicks on Route ___ Six - ty - six! ___

get your kicks on Route ___ Six - ty - six! ___

Natalie Cole (born 1950) is the daughter of the talented Nat "King" Cole. She began her career in 1975 as a soul singer. In the early 1990s she recorded an album that won seven Grammy Awards including Best Album of the Year. Although her father died when she was only fifteen, Natalie was able to perform a duet with her father. This new recording *Unforgettable*, became a great success. Besides singing, Natalie Cole likes roller coasters, comic books, and eating Ritz® crackers with peanut butter.

HISTORIC ROUTE 66

Listen to these recordings by Nat "King" Cole.

 9-26
Unforgettable

by Irving Gordon
as performed by Nat "King" Cole

In 1991, Natalie Cole based her version of *Unforgettable* on her father's original 1951 version.

 9-27
Route 66

by Bobby Troup
as performed by Nat "King" Cole

This recording is very similar to the original 1946 King Cole Trio recording.

Web Site: For additional information about Nat "King" Cole and Natalie Cole, go to *www.sbgmusic.com*.

Give Me Five

How many notes are in a scale? Eight is a correct answer, but not the only correct one. There are many different scales with various numbers of notes. The pentatonic scale has only five notes.

Sing "Pastures of Plenty."

10-1

Pastures of Plenty

Words and Music by Woody Guthrie

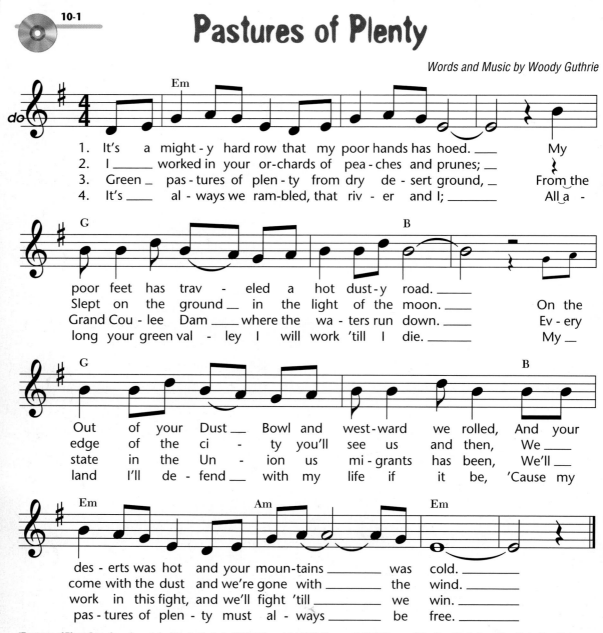

1. It's a might-y hard row that my poor hands has hoed. ___ My
2. I ___ worked in your or-chards of pea-ches and prunes; ___
3. Green ___ pas-tures of plen-ty from dry de-sert ground, ___ From the
4. It's ___ al-ways we ram-bled, that riv-er and I; ___ All a-

poor feet has trav-eled a hot dust-y road. ___
Slept on the ground ___ in the light of the moon. ___ On the
Grand Cou-lee Dam ___ where the wa-ters run down. ___ Ev-ery
long your green val-ley I will work 'till I die. ___ My ___

Out of your Dust ___ Bowl and west-ward we rolled, And your
edge of the ci-ty you'll see us and then, We ___
state in the Un-ion us mi-grants has been, We'll ___
land I'll de-fend ___ with my life if it be, 'Cause my

des-erts was hot and your moun-tains ___ was cold. ___
come with the dust and we're gone with ___ the wind. ___
work in this fight, and we'll fight 'till ___ we win. ___
pas-tures of plen-ty must al-ways ___ be free. ___

Pentatonic Pastures

Listen to Woody Guthrie's "Pastures of Plenty." This song uses the pitches *do, re, mi, so,* and *la.* The tonal center (resting place) is *la.*

Play this accompaniment as you **sing** "Pastures of Plenty."

Woody Guthrie

Woody Guthrie (1912–1967) was named after President Woodrow Wilson. At a very young age, he loved making music. By the end of his life, he had written more than 1,000 songs! Many of his songs were about his love for America and social issues of the times. "Pastures of Plenty" is about the migrant workers and the troubles they faced during the Dustbowl. Woody Guthrie was a great American folk singer, guitarist, and composer. Many people were influenced by Guthrie—Bruce Springsteen, Joan Baez, Bob Dylan, and Guthrie's son, Arlo Guthrie.

THE BEAT GOES ON...

How do you know you are alive? One good answer is that you have a pulse. Music has a pulse called the beat.

The song "I Walk in Beauty" has a very steady pulse like a heart beat. It speaks of the Navajo belief of an inner beauty called *hozho*.

Sing "I Walk in Beauty" and lightly tap the pulse on your chest.

10-3 I WALK IN BEAUTY

Words and Music by Arliene Nofchissey Williams (Navajo)

He ne - ya - na he ya he ya __ na, He ne - ya - na

he ya hi yo _____ he ya hi yo ___ he ya hi yo. I

yearn for beau - ty, yes I do, yes I do; I learn of __ beau - ty

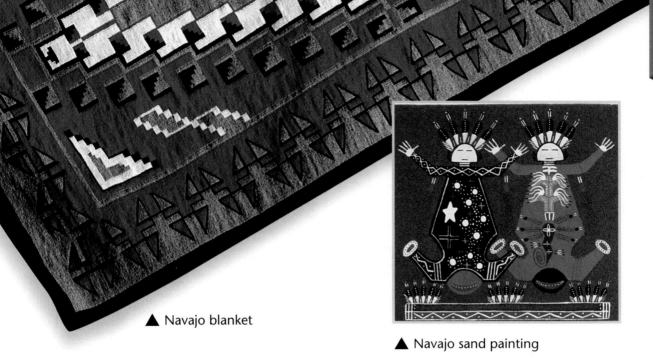

▲ Navajo blanket

▲ Navajo sand painting

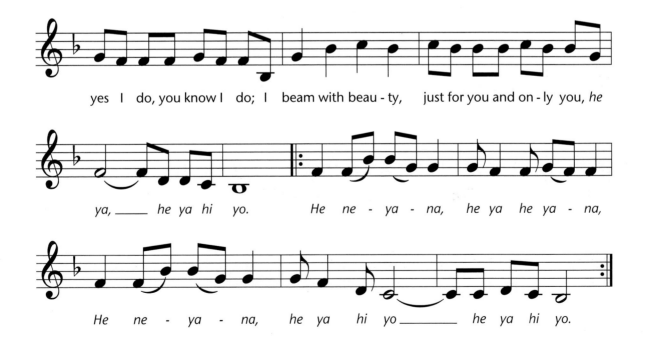

yes I do, you know I do; I beam with beau-ty, just for you and on-ly you, he

ya, _____ he ya hi yo. He ne - ya - na, he ya he ya - na,

He ne - ya - na, he ya hi yo _____ he ya hi yo.

A Changing Meter—A Steady Beat

Look at the notation for "Farewell to the Warriors" and **sing** the song. Notice that the meter changes, but the beat stays the same.

 10-5

FAREWELL TO THE WARRIORS

As sung by Mrs. Charles Mee, about 1908

Native American Song of the Chippewa

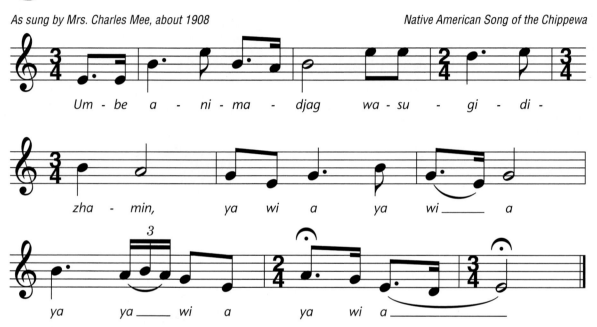

Um - be a - ni - ma - djag wa - su - gi - di -

zha - min, ya wi a ya wi _____ a

ya ya _____ wi a ya wi a _____

The People and Their Songs

The song "Farewell to the Warriors" is a Chippewa song. The Chippewas live near the Great Lakes. After the Revolutionary War, some Chippewas (more commonly called Ojibways) moved to land they were given on the Grand River in Ontario, Canada.

"I Walk in Beauty" was composed by Navajo singer/song writer Arliene Nofchissey Williams. The Navajos are from the southwest region of the United States.

Find the areas of the Chippewa and Navajo Nations on a map.

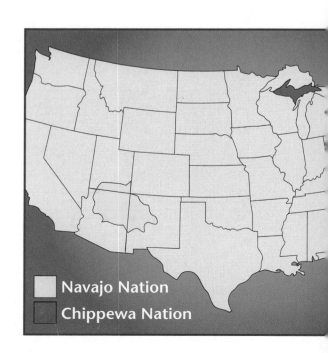

Navajo Nation

Chippewa Nation

M·U·S·I·C M·A·K·E·R·S

J. Bryan Burton

J. Bryan Burton (born 1948) is a music educator of Choctaw and European descent. His interest in Native Americans has led him to learn about many Native American singers and dancers and about their history and culture. Dr. Burton teaches at West Chester University in West Chester, Pennsylvania. He is the author of a collection of songs. His book, *Moving Within the Circle*, is about the history of various Native American people, their customs, and their music.

Listen as J. Bryan Burton talks about his work.

10-8
Interview with J. Bryan Burton

Tune In

There are many Native American instruments such as drums, rattles, and flutes. The Apache play a string instrument called *Tsii' edo a'tl* (the wood that sings). Many of the Eastern Woodland tribes, such as the Chippewa, play drums filled with water!

▲ Chippewa drum and stick

CALIFORNIA, HERE WE COME!

Ever since the Gold Rush in 1849, people have come to California. "Go West" became a common phrase among easterners seeking to make their fortunes. The song "California, Here I Come" captures the spirit of California as a land of opportunity. Al Jolson wrote the song in 1923.

Listen, then **sing** "California, Here I Come." When the same melodic phrase repeats but starts on a different pitch level, we call it a melodic sequence. How many melodic sequences do you hear?

CALIFORNIA OR BUST

MUSIC MAKERS

Al Jolson

Al Jolson (1886–1950) was an entertainer for over 40 years. He started his career dancing on street corners for coins. Eventually, he worked in a carnival, circus, vaudeville theater, on the radio, in recording studios, and in the movies. Al Jolson was known as the "World's Greatest Entertainer."

CALIFORNIA, HERE I COME

*Words and Music by Al Jolson,
Bud Desylva, and Joseph Meyer*

Cal - i - for - nia, here I come. ___

Right back where I start - ed from. ___

Where bow - ers of flow - ers bloom in the spring. ___

Each morn-ing at dawn-ing bird - ies sing and ev - 'ry - thing. A

sun - kissed miss said, "Don't be late." ___

That's why I can hard - ly wait. ___

O - pen up that Gold - en Gate. ___ Cal - i -

for - nia, here I come! ___

United We Sing

The United States is made up of people from all over the world. Many American folk songs were influenced by the musical styles of the settlers in the area. **Sing** "Cotton-Eye Joe." Then **listen** to how it is performed in another style.

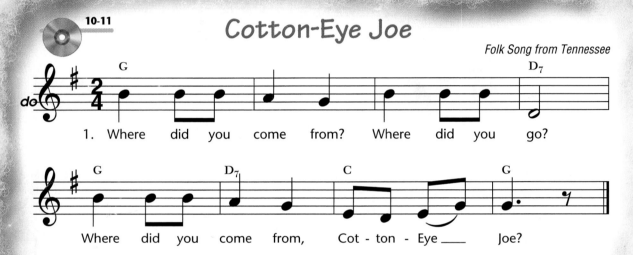

Cotton-Eye Joe

Folk Song from Tennessee

1. Where did you come from? Where did you go?
Where did you come from, Cot-ton-Eye ___ Joe?

2. I've come for to see you,
I've come for to sing,
I've come for to bring you
A song and a ring.

3. When did you leave here?
Where did you go?
When you coming back here,
Cotton-Eye Joe?

4. Left here last winter,
I've wandered through the year.
Seen people dyin',
Seen them with their fear.

5. I've been to the cities,
Buildings cracking down,
Seen the people calling,
Falling to the ground.

6. I'll come back tomorrow,
If I can find a ride,
Or I'll sail in the breezes,
Blowin' on the tide.

7. Well, when you do come back here,
Look what I have brung,
A meadow to be run in,
A song to be sung.

8. Where did you come from?
Where did you go?
Where did you come from,
Cotton-Eye Joe?

Bring Your Passport

A passport identifies you when you travel abroad. The type of music you like is your musical passport. Let's take a trip around the world and learn about people and their cultures through their music.

10-12
Cotton-Eye Joe
Folk Song from the Southern United States

Dancing to *Cotton-Eye Joe*

"Cotton-Eye Joe" is a traditional folk melody that became very popular in dances in the Southwestern United States. Do the dance movements as you **listen** to *Cotton-Eye Joe.*

1. Cross

2. Kick

Bluegrass Listening

Listen to Alison Krauss and the Union Station Band play some country bluegrass music. As you listen, ask yourself these questions: What instrument is featured? What is the meter? How would you dance to this music?

10-14
Dusty Miller

Traditional Fiddle Tune
as performed by Alison Krauss and Union Station band

M·U·S·I·C M·A·K·E·R·S

Alison Krauss

Alison Krauss (born 1971) began learning music by taking classical violin lessons. She first played in a classical style. However, at the age of eight, she decided that she liked playing the country-fiddle style more. In 1983 when she was 12 years old, she won the Illinois State Fiddle Championship. Two years later, Krauss signed her first record contract. In 1990 she received her first of five Grammy awards. Her backup band is called Union Station band and features a banjo, bass, guitar, and Dobro® (a type of acoustic guitar). In 1993 she joined the cast of the Grand Ole Opry making her the youngest cast member.

Russian Music
A Tree with Many Branches

Let's take a musical trip to Russia. Russia is located on the continent of Asia. A small part of Russia is located in Europe.

What do you think this Russian folk song is about? Can you hum the melody? Would you recognize the melody if you heard it again?

St. Basil's Cathedral ▶
in Moscow

Folk Melodies in Classical Music

Listen to *1812 Overture.* Raise your hand when you hear the melody *"Ai, Dunaiĭ moy."*

Fabergé Egg ▶

 10-15
1812 Overture

by Piotr Tchaikovsky

Tchaikovsky's [chai-KOF-skee] *1812 Overture* was written to celebrate Russia's victory over France. In some performances, real cannons are used in the orchestra!

 10-16

Ai Dunaiĭ moy
(Ah, My Merry Dunaii)

English Words by Charles Haywood

Folk Song from Russia

U vo - rot, vo - rot, vo - rot, Da u vo - rot ba -
At their __ fa - ther's gate, they stand, They're gath - ered round, a

tyush - ki - nykh. __ Ai, Du - naiĭ moy, Du - naiĭ, __ Ai, ve - syo -
hap - py __ band. __ Oh, My __ dear Du - naii, __ Oh, my mer -

liy Du - naiĭ! __ Ra - zgu - lya - li - sya re - bya - ta,
ry Du - naii! __ Mer - ry lads are loud - ly __ sing - ing,

Ras - po - te - shi - - lis. __ Ai, Du - naiĭ
Laugh - ing voices hap - pi - ly ring - ing. Oh, my __

moy, Du - naiĭ, __ Ai, ve - syo - liy Du - naiĭ! __
dear Du - naii, __ Oh, my mer - ry Du - naii! __

Russian Tribute to a Tree

The birch tree is often found in the vast forests of Russia. **Listen** to *"Beriozka,"* a tribute to the tree. As you listen, **move** to show the melodic contour.

Beriozka
(The Birch Tree)

Folk Song from Russia

10-20

1. Во по - ле бе - рё - зынь - ка сто - я - ла,
1. See the love - ly birch in the mead - ow,
2. Oh, my lit - tle tree, I need branch - es,
3. From an - oth - er branch I will make now,
4. When I play my new bal - a - lai - ka,

Во по - ле куд - ря - ва - я сто - я - ла.
Curl - y leaves all danc - ing when the wind blows.
For three sil - ver flutes I need three branch - es.
I will make a tin - gling bal - a - lai - ka.
I will think of you, my love - ly birch tree.

Лю - ли, лю - ли, сто - я - ла,
Loo - lee - loo, when the wind blows,
Loo - lee - loo, three ___ branch - es,
Loo - lee - loo, bal - a - lai - ka,
Loo - lee - loo, love - ly birch tree,

Лю - ли, лю - ли, сто - я - ла.
Loo - lee - loo, when the wind blows.
Loo - lee - loo, three ___ branch - es.
Loo - lee - loo, bal - a - lai - ka.
Loo - lee - loo, love - ly birch tree.

Piotr Ilyich Tchaikovsky

Piotr Tchaikovsky (1840–1893) was born in Russia. He started music lessons when he was five years old. During his lifetime, not everyone appreciated his music. Of course this worried him, but he continued to compose. When the famous Carnegie Hall opened in 1891, he was invited to participate in the opening ceremonies. Tchaikovsky wrote many compositions with sweeping melodies. One of his best known works is *The Nutcracker*.

10-24
Symphony No. 4, Movement 4

by Piotr Tchaikovsky
Tchaikovsky used the melody of "*Beriozka*" in this symphony.

To hear an example of a *balalaika,* refer to page 438 in the Sound Bank.

◀ One of the many things made from the birch tree in Russia is the national instrument, the *balalaika* [bah-lah-LIE-kah].

Web Site For more information about Piotr Tchaikovsky, visit *www.sbgmusic.com*.

Bring Your Passport

The Irish Harper

Welcome to Ireland, its people, and its music! One of the first instruments used in playing the music of Ireland was the harp. When you **listen** to the recording of "The Bard of Armagh," you will hear the harp and another ancient instrument. **Identify** the instrument. Why do you think these instruments were among the first created?

10-25

The Bard of Armagh

Words attributed to Thomas Campbell

Folk Tune from Ireland

1. Oh! List to the tale of a poor Ir - ish har - per,
2. At wake or at fair I would twirl my shil - le - lagh,

And scorn not the strings in his old with - er'd ___ hand;
And trip through a jig with my shoes bound with ___ straw;

But __ re - mem - ber those fin - gers could __ once move much sharp - er,
And __ all the __ pret - ty maid - ens from __ vil - lage and val - ley,

To wa - ken the ech - oes of his dear na - tive land.
Love the bold Phel - im Bra - dy, the __ bard of Ar - magh.

The Timbre of Irish Music

Listen to the instruments in these musical selections from Ireland. Remember, an instrument has its own timbre.

10-26
MacAllistrum's March-
Mairseail Alasdroim

Traditional Irish March
as performed by the Chieftains with the Belfast Harp Orchestra

This music was written to honor Alistar MacAllistrum, a Celtic [KEL-tik] hero.

10-27
Crowley's Reel

Traditional Irish Reel
James Galway plays this selection at a fast tempo.

▲ Irish harp

Bring Your Passport

M·U·S·I·C M·A·K·E·R·S
James Galway

James Galway (born 1939), one of the world's greatest flute players, is from Belfast, Ireland. Galway has played with symphony orchestras, jazz artists, and groups like the Chieftains. He enjoys playing many different styles of music from all over the world. He has many flutes. One is made of gold!

Irish Music in America

Irish melodies have found their way around the world and into the United States. Notice the similarities between "The Bard of Armagh" and "Streets of Laredo" on page 264.

Irish dance music is also quite popular. **Listen** to *Crowley's/Jackson's* and **identify** the instruments in the recording.

10-28
Crowley's/Jackson's

Traditional Irish Melody
as performed by Eileen Ivers, John Doyle, and Tommy Hayes

Eileen Ivers is a performer with Riverdance, a show that has performed on Broadway.

▲ Eileen Ivers

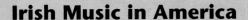

Lord of the Dance has included a variety of performers including Irish folk dancers, solo singers, a flute soloist, and a fiddle duet.

Listen and Look

Listen to *Dúlamán* and follow the form of the piece as it develops.

10-29
Dúlamán

**Traditional Irish Song
as performed by Altan**

The word *dúlamán* means seaweed.

SONG OF SOUTH AFRICA

Africa has many different peoples and countries. "*Tina singu*" is from South Africa, a country located at the southern tip of the continent. The song is often sung at sporting events. **Sing** "*Tina singu*."

10-30

TINA SINGU

Folk Song from South Africa

Introduction (first time only)
Leader

F · Bb · *Group* F · C₇ · F

Ti - na sing - u   le - lu - vu - tae - o.   Wat-sha, wat-sha, wat-sha,
We burn with the   fire __ of life, __ oh,

Leader   *Group*
F · F · Bb

Ti - na,   Ti - na sing - u   le - lu - vu - tae - o.
We burn,   we burn with the   fire ___ of life, ___ oh,

F · C₇ · 1. F · 2. F *Part 2*

Wat - sha,   wat - sha,   wat - sha,   wat - sha,   la - la - la - la - la -

1
F · Bb

Wat - sha, _____   wat - sha, _____

2

la,   la - la - la - la - la - la,   la - la - la - la - la -

290

Playing and Singing Parts

Play the steady beat on a drum. Then play the rhythm of the melody. How are they the same? How are they different? Choose one of these rhythm patterns to accompany *"Tina singu."*

 CD-ROM Use the Africa Studio in *Rock, Rap 'n Roll* to create an accompaniment for *"Tina singu."*

1   wat - sha,   wat - sha,   wat - sha. _____

2   la,   la - la - la - la - la,   la - la - la - la - la -

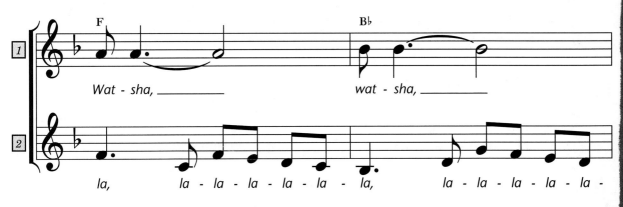

1   Wat - sha, _____   wat - sha, _____

2   la,   la - la - la - la - la - la,   la - la - la - la - la -

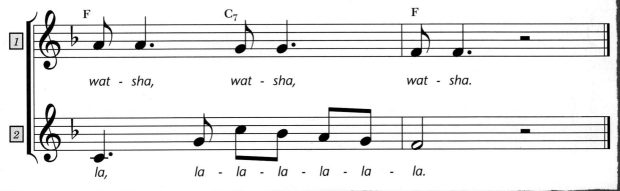

1   wat - sha,   wat - sha,   wat - sha.

2   la,   la - la - la - la - la - la.

Music Flows in Mexico

¡Olé! The people of Mexico have a rich heritage of music in their culture. In Mexico you may hear music played by *mariachi* bands as well as contemporary Latin ensembles. **Sing** "La raspa."

11-1

La raspa

English Words by Kim Williams

Folk Song from Mexico

La ras - pa yo bai - lé   al de - re - cho y al re - vés.
The ras - pa I will dance,   as for-ward and back I go.

Si quie - res tú bai - lar,   em - pie - za a mo - ver los pies.
So if you want to dance,   be - gin with your heel and toe.

Brin - ca, brin - ca, brin - ca tam-bién, mue - ve, mue - ve mu-cho los pies.
Al - ways mov - ing, mov-ing your feet,   back and forth now jump to the beat.

Que la ras - pa vas a bai - lar   al de - re - cho y al re - vés.
This is how the dance we will do,   laugh-ing, laugh-ing all the way through.

Si quie - res tú bai - lar la ras - pa co - mo yo,
So if you want to dance the ras-pa the way I do,

Me tie - nes que se - guir al de - re - cho y al re - vés.
Be - gin to move your feet, and you will be danc - ing, too.

Instrumental

La ras - pa yo bai - lé al de - re - cho y al re - vés.
The ras - pa I will dance, as for - ward and back I go.

Si quie - res tú bai - lar, em - pie - za a mo - ver los pies.
So if you want to dance, be - gin with your heel and toe.

Arts Connection

▲ *Dance in Tehuantepec* (1928) by Diego Rivera

Diego Rivera is sometimes called "the artist of the people." He painted large paintings called murals showing the lives of everyday people.

11-6

El mariachi

Traditional *Mariachi* from Mexico

Mariachi is originally a Coca Indian word meaning musician.

A Poem of the People

Read this poem. Notice how the words paint a picture. What do you think this poem means?

My Song

Toltec Poem from Ancient Mexico
Translated by Toni de Gerez

Like the feathers
of the quetzal bird
my song is beautiful
Now look!
My song is bending over the earth
My song is born
in the house of butterflies

▲ Mayan pottery with *quetzal* birds

Doing the Dance

Move to show rondo form as you **sing** "*La raspa.*"

A
▲ Do the hop step.

B
▲ Take 4 side steps, then reverse.

C
▲ Hook arms with your partner, then spin.

Cherry Blossom Time

In Japan one of the loveliest sights is the cherry blossoms in spring. For more than 1,000 years, the Japanese have been celebrating the cherry blossom ceremony! "*Sakura*" is a song about the beauty of the cherry blossoms.

11-7

Sakura

English Words by Lorene Hoyt

Folk Song from Japan
Modern Arrangement by Henry Burnett

Sa - ku - ra,   Sa - ku - ra,   Ya - yo - i   no
1. Sa - ku - ra,   Sa - ku - ra,   Cher - ry   blos - soms
2. Sa - ku - ra,   Sa - ku - ra,   Blos - soms   wav - ing

so - ra ___ wa,   Mi - wa - ta - su   ka - gi - ri,
ev - 'ry - where.   Clouds of glo - ry   fill the ___ sky,
in the ___ breeze.   Yo - shi - no,   the cher - ry ___ land,

Ka - su - mi ka   ku - mo - ka,   Ni - o - i zo   i - zu - ru;
Mist of beau - ty   in the ___ air,   Love - ly col - ors   float - ing ___ by,
Tat - su - ta,   the ma - ple ___ trees,   Ka - ra - sa - ki,   pine tree ___ grand,

i - za - ya,   i - za - ya   Mi ___ ni   yu - kan. ___
Sa - ku - ra,   Sa - ku - ra,   Let ___ all   come _ sing - ing.
Sa - ku - ra,   Sa - ku - ra,   Let ___ all   come _ sing - ing.

Blossoms in Bloom

Listen to the recording of "Sakura." The song is accompanied by a Japanese string instrument, the koto. **Describe** the dynamics, phrasing, and mood expressed by the performers on the recording. **Sing** "Sakura" with expression. **Play** the following ostinato on the drum to accompany "Sakura."

Play this countermelody for recorder to accompany "Sakura."

House of Spring

by Muso Soseki
Translated by W.S. Merwin and Soiku Shigematsu

Hundreds of open flowers
    all come from
        the one branch
Look
    all their colors
        appear in my garden
I open the clattering gate
    and in the wind
        I see
the spring sunlight
    already it has reached
        worlds without number

MIDI Play each of the first three *koto* tracks in the MIDI song file for *"Sakura."* Play the patterns on glockenspiel or keyboards.

Travel to India

India is a large country with many different geographical regions. India has jungles, forests, large rivers, lakes, oceans, grasslands, and part of the highest mountain range in the world—The Himalayas!

Listen to the Hindu chant *"Shri Ram, jai Ram."* The instrument you hear is called the *sitar*. This Indian instrument has a long neck and metal strings.

"Shri Ram, jai Ram" is sung by a leader and a group. When you think you know the melody, **sing** along with the group.

To hear another example of the *sitar,* turn to the Sound Bank on page 442.

M·U·S·I·C M·A·K·E·R·S

Anoushka Shankar

Anoushka Shankar (born 1981) is one of the world's recognized sitar players. Like her father, Ravi, she is a master of improvisation and an excellent performer. She studied with her father and made her professional debut at age thirteen.

Shri Ram, jai Ram

Hindu Chant

Leader   Group

Shri Ram,   jai Ram, jai   jai   Ram,   Shri Ram,   jai Ram, jai   jai   Ram,

Leader   Group

Shri Ram,   jai Ram, jai   jai   Ram,   Shri Ram,   jai Ram, jai   jai   Ram,

Leader   Group   1.

Shri Ram,   jai Ram, jai   jai   Ram, __   Shri Ram,   jai Ram, jai   jai   Ram __

2.   Leader

jai   Ram,   jai   jai   Ram, __   Shri   Ram,   jai   Ram,   jai   jai   Ram,

Group   All

Shri Ram,   jai Ram, jai   jai Ram.   Shan - ti,   Shan - ti,   Shan - ti.

Listen to *Charukeshi* and **identify** the sound of the *sitar* and the *tabla*. **Describe** their timbre.

Charukeshi

**Raga from India
as performed by Anoushka Shankar**

Shankar plays the traditional music of India.

Web Site For more about Ravi and Anoushka Shankar, visit *www.sbgmusic.com.*

Bring Your Passport

Play a Chinese Treasure

China is a huge country with the largest population in the world.

"*Feng yang hua gu*" is a Chinese folk song about vendors selling their wares. Name some of the things being sold in this song.

Sing "*Feng yang hua gu*," then **play** these parts to accompany the song.

Feng yang hwa gu

(Feng Yang Song)

Folk Song from China

VERSE

Zuo __ shou __ luo,   *you __ shou __ gu,*   *Shou na zhe*
1. Sing the *Feng Yang* Song;   Sing it loud and long.   Clash cym - bals,
2. Gifts for you have I,   Kites that swoop and fly;   Small trin - kets,

luo __ gu lai __ chang __ ge!   *Bie di _____ ge er ___*
beat the drum,   Strike the met - al gong!   We are the ven - dors who
man - y toys,   All of you may buy.   Pa - per of gold shin - ing,

wo ye bu hui chang,   *Zhi hui __ chang _ ge Feng _ Yang _ ge.*
trav - el all day long,   Call-ing our wares _ to the *Feng _ Yang _* Song.
Bam-boo smooth and strong,   Call-ing the clear, _ ringing toy - man's _ song.

REFRAIN

Feng la, ___ feng __ yang __ ge ___ er ___ lai,
Feng yang, feng yang, beat the gong, _ strike the clap - pers well.

Der lang dang piao yi piao,   *Der lang dang piao yi piao,*   *Der piao*
Clash cym - bals, *byah yah yang,*   Clash cym - bals, *byah yah yang!*   *Brrr dong!*

der piao!   *Der piao der piao piao ye der piao piao piao yi piao!*
Brrr dong!   *Brrr dong yah* feng yang, feng yang, *Brrr,* ___ beat the drum!

Chinese Timbres

"*Xiao*" is another Chinese folk melody.
What is this song about?

Sing *"Xiao"* and **listen** to the timbre of the
featured instruments.

11-17

Xiao (Bamboo Flute)

Folk Song from China

Yi   geng   zi ____ zhu   zhi ____ miao ____ miao;
From   the   pur - ple,   straight _ bam - boo;

Sung   yu   bao   bao   zuo   guan   xiao. _____
I   have   made   a   flute   for   you. _____

Xiao   er   dui   zheng   kou   Kou   er   dui   zheng   xiao;
Take   the   bam - boo   flute, Put   it   to   your   lips,

Xiao   zhong   chui ____ chu   shi ____ xin ____ diao;
Play   a   new ____ and   lilt - ing ____ song.

Xiao   bao __ bao   Yi   di   yi   di   xue   hui   liao, _____
My   lit - tle one, Play a   new and lilt - ing   song, _____

Xiao   bao __ bao   Yi   di   yi   di   xue   hui   liao. _____
My   lit - tle one, Play a   new and   lilt - ing   song. _____

▲ Since 1984, Music From China has been sharing both old and new music with American audiences. The performers in the group play instruments invented hundreds to thousands of years ago.

Pipa ▶

▼ *Erhu*

Sheng ▶

Listen to this musical picture of a bird.

11-21
Birds in the Forest

by Yi Jianquan

This selection features Chinese instruments. The sound of the bird is played on the *gao-hu,* a relative of the *erhu.*

Video Library See the video *From Mao to Mozart* for more information on Chinese music.

Israeli Song and Dance

Israel has become one of the most prosperous and modern countries in the Middle East.

"*Yibane amenu*" is an Israeli song sung as a round. **Sing** the song and follow the **repeat signs**.

> The **repeat signs** ‖: and :‖ tell the performer to perform all the music between the signs twice.

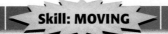

11-22

Yibane amenu

Round from Israel

I — Dm

Yi - ba - ne a - me - nu b - 'ar - tse - nu;
In   our   land   we   shall   re - build   our   na - tion.

II

B - 'ar - tse - nu,   yi - ba - ne,
Build   our   na - tion   in   our   land,

III

Yi - ba - ne,   Yi - ba - ne.
In   our   land,   In   our   land.

Yi - ba - ne.
In   our   land.

Accompaniment Parts

Choose a rhythm instrument and **play** this part to accompany
"*Yibane amenu.*"

Create your own melodic ostinato using these notes:

11-26

Ve' David y'fey enayiam

by M. Shelem

Ve' David y'fey enayiam is one of the oldest and most
popular Israeli dances.

Move to the Steady Beat

This Israeli dance includes steps which
give everyone a chance to dance with a
different partner.

A Flight to the Caribbean

Caribbean is the name given to a large collection of islands located off the coasts of Central and South America.

Listen to the recording "Wings of a Dove," a Caribbean song from the West Indies. The melody pattern in the color boxes below is called a melodic sequence.

11-28

Wings of a Dove

Folk Song from the West Indies

If I had the wings of a dove, If I had the wings of a

dove, I would fly, fly a - way,

Fly _____ a - way _____ and be _____ at rest.

Since I have no wings, Since I have no wings, Since I have no wings, how can I

fly? _____ Since I have no wings, Since I have no wings,

Since I have no wings, I'm gon - na sing, sing, sing, sing.

D.C. al Fine

Play the Caribbean Way

Play the part below on cowbell, drum, claves, or maracas.

Listen to this music from Dominica.

11-30

Mwen boyko samba

Traditional *Samba* from Dominica

This selection is played on steel drums. Like Trinidad and other Caribbean countries, Dominica has a strong tradition of steel drumming.

Revisiting a Dream

"When I was a little boy, I had the same dream over and over again. I would push my tongue against the roof of my mouth, close my eyes, and before I knew it, I'd be floating around in the clouds. I got older and grown up. No matter how hard I pushed my tongue, I couldn't get back to that cloud place. Maybe when I get to be a real old man, I'll have that dream again, because someone told me that real old people and real young people often have the same dreams. I hope so!"

Tomie dePaola, children's book author

Chasing a Dream

Hopes and dreams are very important. As you sing the songs in this unit, think of your hopes and dreams.

Sharing a Song

Some people dream about living in communities where people care for and help each other. Other people dream about their goals and ambitions. **Sing** "Love Can Build a Bridge." Imagine what we could do by sharing and working together.

11-31

Love Can Build a Bridge

Words and Music by Paul Overstreet, Naomi Judd, and John Jarvis

VERSE *mp*

1. I'd glad-ly walk a-cross the des-ert with no shoes up-on my feet to whis-per love so loud-ly, ev-'ry heart would un-der-stand that

share with you the last bite of bread I had to eat. I would
love and on-ly love can join the tribes of man. I would

swim out to save you in your sea of bro-ken dreams. When
give my heart de-si-res so that you might see. The

all your hopes are sink-ing, let me show you what love means.
first step is to re-a-lize that it all be-gins with you and me.

REFRAIN *mf*

Love can build a bridge be-tween your heart and mine.

To Coda ⊕ last time

love can build a bridge, don't you think it's time? Don't you think it's time?

1.
2.

7

2. I would

When we stand to-geth-er, ___ it's our fin-est hour. ___ We can do ___

an-y-thing, ___ an-y-thing, ___ keep be-liev-in' in the pow-er.

Don't you think ___ it's time? Love and on-ly

love, love and on-ly love.

Moving to the Sounds of a Dream

Find the refrain of "Love Can Build a Bridge." Look for repeated words and music. **Create** your own movements to show the meaning of the lyrics of the refrain. **Move** each time the refrain occurs.

Sing FOR FREEDOM

In the 1960s, "We Shall Overcome" was sung by people seeking civil rights in the United States. **Perform** the last two lines of the song using rhythm syllables. Then **sing** this famous freedom song.

11-33

WE SHALL OVERCOME

New Words and Arrangement by
Zilphia Horton, Frank Hamilton, Guy Carawan, and Pete Seeger

Freedom Song from the United States

1. We shall o - ver - come, _____ We shall o - ver - come, _____
2. We'll walk hand in hand, _____ We'll walk hand in hand, _____
3. We are not a - fraid, _____ We are not a - fraid, _____

We shall o - ver - come some - day; _____
We'll walk hand in hand some - day; _____
We are not a - fraid to - day; _____

Oh, _____ deep in my heart I do be - lieve,

(last time)

We shall o - ver - come some day. _____

4. We shall broth-ers be, . . .   5. Truth shall make us free, . . .

What Kind of Land?

For most people, freedom means independence, equality, and justice. **Listen** to *What Kind of Land?*, a song which questions the founding of the United States as a free nation while it held some of its people in slavery.

"What kind of land is this gon' be?

Freedom built on slavery.

How will it stand in time?"

11-35
What Kind of Land?

by Bernice Johnson Reagon

Bernice Johnson Reagon and her daughter Toshi performed *What Kind of Land?* for the PBS television documentary *Africans in America*.

▼ Bernice Johnson Reagon

Chasing a Dream

CIVIL RIGHTS
PLUS

Element: RHYTHM   **Skill: LISTENING**   **Connection: STYLE**

Hope Keeps Dreams Alive

Sometimes it takes work and patience to make a dream come true. Hope keeps us focused on our dreams. **Listen** to "Love Will Guide Us," a song of hope.

◄ These workers are building homes with Habitat for Humanity.

12-1

Love Will Guide Us

Words by Sally Rogers

Traditional Melody

Refrain Love will ____ guide us, peace ____ has
1.   If you ____ can - not sing ____ like

tried _____ us. Hope in - side ____
an - gels, If you ____ can -

us _____ will lead the way, On the ____
not _____ speak be - fore thou - sands, You can ____

Time Signature Review

Identify the time signature at the beginning of "Love Will Guide Us." How many beats are in each measure? Tap the steady beat as you **listen** and **sing** along. **Create** a movement that shows the number of beats in each measure.

Sally Rogers, a folk musician, performs traditional children's songs. She lives in Connecticut and performs throughout the United States. She has sung on radio shows such as *A Prairie Home Companion*. Rogers plays banjo, guitar, and dulcimer. She says, "When we sing together, we can't help but know we are not alone in both our work and our play."

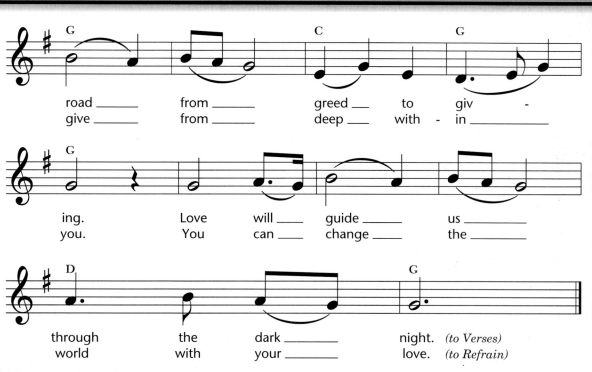

road _____ from _____ greed ___ to giv -
give _____ from _____ deep ___ with - in _____

ing. Love will ____ guide _____ us _____
you. You can ____ change ____ the _____

through the dark _____ night. *(to Verses)*
world with your _____ love. *(to Refrain)*

2. You are like no other being.
   What you can give, no other can give,
   To the future of our precious children.
   To the future of the world where we live.
   (to Refrain)

3. Hear the song of peace within you.
   Heed the song of peace in your heart.
   Spring's new beginning shall lead to the harvest.
   Love will guide us on our way.
   (to Refrain)

▲ This is Martin Luther King, Jr. (1965) speaking to a crowd at the Lincoln Memorial in Washington, D.C.

Dreams of Better Days

Listen to *Better Days* and **sing** along with the refrain.

12-3

Better Days

by Regie Hamm
as performed by Point of Grace

Refrain

Better days are on the way, my friend,
Just a ways on down the line.
I believe that just around the bend everything's gonna be fine.

Better days are just a dream right now;
It's like all you do is pray.
But the world keeps turning, bringing us better days.

Comparing Styles

Compare the sounds and styles of "Love Will Guide Us" and *Better Days*. Which is performed in a folk style? Which is performed in a popular style? How do you know?

Moving and Playing

Move to the beat of *Better Days*. **Improvise** your own movements. Then think of a movement pattern that shows the meter. Is the meter in 2, 3, or 4?

Play these ostinatos with *Better Days*.

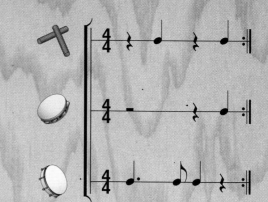

M·U·S·I·C M·A·K·E·R·S

Point of Grace

Denise Jones, Shelley Breen, Heather Floyd, and **Terry Jones** are the group **Point of Grace.** They began performing together in 1991 when they were college students. In 1994 they won the New Artist of the Year award given by the Gospel Music Association. Their album *The Whole Truth* was on the Billboard hit charts for thirteen straight weeks.

Chasing a Dream

A HOPEFUL REFRAIN

During the Great Depression in the 1930s, many people lost their jobs. Some people became hoboes, traveling from place to place in railroad cars looking for work. "Big Rock Candy Mountain" is a famous hobo song— a song of hope for better times.

12-4

BIG ROCK CANDY MOUNTAIN

Traditional

VERSE

1. In the Big Rock Can-dy Moun-tain, There's a land that's fair and bright,
2. In the Big Rock Can-dy Moun-tain, Where the ho-bo nev-er begs,

Where the hand-outs grow on bush-es, And you sleep out ev-'ry night;
And the bull-dogs all are tooth-less, And the hens lay soft-boiled eggs;

Where the box-cars all are emp-ty, And the sun shines ev-'ry day,
All the trees are full of ap-ples, And the barns are full of hay,

Oh, I'm bound to go where there is-n't an-y snow, Where the rain does-n't fall,
There's a lake of stew and ___ so-da pop, _ too, You can paddle all a-round

Rock Candy Rhythms

"Big Rock Candy Mountain" has two sections—a verse and a refrain. Find measures with exactly the same rhythm in both verse and refrain. As you **sing** the song, **move** in one way during the verse and in a different way during the refrain.

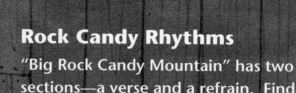

Did you know that there is a place called Rock Candy Mountain in Utah, near the town of Marysvale?

and the wind does-n't blow, In the Big Rock Can - dy Moun - tain.
in a big ca - noe, In the Big Rock Can - dy Moun - tain.

REFRAIN

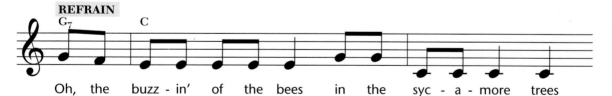

Oh, the buzz - in' of the bees in the syc - a - more trees

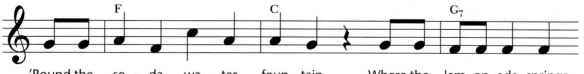

'Round the so - da wa - ter foun - tain, Where the lem - on - ade springs

and the blue - bird sings in the Big Rock Can - dy Moun - tain.

Home Is Where the Heart Is

Pete Seeger, one of America's favorite folk singers, lived in the Hudson River Valley as a child. "Sailing Down My Golden River" is a song about the river, his home, and family.

12-6

Sailing Down My Golden River

Words and Music by Pete Seeger

1. Sail - ing down   my   gol - den   riv - er, _____
2. Sun   and   wa - ter,   old   life   giv - ers, _____
3. Sun - light glanc - ing   on   the   wa - ter, _____
4. Life   to   raise   my   sons   and   daugh - ters, ___

Sun   and   wa - ter _____   all   my   own,
I'll   have them where __   'ere   I   roam,
Life   and   death   are _____   all   my   own,
Gold - en   spar - kles _____   in   the   foam,

And   I   was   nev - er   a - lone.
And   I   was   not   far   from   home.
And   I   was   nev - er   a - lone.
And   I   was   not   far   from   home.

Dreaming About Home

People share their dreams of home in many ways. Musicians write songs, dancers move, and poets write. Think about what makes your home special. Write a poem or story, **compose** a song, or create a dance that tells something about your home.

Playing Melodic Instruments

Identify the notes below by letter name. Then **play** the parts on recorder or mallet instruments. Do the parts move by step, skip, or repeat?

Pete Seeger and other members of the Seeger family have collected and recorded American folk songs. **Listen** to this example.

12-8

She'll Be Coming 'Round the Mountain When She Comes

American Folk Song
as performed by Peggy and Mike Seeger

This selection features banjo and guitar.

Pathway to the Stars

The words of "*Niu lang zhi nü*" come from a Chinese legend. In the legend, a cowherd and a weaving maid are represented by two stars in the sky—Altair and Vega. On July 7th of each year, the Milky Way stretches between the two stars. This is the only day of the year the cowherd and the weaving maid can meet. The rest of the year, they can only dream of each other.

Singing Stars

Vega, the weaving maid in the Chinese legend, is a very bright star in the constellation Lyra. Altair, the cowherd in the Chinese legend, is a star in the constellation Aquila.

Sing this folk song from China, *"Niu lang zhi nü."*
Listen to the timbres of Chinese instruments in the recording.

Niu lang zhi nü
(The Cowherd and the Weaving Maid)

English Words by Mary Shamrock   *Folk Song from China*

1. *Tiau ____ tiau ____ chien niu hsing, jiau ____ jiau ____*
1. High a - bove, the cow - herd star, weav - ing maid, so

hě han nü hsien ____ hsien ien su shou
bright, so far. Grace - ful hands, soft and white,

zha zha nong ji zhu ing ing
weav - ing through each night. Shin - ing

i hsuei jien mu - o mu - o bu de ü
far a - part, weep - ing with a si - lent heart.

2. *Zhong zhru bu cheng zhang,*
   chi ti lei zhru ü
   ne han ching chie chien
   hsiang chü fu ji hsü
   ing ing i hsuei jien
   muo muo bu de ü

2. They must wait throughout the day
   for the moon to light the way.
   Each alone, through the years
   freely flow the tears.
   Shining far apart,
   weeping with a silent heart.

Guiding Stars

Read aloud these Chinese poems about home, family, and friends. Think of ways to **move** as the poem is read. **Create** an instrumental accompaniment to show the meaning and feeling of the poem.

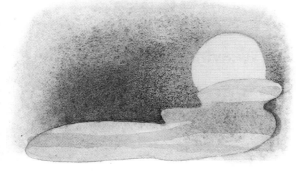

Quiet Night

by Li Bai

A moonbeam on my bed
Or frost on the ground?
I look up at the full moon,
I look down and think of home.

NEWS OF HOME

by Wang Wei

You've just come from my old hometown.
You must have some news of home.
The day you left, was the plum tree
By my window in bloom yet?

Traveler's Song

by Meng Jai

My loving mother, thread in hand,
Mended the coat I have on now.
Stitch by stitch, just before I left home,
Thinking that I might be gone a long time.
How can a blade of young grass
Ever repay the warmth of spring sun?

Music from China

As you follow the listening map below, **listen** for the timbre of the *sheng*.

12-12 Bumper Harvest Celebration

as performed by the Shanghai National Music Orchestra

This recording features the *sheng*, a native instrument of China.

Lost and Found

As settlers moved across the American frontier, they often sang songs about people and places they left behind. **Sing** "My Bonnie Lies Over the Ocean."

How many ties can you find in this song? Which phrases have exactly the same rhythm?

 12-13

My Bonnie Lies Over the Ocean

Folk Song from the United States

VERSE

1. My Bon - nie lies o - ver the o - cean, _____
2. Last night as I lay on my pil - low, _____
3. Oh, blow ye winds o - ver the o - cean, _____
4. The winds have blown o - ver the o - cean, _____

My Bon - nie lies o - ver the sea; _____
Last night as I lay on my bed; _____
Oh, blow ye winds o - ver the sea; _____
The winds have blown o - ver the sea; _____

My Bon - nie lies o - ver the o - cean, _____
Last night as I lay on my pil - low, _____
Oh, blow ye winds o - ver the o - cean, _____
The winds have blown o - ver the o - cean, _____

Oh, bring back my Bon - nie to me. _____
I dreamt that my Bon - nie was dead. _____
And bring back my Bon - nie to me. _____
And brought back my Bon - nie to me. _____

REFRAIN

Bring back, bring back,

bring back my Bon - nie to me, to me;

Bring back, bring back, oh,

bring back my Bon - nie to me. _____

Almost the Same Song

A parody is a comical imitation of a song or story. Here is a parody of "My Bonnie Lies Over the Ocean." The words are different, but the melody is the same. **Sing** this parody. Then write your own.

Cowboy's Dream

Anonymous Parody

Last night as I lay on the prairie,
And looked at the stars in the sky,
I wondered if ever a cowboy,
Could drift to that sweet by and by.

Roll on, roll on,
Roll on, little dogies, roll on, roll on.
Roll on, roll on,
Roll on, little dogies, roll on.

The Original Forty-Niners

Gold was discovered in California in 1848. By 1849, thousands of people traveled to this state, dreaming of gold. They were called "forty-niners."

The trip to California was hard and took a long time. The forty-niners had to cross the prairie in wagons. Others sailed from the east coast of the United States around the tip of South America to reach California. They were willing to do all of this to find gold!

Play an accompaniment for "Clementine" using an autoharp. Find the G and D_7 chords, then strum as you **sing.** Do the verse and refrain have the same chord pattern?

Songs About Life

The forty-niners made up songs about their experiences. Their songs were about the hard work of mining, living in California, or just plain fun. **Sing** "Clementine," a fun song about the gold rush years.

12-17

Clementine

Folk Song from the United States

1. In a cav - ern   by a can - yon, Ex - ca - vat - ing   for a mine,
2. Light she was and   like a feath - er, And her shoes were num - ber nine,

Dwelt a min - er,   for - ty - nin - er, And his daugh - ter, Clem - en - tine.
Her - ring box - es   with - out top - ses, San - dals were   for Clem - en - tine.

Oh, my dar - lin', oh, my dar - lin', Oh, my dar - lin' Clem - en - tine,

You are lost   and gone for - ev - er, Dread - ful sor - ry, Clem - en - tine.

3. Drove she ducklings to the water
   Every morning just at nine;
   Struck her foot against a splinter,
   Fell into the foaming brine. *Refrain*

4. Rosy lips above the water
   Blowing bubbles mighty fine;
   But, alas! I was no swimmer,
   So I lost my Clementine. *Refrain*

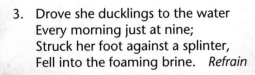

The miners seeking their fortunes were called prospectors. When a large deposit of gold was found, it was called the mother lode.

Back at the Ranch

Some of the forty-niners found gold in the California hills, while some never reached California at all. Eventually, many became farmers, lumberjacks, or ranchers. Having a successful ranch became a new dream. **Listen** to *Saturday Night Waltz* and follow the map of the melody.

12-19
Saturday Night Waltz

from *Rodeo*
by Aaron Copland

In 1942, Aaron Copland wrote music for a ballet called *Rodeo*. The ballet is about life on a ranch. It includes a Saturday night dance scene.

SATURDAY NIGHT WALTZ
LISTENING MAP

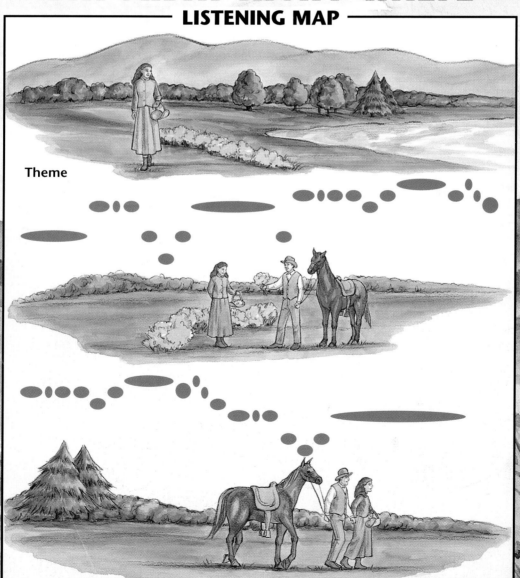

Theme

Aaron Copland

American composer **Aaron Copland** (1900–1990) wrote some of the best-loved and most familiar orchestra music of the 20th century. He developed a distinctly American style by using jazz rhythms and folk melodies in his orchestral music. He wrote two ballets about the American West—*Billy the Kid* and *Rodeo*. He also wrote music based on the poems of Emily Dickinson and a composition about Abraham Lincoln called *Lincoln Portrait*.

Dance with Partners

Learn to do a square dance, one of the kinds of dances done at a hoedown. Choose your partner and get ready to **move**!

12-20
Forked Deer/Fisher's Hornpipe

**Traditional Tune
as performed by Karen Mueller**

This recording features Autoharp, fiddle, and bass—traditional hoedown instruments.

Chasing a Dream

An Appleseed Song

Johnny Appleseed had a dream about a world filled with apple trees, where people would never be hungry. He walked hundreds of miles to make his dream come true. **Sing** this song about Johnny Appleseed.

Johnny Appleseed

From Rosemary and Stephen Vincent Benét

*From an American Folk Hymn
in the Virginia Sacred Musical Repository*

1. Of Jon - a - than Chap - man two things are known, That
2. For fif - ty years o - ver of har - vest and dew, He
3. Con - sid - er, con - sid - er, and think well up - on, The

he ___ loved ___ ap - ples, that he walked a - lone. At
plant - ed his ap - ples where no ap - ples grew. The
mar - vel - ous sto - ry of Ap - ple - seed John. He

sev - en - ty - odd ___ he was gnarled as could be, But ___
winds ___ of the prai - rie might blow through his rags, But he
has ___ no ___ stat - ue, he has no ___ tomb, But he

rud - dy and sound as a good ap - ple tree.
car - ried his seeds in the best deer - skin bags. John - ny
has his ___ apple trees ___ still in ___ bloom.

Ap - ple - seed! John - ny Ap - ple - seed!

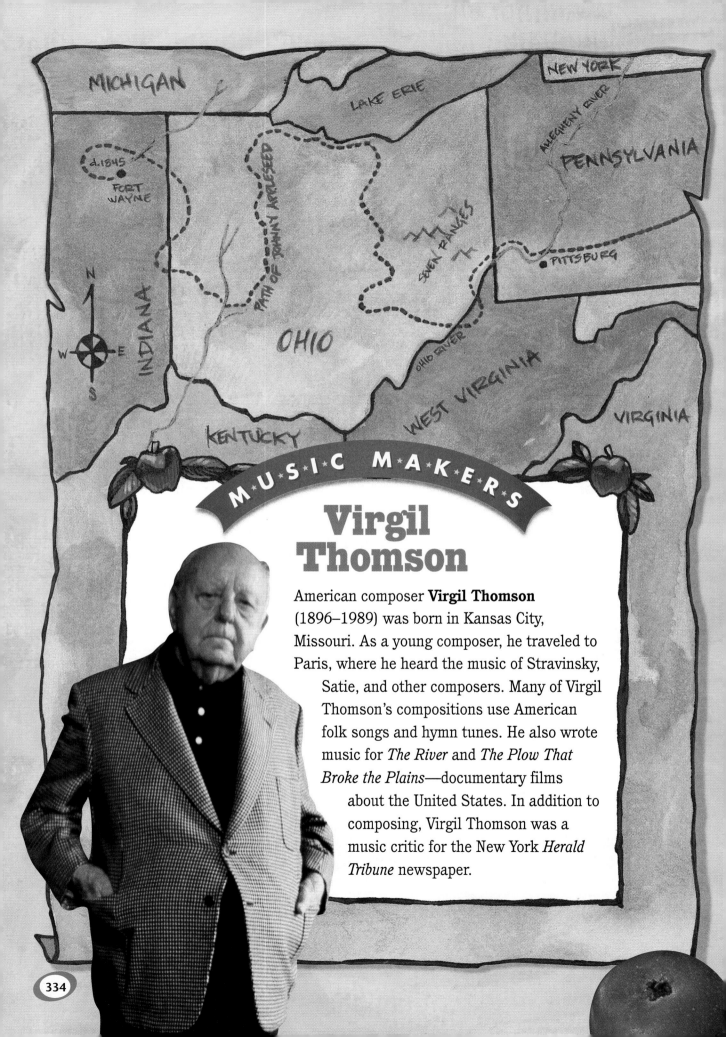

Virgil Thomson

American composer **Virgil Thomson** (1896–1989) was born in Kansas City, Missouri. As a young composer, he traveled to Paris, where he heard the music of Stravinsky, Satie, and other composers. Many of Virgil Thomson's compositions use American folk songs and hymn tunes. He also wrote music for *The River* and *The Plow That Broke the Plains*—documentary films about the United States. In addition to composing, Virgil Thomson was a music critic for the New York *Herald Tribune* newspaper.

Form and Timbre

Johnny Appleseed walked hundreds of miles to make his dream come true. **Identify** the form of the music. What instruments do you hear?

13-5
Walking Song

from *Acadian Songs*
by **Virgil Thomson**

This selection features clarinet, flute, violin, trumpet, and oboe.

Walking Song
LISTENING MAP

Peace AND HARMONY

Peace is the dream of people all over the world. Learning to live together with respect and dignity can help make the dream of peace come true. **Sing** "Peace Round" in unison. Then, sing it as a round or with ostinatos to create harmony. How can you be a peacemaker in your school or community?

13-6

Peace Round

Words by Jean Ritchie

Traditional

What a good-ly thing, if the chil-dren of the world

could live to-geth-er in _____ peace.

▲ On May 25, 1986, over five million Americans participated in Hands Across America. At a designated time, participants across sixteen states joined hands to raise money for hungry and homeless people.

Sing for Peace

Below are two ostinatos from "Peace Round." Look up words for peace in different languages and **sing** them as ostinatos. Choose the one you like best, and add the ostinato to your performance of "Peace Round."

Move for Peace

Move to the half-note beat as you **sing** "Peace Round." Then **perform** a movement round.

13-8

Interview with Jean Ritchie

M·U·S·I·C M·A·K·E·R·S

Jean Ritchie

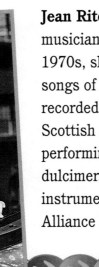

Jean Ritchie (born 1922) is one of the most famous folk musicians in the United States. During the 1960s and 1970s, she introduced thousands of people to the folk songs of Kentucky. Some of the music she performed and recorded was passed down from her Irish, English, and Scottish ancestors. Before Jean Ritchie began performing, few people were familiar with the mountain dulcimer. Because of her music, people began to play the instrument again. In 1998, Jean Ritchie won the Folk Alliance Lifetime Achievement Award.

Chasing a Dream

Earth Speaks

Read this poem and think about
what you heard Earth say today.

Prayer for Earth
by Myra Cohn Livingston

Last night
an owl
called from the hill.
Coyotes howled.
A deer stood still
nibbling at bushes far away.
The moon shone silver.
Let this stay.

Today
two noisy crows
flew by,
their shadows pasted to the sky.
The sun broke out
through the clouds of gray.
An iris opened.
Let this stay.

Earth, Sea, and Sky

Earth is a home for everyone. It sustains us, providing all that we need to live. Its beauty and wonder inspire our hearts and minds. We are learning that it is also our responsibility to protect our precious Earth.

We Sail Together

The song *"Somos el barco"* is about our connection with the world around us.
Sing this song and think of how you are connected to the world.

Somos el barco
(We Are the Boat)

Words and Music by Lorre Wyatt

So-mos el bar-co ___ So-mos el mar
yo na-ve-go en ti Tu na-ve-gas en mí
We are the boat, we are the sea.
I sail in you, you sail in me.
1. The stream sings __ it to the riv-er, ___ The
riv-er sings __ it to the sea. The sea sings it
to the boat __ that car-ries you __ and me. ___ So-mos el

2.–4.

2. The boat we are ___ sail - ing in ___ was
3. With our hopes we _____ raise the sails _ to
4. The voy - age has been _ long and hard _ and

built by man - y _____ hands. The sea we are
face the wind once _ more. With our hearts _____ we
yet we're sail - ing ___ still. With a song to help us

sail - ing on _____ touch-es ev - 'ry sand. _
chart the wa - ters _ nev - er sailed be - fore. _
pull to - geth - er ___ if we on - ly will. ___

D.S. al Fine

So-mos el

Play a Countermelody

Perform this recorder part during the refrain of "*Somos el barco.*"

Countermelody Refrain

Our Planet

How would you describe our planet? You could use facts such as "the planet Earth is a sphere and revolves around the sun." You could use feelings like "our planet is very beautiful and exciting." Maybe you would use both.

Read this poem. Does the author use facts, feelings, or both to describe our planet?

Written in March

by William Wordsworth

The cock is crowing,
The stream is flowing,
The small birds twitter,
The green field sleeps in the sun;
The oldest and youngest
Are at work with the strongest;
The cattle are grazing,
Their heads never raising;
There are forty feeding like one!
Like an army defeated
The snow hath retreated,
And now doth fare ill
On the top of the bare hill;
The ploughboy is whooping—anon—anon;
There's joy in the mountains;
There's life in the fountains;
Small clouds are sailing,
Blue sky prevailing;
The rain is over and gone!

Often a composer will use only a few lines from a text to create a song. What lines from this poem would you use?

Sing "This Pretty Planet." Is this a song with facts, feelings, or both?

This Pretty Planet

Words and Music by John Forster and Tom Chapin

This pret-ty plan-et spin-ning through space. You're a gar-den. You're a har-bor. You're a ho-ly place. Gold-en sun go-ing down. Gen-tle blue gi-ant. spin us a-round. All through the night Safe till the morn-ing light.

The Beautiful Earth

What feelings about Earth are expressed in this song?

Read this song using rhythm syllables. Now use pitch syllables and hand signs to **read** measures 9 and 10.

For the Beauty of the Earth

Words by Folliott S. Pierpoint

Music by Conrad Kocher

1. For the _beau-ty of the earth, For the beau-ty of the skies,
2. For the _beau-ty of each hour Of the day and of the night,
3. For the _ joy of ear and eye, For the heart and mind's de-light,
4. For the _ joy of hu-man love, Broth-er, sis-ter, par-ent, child,

For the _ love which from our birth, O-ver and a-round us lies.
Hill and _ vale and tree and flower, Sun and moon and stars of light.
For the _ mys-tic har-mo-ny Link-ing sense to sound and sight.
Friends on _ earth and friends a-bove, For all gen-tle thoughts and mild.

Lord of all, to Thee we raise This our hymn of grate-ful praise.

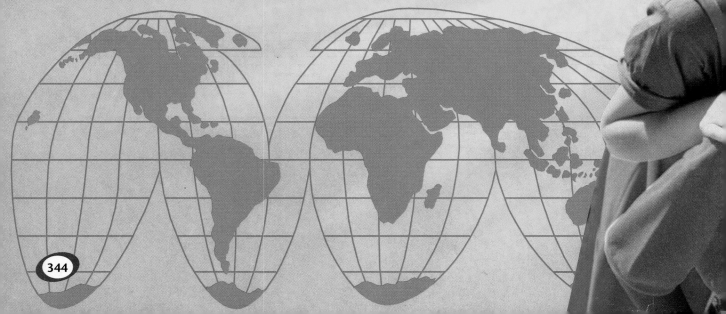

Name the Continents

The largest land masses on Earth are called continents. Here's a great way to remember them!

Read "The Continents" using rhythm syllables. Then **perform** it as a **canon**.

A **canon** is a musical form in which the parts imitate each other. One part begins, or leads, and the other parts follow.

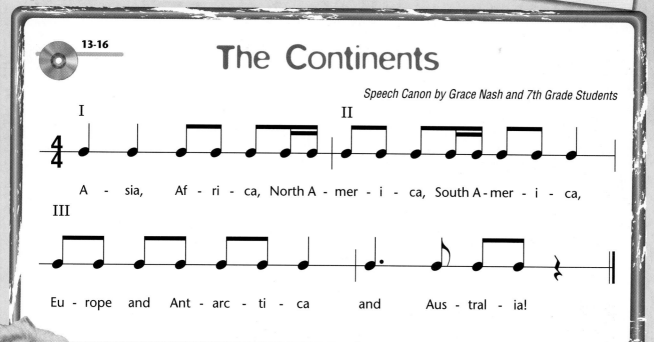

13-16

The Continents

Speech Canon by Grace Nash and 7th Grade Students

I
II

A - sia, Af - ri - ca, North A - mer - i - ca, South A - mer - i - ca,

III

Eu - rope and Ant - arc - ti - ca and Aus - tral - ia!

OUR PLANET— Our Home

We are all together on planet Earth, spinning through space. The Earth is our home and our protector, so we all must take care of it. This Cherokee song puts these ideas into music. **Sing** the melody, and then the harmony part. Then, sing both parts together.

13-18
The Earth Is Our Mother

Cherokee Song
Arranged by Barbara Sletto

1.,3. The Earth ___ is our Moth - er, we must take care of her. The
2. Her sa - cred ground we walk u - pon with ev - ery step we take. Her

Earth ___ is our Moth - er, we must take care of her.
sa - cred ground we walk up - on with ev - ery step we take.

Hey ___ yan - na, ho ___ yan - na, hey ___ yan yan.

Hey ___ yan - na, ho ___ yan - na hey ___ yan yan.

Protecting Earth

In the twentieth century, the United States government formed the Environmental Protection Agency (EPA) to protect our planet from damage caused by humans. For centuries, Native American traditions have considered Earth to be precious, to be cared for rather than consumed. This poem by Chief Dan George expresses this sentiment.

And My Heart Soars

by Chief Dan George

The beauty of the trees,
The softness of the air,
The fragrance of the grass,
   speaks to me.

The summit of the mountain,
The thunder of the sky,
The rhythm of the sea,
   speaks to me.

The faintness of the stars,
The freshness of the morning,
The dew drop on the flower,
   speaks to me.

The strength of fire,
The taste of salmon,
The trail of the sun,

And the life that never goes away,
   They speak to me.

And my heart soars.

Water, Water Everywhere

"Singin' in the Rain" is a song from the movie *Singin' in the Rain*. In the movie, Gene Kelly is singing about being happy in love despite the rain and cloudy skies.

As you **sing** the song, think about times you were happy even when skies were gray.

Sing this song about enjoying the rain.

13-22

Singin' in the Rain

Words by Arthur Freed

Music by Nacio Herb Brown

I'm sing - in' in the rain, just sing - in' in the

rain. What a glo - ri-ous feel - ing, I'm hap - py a -

gain! I'm laugh - ing at clouds so dark up a -

bove. The sun's ___ in my heart ___ and I'm read - y for

Experiment with Sound

Create an introduction to this song using percussion instruments to sound like a rainstorm. Start with distant rolls of thunder on the drums. As the thunder gets louder, add lightning by using an instrument such as the slapstick. Gradually make the sound of raindrops by using light finger taps on a hand drum or desktop. Have the raindrops get louder and faster. At the end, add a *coda* by gradually having the rain come to a stop. Then find a way to **create** a rainbow.

▲ Gene Kelly

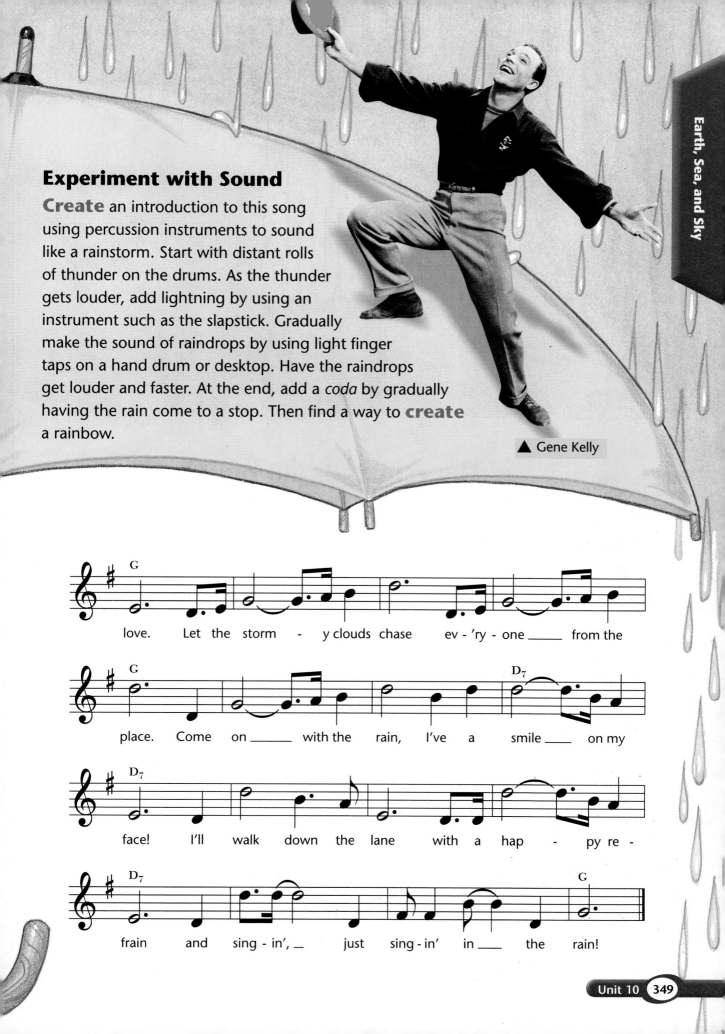

love. Let the storm - y clouds chase ev - 'ry - one _____ from the

place. Come on _____ with the rain, I've a smile _____ on my

face! I'll walk down the lane with a hap - py re -

frain and sing - in', _ just sing - in' in _____ the rain!

When It Rains, It POURS

"The Wheel of the Water" is a song about a scientific process. Read the text of the song and name the process.

13-24

The Wheel of the Water

Words and Music by John Forster and Tom Chapin

The wheel of the wa-ter go 'round and 'round, And the

wheel of the wa-ter go 'round. And the

Voice 2

Wa-ter flow down, down, trick-le, trick-le down,

Down to the o - cean, trick-le, trick-le down.

350

A Piece of the Cake

This song is layered, just like a layer cake! It has five different voice parts, one on top of the other. When the song is put together, all five parts are sung at the same time. Practice each voice part separately. **Sing** the song by adding one voice part at a time.

Voice 3

See the va-pors rise. See them cloud the skies.

Voice 4

Clouds rain down. Thun-der and light-ning sound.

Voice 5

Springs bub-ble, bub-ble up. Springs bub-ble, bub-ble up.

Icing on the Cake

Create movements for each song layer and make your movements express the text. How many sets of movements do you need? **Listen** to the song and **perform** your movements.

Our Cake Is Baked

Now it's time to put our piece together. To perform our creation we need five different voice groups and five different movement groups.

Now with all the layers we've created, **perform** the song. Good luck!

Arts Connection

▲ *Wooded Landscape* (1851) by Jean François Millet

Back to Nature

In the 1700s and early 1800s, many Europeans felt they had moved too far away from nature. As a result, the Pastoral Movement developed in the arts. During this time, many artists created works to express their feelings about nature.

Listen for the storm in this music by Ludwig van Beethoven. He composed this music to describe his love of nature.

13-25
Symphony No. 6, Movement 4

by Ludwig van Beethoven
This symphony was first published in 1809.

Why Is There Day and Night?

Long, long ago before people had developed the science of astronomy, the Hmong people had their own system for explaining the stars, the sun, the moon, and other natural events. This is the ancient Hmong story of how day and night might have come to pass.

13-26
Nruab hnub thiab hmo ntuj

Hmong Folk Tale

Listen to the story. Then using the script, "Vocal Part," "Daytime Music," and "Nighttime Music," **create** a musical play. **Compare** the melodic contour of the musical parts.

Long ago, there were nine suns and nine moons. When it was night, it was nighttime for a very long time. When it was day, it was daytime for a very long time. However, the people of the world worked very hard and still did not have enough food to eat, and they were angry.

Arts Connection

▲ *Paj ntaub* story-telling quilt (1999) by May Chao Lor. The Hmong people use quilts to document folklore and history.

So the people made a crossbow and went to shoot the suns. But the suns and moons would not come out. They were very afraid and were not willing to come out. The people asked what kind of animal could go and call the suns and the moons to come out.

The people asked a bull to call out the suns and moons. A bull came out huffing, puffing, and snorting. "Come out!" he shouted. But the suns and moons would not come out.

Then the people asked a tiger to try. A tiger came out growling and roaring. "Come out!" he shouted. But the suns and moons would not come out.

All instruments

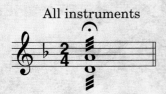

Vocal Part

But the suns and moons would not come out!

ext the people asked a lee-nyu bird. The lee-nyu bird came out flapping, hooting, and squawking. "Come out!" she shouted. But the suns and moons would not come out.

Finally, the people asked the rooster to try. The rooster came out puffing up his chest very proudly, and started to crow.

Daytime Music

And then . . . the sun came out for a little while. And then . . . the moon came out for a little while. Since that time, there has been daytime and nighttime, so the people can work and have enough to eat. They have lived that way until now.

Nighttime Music

Alto Glockenspiel *(moderate tempo)*

Alto Metallophone

The Seasons

In what seasons do you begin and end the school year? This song is about the cycles of nature. **Sing** "Cycle Song of Life." Notice how the **descant** adds another layer to the texture.

A **descant** is a countermelody that decorates the main melody, often soaring above the melody of the song.

14-1

Cycle Song of Life (The River Song)

Words and Music by James Durst

1. The riv-er casts her murk-y eyes _toward heav-en, __
2. Just when it seems the night will last __ for-ev-er, __
3. To un-der-stand the laugh-ter of __ the spring-time, _

but nev-er stops to doubt that she must roll out to the sea.
the sun ap-pears to kiss a-wake the dark-ness in-to day.
you have to see the sum-mer melt a-way in-to the fall.

And the se-cret of what takes her to her si-lence _
And __ though his life is short, he makes the jour-ney __
But __ 'til you've known the end-less sleep of win-ter, __

goes with her to her death be-yond e-ter-ni-ty.
and knows deep in his heart that there's no oth-er way.
you'll nev-er hear the cy-cle song of life at all.

REFRAIN
Descant last time only

The riv-er just keeps flow-in' on and

And the riv-er just keeps flow-in' on and on. The

on. The sun keeps go-in' 'round,

sun keeps go-in' 'round to bring the dawn. And

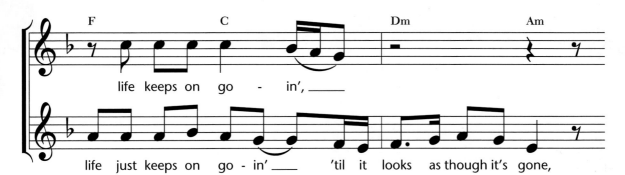

life keeps on go - in', _____

life just keeps on go-in' _____ 'til it looks as though it's gone,

repeat refrain last time

but it real-ly just keeps flow-in' on and on.

More of the Seasons

The Seasons by Antonio Vivaldi is probably the most famous piece of music about the seasons. Why do you think there are four sections in this piece?

Listen to this piece by Antonio Vivaldi.

14-3
Spring

**from *The Four Seasons*
by Antonio Vivaldi**

This piece was written for small orchestra and solo violin.

Seeing Stars

When the first star of the evening appears, make a wish. What did you wish for? In the song "Starlight, Star Bright," what does the composer wish for the world?

Look at the music for "Starlight, Star Bright." Do verses one and two have the same notation? Identify the form of the song. Then sing "Starlight, Star Bright."

M·U·S·I·C M·A·K·E·R·S

James Durst

James Durst is a composer, singer, and guitar player. Durst was born and raised in California. Now he spends his life traveling the world, bringing his music and the message of harmony and understanding to people everywhere. In each country he learns new songs. Recently he has started going into schools to work with students.

Starlight, Star Bright

Words and Music by James Durst

A C REFRAIN — F — C

Star - light, star bright, first star I

Gsus₄ — G — Am₇ — Em — F — C

see to - night. I wish I may, I wish I might. _

C — Dm₇ — Gsus₄ — G — C — Csus₄ — C — *Fine*

Have the wish I wish to - night.

B F VERSE — G — C — F — G

1. Shine __ on peo-ple of the earth; __ make us wor - thy
   Shine __ on chil-dren ev - 'ry - where; _ keep them safe and
2. Shine __ on an - i - mals and plants; _ il - lu - mi - nate their
   Lit - tle bea-con out in space; _ shine up - on the

Am₇ — Em — B♭ — Dm₇ — A♭

of our birth. Bright-en paths thru dark of night;
free from care. Feed their bod - ies, souls and minds;
life - long dance. Light the land, the sky, and sea;
hu - man race. Grant this hum - ble, hope - ful prayer;

Gsus₄ — G₇ — *D.C. after each verse*

that we might walk in truth and light.
that they might bless this world in kind.
and all that share life's mys - ter - y.
for peace to flour - ish ev - 'ry - where.

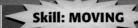

The Moving Moon

In this song, the words describe the Korean idea of what can be seen in the moon. What shapes have you discovered while gazing at the moon?

Sing "Sailboat in the Sky."

 14-6

Sailboat in the Sky

English Words by Aura Kontra   *Folk Song from Korea*

푸 른 하 늘 은__ 하 수 하 얀 쪽 배 에
Pu reun ha nul eun - ha su ha yan jjok bae ae,
See the small white boat in the sky, sail - ing toward the west,

계 수 나 무 한__ 나 무 토 끼 한 마 리
Gae su na mu han - na mu to kki han ma ri,
High a - bove the cin - na - mon tree where a rab - bit rests.

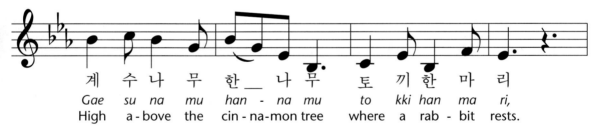

돛 대 도 아 니 달 고 삿 대 도 없 이
Dot dae do ah ni dal go sat dae do up si,
With no sails or oars, it skims o'er the Mil - ky Way,

가 기 도 잘 도 간 다 서__ 쪽 나 라 로
Ga gi do jal do gahn da so - jjok na ra ro.
Float - ing a - mong the clouds as slow - ly it fades a - way.

Strong and Weak Beats

Sing the song again. Clap on the first beat of each measure and pat on the fourth beat of each measure.

Korean Hand Game

Below is a picture of a traditional Korean hand game often played while singing the song. The game is played quickly. To learn it, **move** slowly and then speed up.

The Planets

The planets in our solar system have long inspired people's imagination. **Listen** to this recording of "Mars, the Bringer of War" from *The Planets*.

M·U·S·I·C M·A·K·E·R·S

Gustav Holst

Gustav Holst (1874–1934) was a musician, composer, and teacher. As a child he studied piano. Later, he went to the Royal College of Music and studied composition and trombone. As a teacher, Holst was known for encouraging beginners. He was a believer in learning music by "doing" music. Holst composed for both orchestra and wind bands. Perhaps his most famous work is *The Planets*.

Moving Through Space

As you learn more about space, the planets begin to seem like friends. If you had the chance, which planet would you visit first?

Perform this rhythm game to learn the names of the planets.

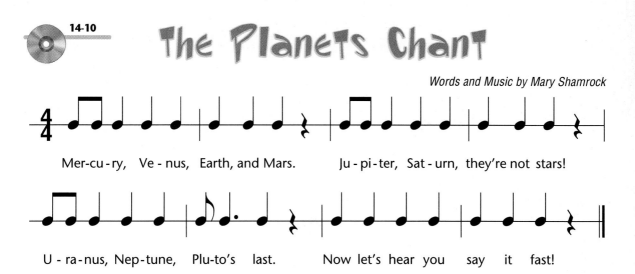

14-10

The Planets Chant

Words and Music by Mary Shamrock

Mer-cu-ry, Ve - nus, Earth, and Mars.   Ju - pi-ter, Sat - urn, they're not stars!

U - ra-nus, Nep-tune, Plu-to's   last.   Now let's hear you   say   it   fast!

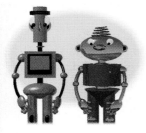

Pat thighs

Clap.

Clap right hands.

Clap.

Clap left hands

Clap.

Clap with partner.

Clap.

14–12

Mars, The Bringer of War

from *The Planets, Suite for Large Orchestra, Opus 32*
by Gustav Holst

This selection is one of seven pieces in this suite. The other planets included in the entire work are Mercury, Venus, Jupiter, Saturn, Uranus, and Neptune.

We'll begin our choral adventure by singing the calypso song, "Shake the Papaya Down."

14-13

Shake the Papaya Down

Calypso Song
Arranged by Ruth E. Dwyer and Judith M. Waller
Edited by Henry H. Leck

Ma - ma says no play; This is a work - day.
Sweet, sweet pa - pa - ya, Fruit of the Is - land,

Up with the bright sun; Get all the work done. If you will help me,
When all the work's done, Dance on the white sands. If you will help me,

Climb up the tall tree, Shake the pa - pa - ya down.
Climb up the tall tree, Shake the pa - pa - ya down.

Shake them down, _ Shake them down, _ Climb the tall _ tree, Shake them down. _

Shake them down, _ Shake them down, _ Shake the pa - pa - ya down.

UNIT 11

Sing Out!

Welcome to the wonderful world of choral music. Experience the world around you in a way that can only happen when you sing.

Part 1: Ma-ma says no play; This is a work-day. Up with the bright sun; Get all the work done. If you will help me, Climb up the tall tree, Shake the pa-pa-ya down.

Part 2: Shake them down, Shake them down, Climb the tall tree, shake them down. Shake them down, Shake them down, Shake the pa-pa-ya down.

Get It Together

"Lullaby and Dance" is a song with two very different sections. "Lullaby" is Cajun. The Cajuns are descendants of early French settlers in Nova Scotia and New Brunswick in Canada and later in Louisiana and Texas. "Dance" is based on a traditional American play-party song.

𝒜rts Connection

◀ *Fiddling Sailor* by Christian Pierre, a contemporary Cajun American artist

Singing Tips

Sing the vowel *e* in words such as *sweep, dreams,* and *seems* with slightly rounded lips to avoid a wide vowel quality. When singing the word *away,* prolong the *a* vowel sound in *way* for four beats.

Reading Music Tips

Identify and **sing** the *do, mi,* and *so* pattern in measures 4–5. Find and sing all the other *do, mi,* and *so* patterns in "Lullaby and Dance."

Knowing the Score

Which voice part has the melody in measures 11–14 and in measures 22–25? Where do Voice 1 and Voice 2 sing the same rhythms and pitches together? To discover when the texture and harmony of this composition change, find the measures where Voice 1 has different rhythms and pitches from those found in Voice 2.

The proper *e* vowel mouth position ▶

14-15

Lullaby and Dance

Traditional
Arranged by Ruth E. Dwyer

Sweep, sweep, sweep a - way. Sweep the road of dreams. Peo-ple say that in the

night, The tur-tle will talk it seems. The tur-tle will talk it seems.

Sweep, sweep a - way. Sweep the road of

Sweep, sweep, sweep a - way. Sweep the road of

dreams. Peo-ple say that in the night, The tur-tle will talk it

dreams. Peo-ple say ____ that in the night, ____ The tur-tle will

seems. The tur - tle will talk it seems. _____

talk it seems. _____ Will talk it seems. _____

1 Come out to-night, Come out to-night, Come out to - night. _____

2 Come out to-night, Come out to-night, Come out to - night. _____

unison

Al - a - bam - a Gal, won't you come out to - night,

Come out to - night, Come out to - night. Al - a - bam - a Gal, won't you

come out to - night and dance by the light of the moon. The

moon shines bright the wind blows cool, I set my wag-on and un-hitched my mule.

Fid - dles tune a might bit high'r, Set your heels kick-in' 'round the fire.

Arts Connection

◄ Horse and Rider weather vane (1870)

46 F / C

1. Al - a - bam - a Gal, won't you come out to-night, Come out to-night,

2. Al - a - bam - a Gal, Come out to-night, Come out to-night,

49 F

1. Come out to - night. Al - a - bam - a Gal, won't you

2. Come out to - night. Al - a - bam - a Gal,

51 F / C / F / *div.*

1. come out to - night and dance by the light of the moon. And

2. Come out to - night and dance by the light of the moon.

54 dance by the light _____

F/ C / C₇ / F

1. dance by the light of the moon.

2. dance by the light of the moon.

Listen to an American Folk Tune

Here is another example of a folk tune from the southern United States.

Listen to *Jolie Blonde*.

14-17
Jolie Blonde

**Cajun Folk Melody
as performed by the Hackberry Ramblers**

This song is a favorite at country and western dances.

Singing Phrases

"*Einini*" is a Gaelic lullaby. Feel the rocking movement as you **sing** the song. Give the first note of each measure a little extra weight to create a swinging motion.

Singing Tips

This song uses many *e* and *a* vowels. They are similar and should be sung in almost the same way. Place the tip of your tongue against your lower teeth inside your mouth.

Reading Music Tips

Find *do* in the song and **identify** the key. Notice *mi, re,* and *do* are highlighted in the music. What is the first pitch syllable of the song? The composer suggests the song be sung *andante,* which means "walking tempo." The dynamic marking indicated is *mf.* Why were these expressions chosen?

Knowing the Score

On what beat of the measure does each phrase start? You already know the name for this. It is called an upbeat. How many are there in this song? Each upbeat in the song is the same note. Name the pitch.

Einini

Gaelic Folk Song
Arranged by Cyndee Giebler

Ein - in - i, ein - in - i, cod - al -

ai - gi, cod - al - ai - gi, ein - in - i, ein - in - i, cod - al -

ai - gi, cod - al - ai - gi. Cod - al - ai - gi, cod - al - ai - gi, cois an

chlai amuigh, cois an chlai amuigh, cod - al - ai - gi, cod - al -

ai - gi, cois an chlai amuigh, cois an chlai amuigh.

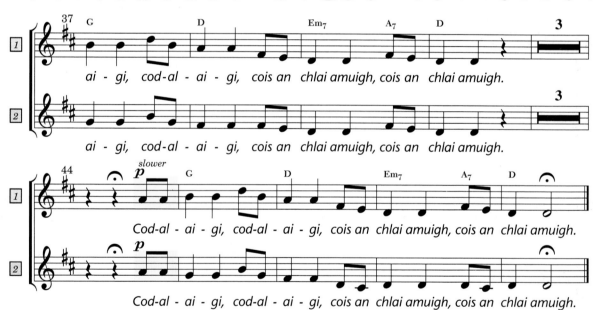

ai - gi, cod-al - ai - gi, cois an chlai amuigh, cois an chlai amuigh.

ai - gi, cod-al - ai - gi, cois an chlai amuigh, cois an chlai amuigh.

Cod-al - ai - gi, cod-al - ai - gi, cois an chlai amuigh, cois an chlai amuigh.

Cod-al - ai - gi, cod-al - ai - gi, cois an chlai amuigh, cois an chlai amuigh.

Singing in Layers

"Little David Play on Your Harp" is an African American spiritual.

Singing Tips

As you **sing** the words *play on your harp, hallelu,* make certain the *p* in the word *harp* is not connected to the *h* in *hallelu.*

Reading Music Tips

Practice speaking the syncopated rhythm pattern in the words *play on your.* Then practice the word *hallelu* with an accent on the *h.*

Knowing the Score

Find the words *Refrain, Verse,* and *ostinato.* What do these words mean? Is the melodic ostinato sung with the verse or refrain?

14-21

Little David, Play on Your Harp

African American Spiritual
Arranged by Shirley McRae

REFRAIN

Lit - tle Da - vid, play on your harp, hal - le - lu, hal - le - lu, Lit - tle Da - vid, play on your harp, hal - le - lu.

VERSE

1., 4. Lit - tle Da - vid was a shep - herd boy, he
2. Old Dan - iel in the li - on's den, but
3. Lit - tle Da - vid was a might - y king, and

slew Go - li - ath and sang for joy.
he came out all whole a - gain.
all the peo - ple came to sing.

Refrain ostinato 1

Play on your harp, ___ sing hal - le - lu.

Refrain ostinato 2

Play, play, sing hal - le - lu.

Refrain ostinato 3

Play on your harp, sing hal - le - lu - jah. ___

Listen for the melody as the Moses Hogan Chorale performs its version of *Little David, Play on Your Harp.* Then listen to Moses Hogan talk about his experiences in music.

14-23
Little David, Play on Your Harp

African American Spiritual
as performed by the Moses Hogan Chorale
This version is performed *a cappella*.

Sing Out!

M·U·S·I·C M·A·K·E·R·S
Moses Hogan

Moses Hogan (1957–2003) was an accomplished pianist, conductor, and arranger. His awards included winning the Kosciuszko Foundation Chopin Competition. He was also the founder of the Moses Hogan Chorale, a group famous for its high quality choral performances.

14-24
Interview with Moses Hogan

Two Melodies — One Song

Brazil is the largest South American country in both size and population, and the official language is Portuguese. *"Sambalele"* is a song that has two folk melodies that may be performed together. Melodies that can be performed in this way are called partner songs.

Singing Tips

Learn each melody of the song separately, then **sing** *"Sambalele."* Practice singing the song on the neutral syllable *pah,* accenting the initial consonant *p* for the rhythm pattern in measure 6.

Reading Music Tips

The rhythm of *"Sambalele"* is syncopated. Find this pattern in the song.

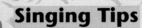

Practice this pattern before you **sing** the song. Both melodies use only four rhythmic note values. What are they?

Knowing the Score

What is the purpose of the five-measure rest at the beginning of the song? In which part of the song does the arranger create texture and harmony? Explain your answer.

14-25

Sambalele

English Words by Henry Leck

Folk Song from Brazil
Arranged by Henry Leck

Sam-ba - le - le ta do-en - te, tac-oa ca-be-ça que
Sam-ba - le - le is a fel - low, Who rare - ly gets to his

bra - da Sam-ba - le - le pre-ci-sa - va de u-mas de zoi-to lam-
pil - low, He spends his time loud-ly play - ing. No one can tell where he's

ba - das, Sam - ba - le - le ta do-en - te, tac-oa ca - be-ça, que
stay - ing, Sam - ba - le - le went out danc - ing, With his new cart he went

bra - da Sam - ba - le - le pre - ci - sa - va
pran - cing, then he ar - rived at the mar - ket,

de u-mas de zoi-to lam - ba - das, Sam - ba sam - ba
but he for-got how to park it. Sam - ba sam - ba

sam - ba - le - le Pi-sa - na ba - ra da sa - ia le - le!
sam - ba - le - le We wish your neigh-bors could tell where you stay.

Samba samba samba-le-le! Pi-sa na bar-ra da

Samba samba samba-le-le! Of-ten we just can-not

sa - ia Ba - la - io meu bem, Ba - la - io sin - ha ba -

find you. Ba - la - io the brave, Ba - la - io the fair ba -

la - io do co-ra-ção Mo - ça - que não tem ba - la - io sin - ha bo-taa

la - io whom we a - dore. I know your dark hair and pret-ty dark eyes are the

cos - tu - ra no chão. Ba - la - io meu bem, ba -

en - vy of us all. Ba - la - io so sweet ba -

la - io sin - ha ba - la - io do co - ra - ção Mo -

la - io so kind ba - la - io we can't ig - nore. The

ça - que não tem ba - la - io sin - ha bo-taa cos - tu - ra no

beau-ty you bring how hap-py you sing we all want to see you

46 F *div.* Gm

1 chão! Ba - la - io meu bem, ba - la - io sin - ha, ba -
more. Ba - la - io so nice, ba - la - io pre - cise ba -

2 chão! Sam - ba - le - le ta do - en - te,
more. Sam - ba - le - le is a fel - low,

49 C₇ F

1 la - io do co - ra - ção Mo - ça - que não tem ba -
la - io you live next door. We hope that you stay, so

2 tac - ao ca - be - ça que bra - da! Sam - ba - le - le pre - ci -
who rare - ly gets to his pil - low, He spends his time loud - ly

52 Gm   C₇   F

1
la - io sin - ha bo - taa cos - tu - ra no chão! Ba -
we can all say that you are our friend some more. Ba -

2
sa - va de u-mas de zoi - to lam - ba - das! Sam -
play - ing. No one can tell where he's stay - ing. Sam -

55 F   Gm   C₇

1
la - io meu bem, ba - la - io sin - ha, ba - la - io do co - ra -
la - io the brave, ba - la - io the fair ba - la - io whom we a -

2
- ba, sam - ba sam-ba - le - le! Pi - sa - na ba - ra da
- ba, sam - ba sam-ba - le - le! We wish your neigh-bors could

Sound of the *Samba*

One of the most beloved kinds of music in Brazil is the *samba*. Every year a big celebration called *Carnaval* takes place. Many people parade through the streets singing and dancing to *samba* music.

Listen for the *samba* rhythms in this recording of *Bate-papo*.

14-29

Bate-papo

Batucada Street Samba **from Brazil**
as performed by Bateria Nota 10

The *batucada samba* is the rhythmic foundation for *Carnaval*.

what's the score?

The beauty of nature is all around us. Read the words to "Circle 'Round the Moon." What do they mean? One challenge in reading music is to follow your part in a complete score. As you **listen** to "Circle 'Round the Moon," trace your part in the score.

Singing Tips

Learn the first phrase of "Circle 'Round the Moon." **Sing** this phrase wherever it appears in the song. Next, learn measures 13–15 and **sing** this phrase wherever it appears in the song. Now **sing** each phrase without taking a breath in the middle.

Reading Music Tips

Read measures 5–8 using pitch syllables. The melody often uses pitch syllables *do, mi,* and *so.* The melody also uses a ♪♪ ♪♪ rhythm pattern. Why does this rhythm pattern change to larger note values? How does this make the music feel?

Knowing the Score

The composer of "Circle 'Round the Moon" uses **word painting** to help create mood. An example of word painting appears in measure 13. Notice in the words *high above the trees,* the note for the word *high* is the highest note in the measure and the lowest note is for *trees.* How many other examples of word painting can you find?

Word painting is the positioning of pitch and rhythm patterns to resemble the meaning of words.

Circle 'Round the Moon
(From "Reflections of Youth")

Words and Music by
Mark Hierholzer

Cir-cle 'round the moon in-vites me to stay out in the win-ter - time. _____

Crys-tals in the air sug-gest that I pre-pare for the cold night air. _____

High a-bove the trees you will make me see that with such a sight

Sing Out!

sheer de - light is hid - den ev' - ry - where for those who care to see. ____

____ Cav-erns down be-low in - vite me to come down on the

slip - p'ry rock. _____ I - ci - cles of stone and

hor-rid moun-tain gnomes hid-den in the dark. _____

In the ground be - low you will make me know that with

In the ground be - low you will make me

such a sight sheer de - light is hid - den ev' - ry -

know that with such a sight sheer de - light ev' - ry -

hear the sea-gulls screech   in the hot dry air. _____

beach,   hear them in the hot   dry   air. _____

What great mind be - hind it   dreamed it and de - signed it?

What great mind be - hind it   dreamed it and de - signed it?

Snow - y night,   sum - mer flight,   pain - ful beau - ty

in my sight mak - ing me long for you. _____

Music to My Ears

The words of "Circle 'Round the Moon" have a specific mood. This poem by James Whitcomb Riley also has a specific mood. If you set "Extremes" to music, what dynamics would you choose? What tempo? What instruments might you choose for the accompaniment?

Extremes

by James Whitcomb Riley

A little boy once played so loud
That the thunder, up in a thundercloud,
Said, "Since I can't be heard, why, then
I'll never, never thunder again!"

And a little girl once kept so still
That she heard a fly on the sill
Whisper and say to a ladybird,
"She's the stillest child I ever heard."

Carols in Harmony

"A Merry Modal Christmas" is a collection of three European Christmas carols.

Singing Tips

Sing *"Pat-a-Pan"* and *"La marche des rois"* on the neutral syllable *to* to create a pointed attack on each note. On "Coventry Carol," **sing** the melody on *loo* to create a *legato* feeling.

Reading Music Tips

For *"Pat-a-pan,"* **sing** low *la*-low *ti-do-re-mi* up the scale and *mi-re-do*-low *ti*-low *la* down. Perform the pattern slowly and quickly. Tap the rhythms in measures 46–49. This is a repeated rhythm pattern in *"La marche des rois."*

Knowing the Score

Identify the ostinato in *"Pat-a-pan."* Find the melody and harmony parts in "Coventry Carol" and *"La marche des rois."*

A Merry Modal Christmas

15-3

Words and Music by Bernard de la Monnoye (Pat-a-Pan)
Carols from France and England
Arranged by Buryl Red

Pat-a-Pan

Part 1:
Prum, pum, pum! Prum, pum, pum! Gui - lo, prends ton tam - bou - rin, Toi, prends ta flú - te, Ro - bin; Au son de cés in - stru - ments, Tu - re - lu - re - lu, pat - a - pat - a - pan; Au son de cés in - stru - ments, Je di - rai No - ël gai - ment.

Wil - lie, get your lit - tle drum, Ro - bin, bring your flute, and come. Aren't they fun to play up - on? Tu - re - lu - re - lu, pat - a - pat - a - pan; When you play your fife and drum, How can an - y - one be glum?

Part 2:
pum! Prum, pum, pum! Prum, pum, pum! Prum, pum, pum! Prum, pum, pum! Prum, pum, pum!

Coventry Carol

Part 1 & 2:
Lul - lay, Lul - lay,

Part 1:
Lul - lay, Lul - lay,

Part 2:
Lul - lay, Thou lit - tle ti - ny Child,

Sing Out!

Unit 11   **395**

1 By, by, lul - ly, lul - lay, lul - lay.

2 By, by, lul - ly, lul - lay; _____ Lul -

1 Lul - lay, Thou ti - ny Child,

2 lay, Thou lit - tle ti - ny Child,

1 By, by, lul - ly, lul - lay. _____

2 By, by, lul - ly, lul - lay. _____

2 *f La Marche des Rois*

1 2 Ce mat - in, Ce mat - in, Ce mat - in, J'ai
This great day, This great day, This great day, I

ren - con - tré le train, De trois grands rois qui al - laient en - voy - a - ge __
met up - on the way, The Kings of East as they came rid - ing proud - ly, __

Ce ma - tin, j'ai ren - con - tré le train, De trois grands rois des - sus le
This great day, I met up - on the way, The Kings of East with all their

grand che - min. Tout char - gés d'or les sui - vant d'a - bord, De
fine ar - ray. The gifts of gold, frank - in - cense, and myrrh, Were

Join the Celebration

Some music just seems to be made for a celebration. *"La copa de la vida"* was sung by Ricky Martin for the 1998 World Cup in France. **Sing** the song and be part of the celebration.

15-8

La copa de la vida (The Cup of Life)

Words and Music by Desmond Child and Robi Rosa

Do you real - ly want _ it? ____ Yeah! Do you real - ly want _

____ it? ___ Yeah! Do you real - ly want _ it? ___ Yeah!

Go, go, go.   Go, go, go.   Al - lez, al - lez, al-lez.   Al - lez, al - lez, al-lez.

Sing and celebrate

Music is an important part of our lives. We use music to celebrate special times.

Call   Response   Call   Response   C   R   C   R   Tutti   8

Em

Go,   go,   go,   go.   Go, go, go, go. Here we go, yeah!

VERSE   *Solo*

Em   C   Em

1. The cup of life,   this ___ is the one. _   Now is the time,   don't _
2. *La   vi - da es   com - pe - ti - ción. _   Hay que so - ñar,   ser ___*

C   Em   C

_____ ev - er stop.   Push it a - long,   got - ta be strong. _
_____ *cam - pe - ón.*   *La   co - pa es   la _____ ben - di - ción, _*

Push it a-long, right __ to the top. Co - mo Cain y A - bel es un par -
la ga-na-rás, go, __ go, __ go. And when you feel the __ heat the world is

ti - do __ cruel. __ Tie-nes que pe - le - ar __ por un - a es - tre -
at your __ feet. __ No one can hold you down __ if you real - ly want __

- lla. __ Con - si - gue con hon - or la co - pa
__ it. __ Just steal your des - ti - ny right from the

del a - mor. __ Pa - ra so - bre - vi - vir __ y lu - char por e -
hands of __ fate. __ Reach for the cup of life __ 'cause your name is on __

Response   *Response*
- lla. __ Lu - char por e - lla. __Yeah! Do you real-ly want __ it? __Yeah!
__ it. __ Do you real - ly want __ it?

REFRAIN *Tutti*

Here we go. Al - lez, al - lez, al - lez. Go, go, go. Al -
Uno, dos, tres, o - lé, o - lé, o - lé. Un, deux, trois, Al -

lez, al - lez, al-lez. __ To-night's the night we're gon-na cel-e-brate. The
lez, al - lez, al-lez. __

To Coda 2nd time ⊕

3

cup of life, al - lez, al - lez, al - lez. __

Tune In

Every four years, the best soccer teams from around the world play in a month long tournament called the World Cup. The first World Cup took place in 1930 and was won by Uruguay.

Al - lez, al - lez, al - lez, al - lez. Al - lez, al - lez, al - lez, al - lez. Al -

lez, al - lez, al - lez, al - lez. Al - lez, al - lez, al - lez. _____ Al -

lez, al-lez, al-lez. _____ Yeah!   Do you real-ly want _it? ___ Yeah!

Yitzhak Rabin
▼ Nobel Peace Prize, 199[4]

SING in Peace

▲ Jane Addams
Nobel Peace Prize, 1931

This song from Israel could be from any country. The message is universal—peace in our world. Israel's Prime Minister, Yitzhak Rabin, was working for peace when he was assassinated. A copy of this song was found in his pocket.

Look at the song *"Shir l'shalom."* Notice the melodic rhythm is repeated many times. Clap the rhythm of the first phrase.

Now we're ready to **sing** the song.

 15-11

Shir l'shalom
(Hand in Hand–A Song for Peace)

Hebrew Words by Jacob Rotblitt
English Adaptation by Stanley Ralph Ross and Michael Isaacson

Music by Yair Rosenblum
Arranged by Michael Isaacson

1. Tnu la - she - mesh la - a - lot, la - bo - ker l' - ha -
2. Tnu la - she - mesh la - cha - dor mi - ba - 'ad la - pra -
1. Ev - 'ry day, the sun will rise and shine u - pon our __
2. As we gath - er side by side to plead for what we __

ir. Ha - za - kah she - ba - tfi - lot ____ o -
chim. Al ta - bi - tu l' - a - chor, __ ha -
land, Urg - ing us to re - a - lize ____ we
need, Throw a - way mis - ta - ken pride __ and

ta - nu lo tach __ zir. Mi a - sher ka -
ni - chu la - hol - chim. Su ey - na - yim
must walk hand - in - hand. Peo - ple who were
peace will then suc - ceed. Broth - ers will em -

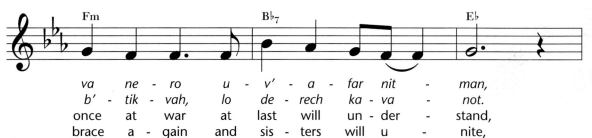

va ne - ro u - v' - a - far nit - man,
b' - tik - vah, lo de - rech ka - va - not.
once at war at last will un - der - stand,
brace a - gain and sis - ters will u - nite,

Be - chi mar lo ya - i - ro _____ lo
Shi - ru shir la - a - ha - vah, ____ v' -
It's a sign we can't ig - nore, ___ we
Ev - 'ry day we live in peace __ will

yach - zi - ro l' - chan. Ish o - ta - nu
lo la - mil - cha - mot. Al ta - gi - du
must walk hand - in - hand. In this world we
shine with rad - iant __ light. On - ly when we're

lo ya - shiv mi - bor tach - teet a -
yom ya - vo, ha vi - u et ha -
will sur - vive, give thanks to God a -
hand - in - hand can san - i - ty be __

fel. Kan lo yo - i - lu lo shi - rey ha -
yom! Ki lo - cha - lom hu. U - v' - chol ha -
bove, be - cause we know the rea - son we are
near, let's strive to do our best to make sure

ni - tsa - chon __ v' - lo shi - rey ha - lel.
ki - ka - rot __ ha - ri - u l' - sha - lom!
all a - live, __ is God's e - ter - nal __ love.
war is banned _ and peace will con - quer __ fear.

La' chen rak shi - ru shir l' - sha - lom, __ al
And so we sing, sing, sing of a day __ when

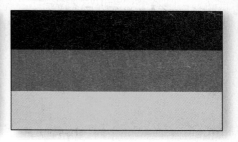

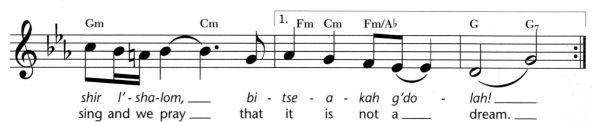

| Fm | Dm | G | | A♭ | B♭ |

til - cha - shu   tfi - la.   La' chen rak   shi - ru
peace   will   reign   su - preme;   And   so   we   sing,   sing,

| Gm | Cm | 1. Fm Cm | Fm/A♭ | G | G₇ |

shir   l' - sha-lom, ___   bi - tse - a - kah g'do - lah! _____
sing and we pray ___   that   it   is   not a ____   dream. ___

2.

| Fm | G | A♭ | B♭ | Gm | Cm | A♭ | B♭ | Cm |

tse - a - kah g'do - lah! _____   g' - do - lah! _____
it   is   not a ___   dream, ___   Not   a   dream. _____

Mother Teresa ▶
Nobel Peace Prize,
1979

◀ Nelson Mandela
Nobel Peace Prize,
1993

Aung San Suu Kyi ▶
Nobel Peace Prize,
1991

Movin' and Groovin' Is a "Boo"tiful Thing

Originally a Celtic holiday, Halloween has come to mean costumes, trick or treating, and horror stories for children. *Little Shop of Horrors* was an Off-Broadway musical hit. It is about a flower shop employee and his plant, Audrey II, which is from outer space.

Sing "Little Shop of Horrors." Then choose an instrument and **play** the melody.

Little Shop of Horrors

Words by Howard Ashman

Music by Alan Menken

Holiday Harmony

The shortest day of the year occurs on the winter solstice, December 21 or 22. In the northern parts of the world, snow, ice, and cold are associated with winter. This song paints a picture of a cold winter day. **Sing** the partner song "Winter Fantasy" and imagine the picture the song creates.

15-17

Winter Fantasy

Words and Music by Jill Gallina

Snow-flakes fall-ing all o-ver town, slip-ping slid-ing
There's an i-cy chill in the air, tell-ing us that

1.
ev-'ry-bod-y rush-in' 'round.

2.
win-ter's real-ly here. Oh!

I'm so glad that win-ter is here. Grab your sled and

let out a hap-py cheer be-cause it's snow-ing, blow-ing, all through the day.

Win-ter winds will sure-ly blow all your cares a-way.

A Cool Holiday Song

Many popular performers enjoy recording holiday music. **Listen** to this version of *Let It Snow! Let It Snow! Let It Snow!* by Harry Connick, Jr. Then **sing** your own version of the song.

15-19

Let It Snow! Let It Snow! Let It Snow!

Words by Sammy Cahn

Music by Jule Styne

The snow-man in the yard is fro-zen hard; He's a sor-ry sight to see,

If he had a brain he'd com-plain, Bet he wish-es he were me.

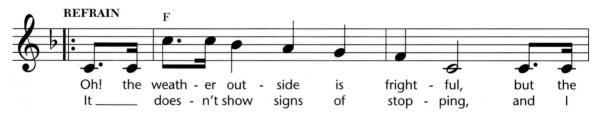

Oh! the weath-er out-side is fright-ful, but the
It _____ does-n't show signs of stop-ping, and I

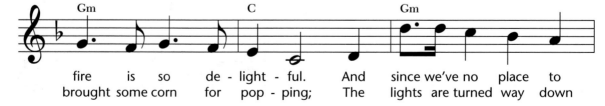

fire is so de-light-ful. And since we've no place to
brought some corn for pop-ping; The lights are turned way down

go, Let it snow! Let it snow! Let it snow!
low. Let it snow! Let it snow! Let it snow!

Harry Connick, Jr.

Harry Connick, Jr. (born 1967) has had a wonderful career in music and acting. Born in New Orleans, his musical style is rooted in New Orleans jazz. He started playing the piano at age three. Before Connick was 10 years old, he played with a professional jazz band and later with the New Orleans Symphony.

15-21
Let It Snow! Let It Snow! Let It Snow!

by Jule Styne and Sammy Cahn
as performed by Harry Connick, Jr.

This recording features a jazz ensemble and an orchestra.

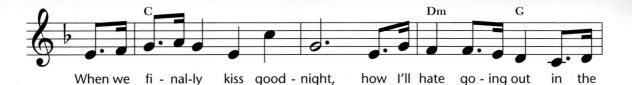

When we fi-nal-ly kiss good-night, how I'll hate go-ing out in the

storm! But if you'll real-ly hold me tight, all the way home I'll be warm. The

fire is slow-ly dy-ing, and, my dear, we're still good-bye-ing. But as

long as you love me so, Let it snow! Let it snow! Let it snow!

Sing and Celebrate

Harmony in Chanukah

Chanukah is a holiday observed by Jewish people. It is also called "The Festival of Lights." This holiday is celebrated by lighting candles on a *menorah*, exchanging gifts, and eating traditional foods such as *latkes* (potato pancakes). Families and friends exchange gifts and play games during the eight days of Chanukah.

Accompany *"Ocho kandelikas"* on the guitar. Practice playing the E string and the B string on the guitar. Then follow the music on page 413 and **play** E or B as you sing the song.

412

Singing in Ladino

When the Jews left Spain in 1492, they took with them a local Spanish language. It is called Judeo-Spanish or Ladino. This language is still known in many countries of the world where Jews have settled. **Sing** this Ladino song.

15-22

Ocho kandelikas
(Eight Little Candles)

Words and Music by Flory Jagoda

VERSE

1. Ha - nu - ka lin - da sta a - ki   o - cho kan - de - las pa - ra mi.
2. Mu - chas fi - e - stas vo fa - zer   kon a - le - gri - as i pla - zer.
1. O love-ly Cha-nu-kah is here,   eight can-dles' light to bring me cheer.
2. Cha-nu-kah par-ties ev-'ry day,   drei-del games for all to play.

Ha - nu - ka lin - da sta a - ki   o - cho kan - de - las pa - ra mi.
Mu - chas fi - e - stas vo fa - zer   kon a - le - gri - as i pla - zer.
O love-ly Cha-nu-kah is here,   eight can-dles' light to bring me cheer.
Cha-nu-kah par-ties ev-'ry day,   drei-del games for all to play.

REFRAIN

O _____ u - na kan - de - li - ka, dos kan - de - li - kas, tres kan - de - li - kas,
O _____ one _ lit - tle can - dle, two lit - tle can - dles, three lit - tle can - dles,

kuat - ro kan - de - li - kas, sin - ko kan - de - li - kas, sej kan - de - li - kas,
four _ lit - tle can - dles, five _ lit - tle can - dles, six lit - tle can - dles,

sie - te kan - de - li - kas, o - cho kan - de - las pa - ra mi.
sev - en lit - tle can - dles, eight lit - tle can - dles all for me.

3. *Los pastelikos vo komer*
   kon almendrikas i la myel.
   Los pastelikos vo komer
   kon almendrikas i la myel.
   Refrain

3. Sweet little pastries we will eat,
   filled with almonds and honey.
   Sweet little pastries we will eat,
   filled with almonds and honey.
   Refrain

Sing and Celebrate

CHRISTMAS RHYTHMS

Christmas is a holiday celebrated by Christians all over the world. Christmas traditions differ from country to country. Although only one day is celebrated as Christmas Day, the Christmas season is actually twelve days.

Sing the song and notice the changes in meter.

THE TWELVE DAYS OF CHRISTMAS

Christmas Song from England

On the first day of Christ-mas my true love gave to me, a
par - tridge _____ in a pear tree.

On the se-cond day of Christ-mas my true love gave to me,
third
fourth

3. *on to next ending* 2. *on to next ending* 1.
four call-ing birds, three French _ hens, two tur-tle doves,

and a par - tridge __ in a pear tree.

On the fifth day of Christ-mas my true love gave to me,
sixth
seventh
eighth
ninth
tenth
eleventh
twelfth

twelve drum-mers drum-ming, eleven pip-ers pip-ing, ten lords a leap-ing,

nine la-dies danc-ing, eight maids a milk-ing, seven swans a swim-ming,

six geese a lay-ing, five gold-en rings, four _ call-ing birds,

three French hens, two _ tur-tle doves, and a par-tridge _ in a pear tree.

Listen to *Good King Wenceslas* [WEN-ses-lahs].
What story does the song tell?

16-1

Good King Wenceslas

**Traditional Carol
as performed by the Westminster Choir**

This traditional carol may have come from Bohemia, a
section of the former Czechoslovakia.

Sing and Celebrate

Nine-Day Celebration

In Mexico, Christmas is celebrated for nine days and is called *Las posadas*. **Create** ostinatos in meter in 3 and meter in 2. **Perform** them while you sing *"Al quebrar la piñata."*

16-2

AL QUEBRAR LA PIÑATA
(Piñata Song)

English Words by Verne Muñoz

Christmas Song from Mexico

En las no - ches de po - sa - das, _____
In the hap - py days of Christ - mas, _____

La pi - ña - ta es lo me - jor; _____
Sounds of glad - ness fill the air; _____

La ni - ña más re - mil - ga - da _____
When it's time for the pi - ña - ta, _____

Se al - bo - ro - ta con ar - dor. _____
There's ex - cite - ment ev - 'ry - where. _____

Da - le, da - le, da - le, no pier - das el ti - no,
Take a stick and whack it, Be the one to crack it;

Que de la dis - tan - cia se pier - de_el ca - mi - no.
Win pi - ña - ta's treas - ure, Can - dies for your pleas - ure.

A Seasonal Song

Listen to *Feliz Navidad,* a song in Spanish and English. **Create** an ostinato pattern to play while you listen.

16-6
Feliz Navidad

by José Feliciano
Feliciano's arrangement of *Feliz Navidad* made the song popular across the United States.

KWANZAA
Hello and Goodbye

Kwanzaa is a Swahili word that means "first." The holiday, *Kwanzaa*, was created by Dr. Maulana Karenga to remind African Americans of their heritage. It is celebrated from December 26 through January 1.

Identify the phrases as you **listen** to "*Harambee*." **Sing** the song, and **perform** a slight *crescendo* at the beginning and a slight *decrescendo* at the end of each phrase.

16-7

Harambee

Words and Music by James McBride

1. We gath-er for the Kwan-zaa hol-i-day this time each year __ With
2. ⅞ Sev-en dif-f'rent prin - ci-ples that help us learn to grow __ We
3. ⅞ Build-ing as a na - tion with our hon-or and our pride, __ We

rel - a - tives and friends from far and wide, __
cel - e - brate our faith and u - ni - ty, ____
learn to hon - or truth and show our love, __

Shar-ing in a peace-ful time of trust and love and song, __ With
Hop-ing that the best __ of all your wish-es do come true, __ We
Car-ing is a part __ of our re-spon-si-bil-i-ty. __ We

418

joy e - nough to last __ the whole year long.
wish a hap - py Kwan - zaa to you.
want the world to live __ in har - mo - ny.

REFRAIN Fm₇ E♭

A Kwan-zaa hol - i - day _ is a spe-cial hol - i - day, _ A
Ha - ram - bee __ means __ hel - lo and good-bye, too, _ A

1. Fm₇ B♭

time to cel - e - brate __ our his - to - ry.

2. A♭ B♭ E♭

way of show - ing that __ I care for you.

Guide Our Hope

Singing brings people together during times of struggle. "We Shall Not Be Moved" is associated with the Civil Rights Movement in this country. This song reminds us of Dr. Martin Luther King's fight for the rights of African Americans.

Sing the song and then **play** it on a melody instrument.

▲ Martin Luther King, Jr., his wife Coretta, and marchers in Selma, Alabama in 1965.

16-9

We Shall Not Be Moved

Traditional Freedom Song

do

| G | C | D₇ |

1. We   shall   not,   we shall not be
2. We're   on our way   to   vic-tor-y, ____   we shall not be
3. Segre - ga-tion is __ our   en-e-my, __   it must be re-

D₇   G   G₇

moved. ___ We   shall   not,   we shall not be moved.
moved.__ We're on our way __ to   vic-tor-y, ____   we shall not be moved.
moved. Segre - ga-tion is __ our   en-e-my, __   it must be re-moved.

C

Just   like   a   tree,   that's   plant - ed   by   the

G   B₇   Em   G   D₇   G

wa   -   ter.   We   shall   not   be   moved.

In 1963 Dr. King gave his famous "I Have a Dream" speech to a huge gathering in Washington D.C. This event is called the March on Washington. ▶

Sing and Celebrate

CREATING LIVING TRADITIONS

During the eight days of Passover, Jews remember the freeing of Jewish slaves in Egypt thousands of years ago. They celebrate by having traditional services called *seders* and reading from the *Haggadah*. Symbolic foods are eaten and traditional songs are sung. **Sing** "*Dayenu,*" a traditional song.

A Refrain to Remember

Analyze the form of this song. Which of these two sections is always sung with the same words? Which section has different words each time it is sung?

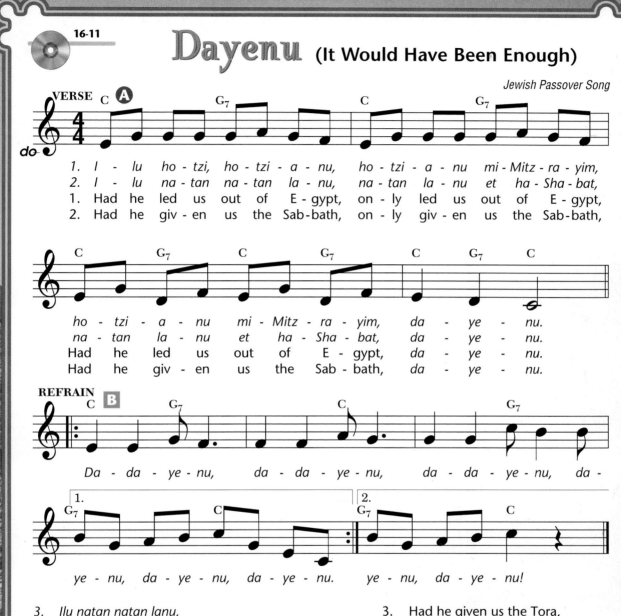

Dayenu (It Would Have Been Enough)

Jewish Passover Song

VERSE A

1. I - lu ho - tzi, ho - tzi - a - nu, ho - tzi - a - nu mi - Mitz - ra - yim,
2. I - lu na - tan na - tan la - nu, na - tan la - nu et ha - Sha - bat,
1. Had he led us out of E - gypt, on - ly led us out of E - gypt,
2. Had he giv - en us the Sab-bath, on - ly giv - en us the Sab-bath,

ho - tzi - a - nu mi - Mitz - ra - yim, da - ye - nu.
na - tan la - nu et ha - Sha - bat, da - ye - nu.
Had he led us out of E - gypt, da - ye - nu.
Had he giv - en us the Sab - bath, da - ye - nu.

REFRAIN B

Da - da - ye - nu, da - da - ye - nu, da - da - ye - nu, da -

1.
ye - nu, da - ye - nu, da - ye - nu.

2.
ye - nu, da - ye - nu!

3. Ilu natan natan lanu,
natan lanu et haTora,
natan lanu et haTora, dayenu.
Refrain

3. Had he given us the Tora,
only given us the Tora,
Had he given us the Tora, *dayenu*.
Refrain

Sing and Celebrate

Heartbeat OF A Nation

Patriotic songs are songs that express love of and loyalty to one's country. During war time, the armed forces defend our country and our freedom.
Conduct "America" while the rest of the class sings the song.

16-15

America

Words by Samuel Francis Smith

Traditional Melody

1. My coun - try! 'tis of thee, Sweet land of
2. My na - tive coun - try, thee, Land of the
3. Let mu - sic swell the breeze, And ring from
4. Our fa - thers' God, to Thee, Au - thor of

lib - er - ty, Of thee I sing; Land where my
no - ble free, Thy name I love; I love thy
all the trees Sweet Free - dom's song; Let mor - tal
lib - er - ty, To Thee we sing; Long may our

fa - thers died, Land of the Pil - grims' pride,
rocks and rills, Thy woods and tem - pled hills;
tongues a - wake, Let all that breathe par - take,
land be bright With Free - dom's ho - ly light;

From ev - 'ry ___ moun - tain - side Let ___ free - dom ring!
My heart _ with _ rap - ture thrills Like _ that a - bove.
Let rocks _ their _ si - lence break, The _ sound pro - long.
Pro - tect _ us ___ by Thy might, Great _ God, our King!

Our National Anthem

Sing "The Star-Spangled Banner" with pride. People stand to show respect for our country while they sing the National Anthem.

16-17

The Star-Spangled Banner

Words by Francis Scott Key

Music by John Stafford Smith

Oh, __ say! can you see, by the dawn's ear - ly light, What so
stripes and bright stars, through the per - il - ous fight, O'er the

proud - ly we hailed at the twi - light's last gleam-ing, Whose broad
ram - parts we watched were so gal - lant - ly

stream-ing? And the rock - ets' red glare, the bombs burst - ing in

air, Gave proof through the night that our flag was still

there. Oh, say, does that __ Star - Span - gled Ban - ner __ yet __

wave __ O'er the land __ of the free and the home of the brave?

Playing the Recorder

This section of your book will help you learn to **play** the soprano recorder, a small wind instrument.

Getting Ready

Extend your hand forward with palm upward. Pretend you have a small feather on your palm. Blow the "feather" gently so it moves across your palm without falling. This is all the air you need to produce a good sound.

Covering the Holes

Using your left hand, cover the holes shown in the picture. Be sure to press just hard enough so that the holes make a light mark on your fingers. Remove your hand to check that there is an outline of a circle on each finger.

Let's Play G and A

Put your hands back in
position to play G. Cover
the tip of the mouthpiece
with your lips. Blow
gently as you whisper
daah. Practice playing G
using a steady beat.

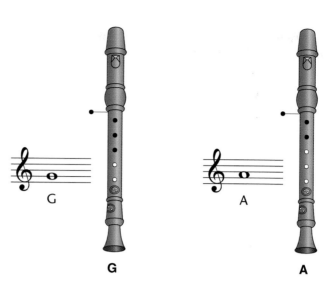

G

A

Counter this Melody

Play this countermelody throughout the first section of "Oh, Susanna."
Create a hand jive to perform as you **sing** the refrain.

A

G

A

G

Adding B

Now you are ready to learn to play B. Cover the holes shown in the diagram. Before playing, predict if B will sound higher or lower than G or A. Here is a recorder part that you can **play** while others **sing** "Missy-La, Massa-La" on page 184. Make sure you observe the repeat bars at the end of each phrase.

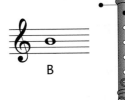

B

G   A

B

Three New Notes

Here are three new notes. Cover the holes securely with your fingers arched and whisper *daah*.

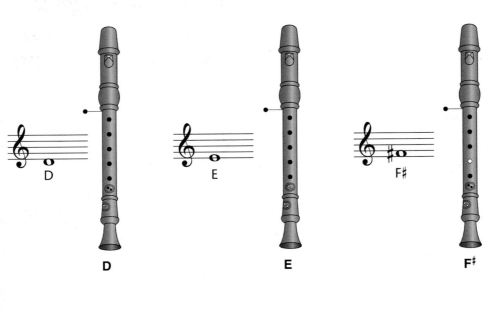

D   E   F♯

Now you are ready to **play** a countermelody to accompany the singing of "The Keel Row" on page 236. Does the countermelody have mostly leaps or steps?

"B-A-G" Songs Plus

Now that you can play G, A, B, D, and E you will be able to **play** some of the songs in your book. Look at "See the Children Playin'" page 103, "Old House, Tear It Down" page 174, and "Love Will Guide Us" page 314. Practice individual phrases before playing the entire song.

Ready for High C and High D

Practice **playing** two new notes. Move your thumb slightly away from the hole when playing D.

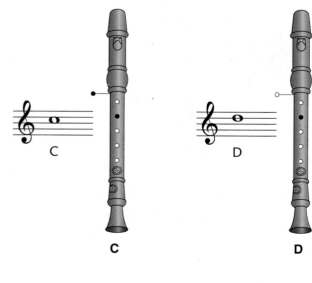

Going Up the Scale

The recorder part below for "Frog Music" on page 196 uses the first 5 notes of the G scale. Can you name these notes? After playing the recorder melody as written, **create** a new one. Keep the same melody but change the rhythm patterns. Before beginning, think of some patterns that can be used in place of quarter notes.

Pipes Around the World

Listen to these musical examples. Point to each instrument as you hear it being played.

🔊 **16-19**

Pipes Around the World

Sound Montage

As you **read** the captions, study the pictures of these **aerophones** from around the world. How do you think each instrument will sound?

Aerophones are instruments that produce sound by vibrating air.

Didgeridoo, a 5 feet long wooden instrument from Australia, is played by Aboriginals during various ceremonies and rituals. ▶

▲ *Shakuhachi*, an end-blown bamboo flute from Japan, can be found in various lengths, but most only have four finger holes and one thumb hole.

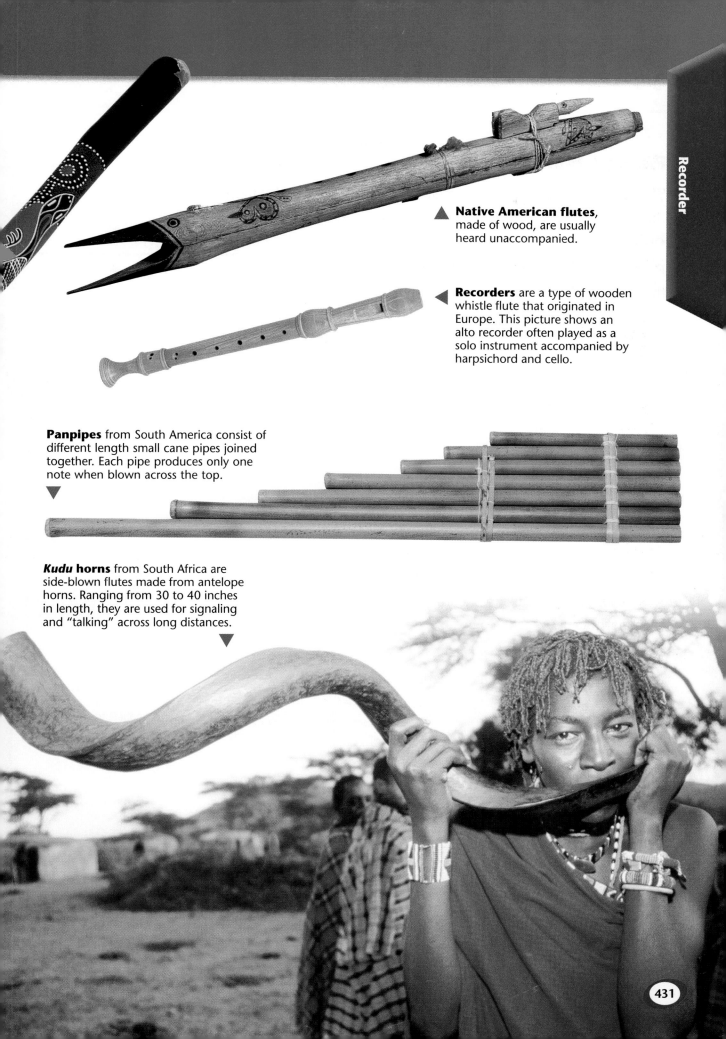

Native American flutes, made of wood, are usually heard unaccompanied.

Recorders are a type of wooden whistle flute that originated in Europe. This picture shows an alto recorder often played as a solo instrument accompanied by harpsichord and cello.

Panpipes from South America consist of different length small cane pipes joined together. Each pipe produces only one note when blown across the top.

***Kudu* horns** from South Africa are side-blown flutes made from antelope horns. Ranging from 30 to 40 inches in length, they are used for signaling and "talking" across long distances.

431

Mallet Instruments

Playing Mallets

When using mallets to play instruments, follow these simple suggestions.

Holding the Mallets

Fold your fingers and thumbs around the mallet handle—the thumb should lie alongside the handle, but the pointer finger should not sit on top of the mallet. The backs of your hands should face the ceiling. Grip the handles on the hand grips, but not at the very end. (Smaller hands may need to grip further up toward the mallet head.) Elbows should hang easily at your sides. Avoid elbows that stick out to the side or hug the body.

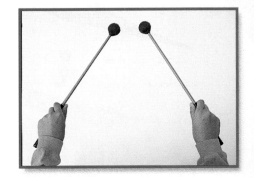

Striking the Bars

Strike each bar at its center, not at either end. Let your mallet strike quickly and then bounce away. If you let the mallet stay on the bar, the sound is stopped.

Matching Mallets to Instruments

It is important to choose the appropriate mallet for each instrument to make its best sound.

For special effects, use hard wood mallets or mallet handles. Avoid anything that would damage the surface of the bars.

Bass instruments need large felt or yarn heads. Choose softer mallets for metallophones, and harder mallets for xylophones. ▼

Alto/soprano xylophones need medium-sized felt or yarn heads with a hard core. Alto/soprano metallophones need the same, but with a softer core. ▼

Glockenspiels need small wood, hard rubber, or composition heads. ▼

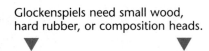

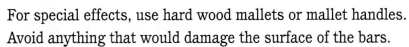

Playing Position

You may sit or stand while playing mallet instruments. This depends on the distance of the top of the instrument from the floor. Your body should stay straight with your arms placed easily in front of you to strike the bars.

Sit on the floor. ▶

Sit in a chair to play bass instruments. ▶

◀ Stand

Sit in a chair. ▶

Mallet Instruments

433

Playing the Guitar

Playing the Guitar

There are three types of guitars—nylon-string classical, steel-string acoustic, and electric. Look at these photographs and learn the names of their parts.

tuning keys

nut

fret

neck and fingerboard

soundhole

pick-ups

tremelo arm

tone and volume controls

toggle switch

▲ Nylon-String Classical Guitar

▲ Steel-String Acoustic Guitar

▲ Electric Guitar

Tuning the Guitar

The strings on a Guitar need to be tuned to certain pitches. It is also necessary to fine-tune and re-tune during long periods of performance. Follow these steps to tune the guitar.

- To get started quickly, you may ask your teacher to tune the guitar for you.
- Guitar strings are numbered 1, 2, 3, 4, 5, and 6, with string number 6 being the lowest (or largest).
- You can tune the guitar using the keys of the piano. The illustration at right shows what keys to use for tuning each guitar string.

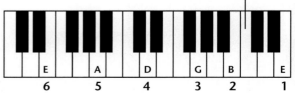

middle C

| E | A | D | G | B | E |
| 6 | 5 | 4 | 3 | 2 | 1 |

Getting Ready to Play

Follow these directions to learn how to **play** the guitar.

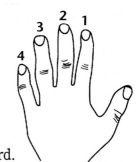

- The left-hand fingers press the strings on the frets to produce chords.
- The right-hand thumb brushes the strings in order to make the sound.
- Use the left-hand finger numbers when you read guitar chords.
- Always relax your body. The guitar neck should be slanted slightly upward.

Playing Your First Chords

Chords are indicated in most songs in this book. The chord names tell you which chords to play, and when to play them.

To play chords on the guitar

- Place the thumb of your left hand behind the neck.
- Keep your fingers arched as you reach around the neck to press the strings.
- Press the strings down onto the fingerboard.
- Keep your palm away from the neck.

Guitar Chords

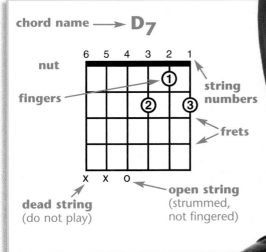

Playing the Keyboard

In this section of your book, we will learn to **play** keyboard instruments.

Sitting Position

For maximum support from your arms, shoulders, and back, sit slightly forward on the bench with your feet resting on the floor at all times. Your knees should be just under the front edge of the keyboard. You should feel a center of gravity which will allow you to lean from side to side if necessary.

Hand Position

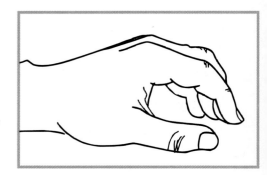

The best hand position is the shape of your hand as it hangs at your side. When you bring your hand up to the keyboard, curve your fingers at the middle joint and make your wrist parallel to the keyboard. You should feel "flexibility" in your elbows as they hang near your side. The elbow should follow through with the natural movement of your wrist.

Finger Numbers

The fingers are numbered as pictured here.

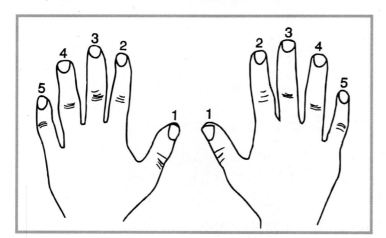

Fingerings for Melodies

How a melody moves determines the fingering on the keyboard. Look at the diagrams at the top of page 437. By translating the keyboard examples to one- and two-line staves, it is easy to see how right/left movement on the keyboard relates to up/down movement on the staff.

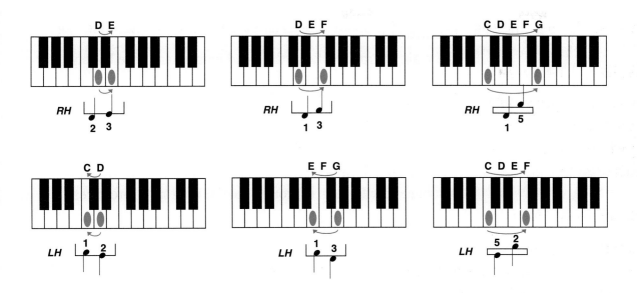

Three-Line Reading

Play these examples. Determine the fingering before you begin each one.

RH   Begin on G:

LH   Begin on C:

Playing from Treble and Bass Clefs

When singing and playing music, you must follow the upward and downward direction of a melody to determine if it moves by step, by leap, or if it stays on a repeated tone. When playing music, you must also determine where to play the notes on the keyboard. Each note in printed music indicates one place and only one place where it can be played.

Sound Bank

Most instruments appear on the page indicated. In a few instances, the reference is to a family of instruments.

◀ **Bagpipes** An air reservoir contained in an animal skin bag is the main characteristic of this reed instrument. The bagpipe is common in Arabic and European countries. p. 252 CD 16-20

◀ *Balalaika* [bah-lah-LIE-kah] A flat, triangular, long-necked instrument with a small, round hole at the top. It produces sound when any of the three metal strings are plucked. The balalaika is popular in Russian folk music and is a member of the lute family. p. 285 CD 16-21

◀ **Bassoon** A large, tube-shaped, woodwind instrument with a double-reed. Lower notes on the bassoon can be gruff or comical. Higher notes are softer, sweeter, and gentler sounding. p. 68 CD 16-22

◀ **Cello** A large wooden string instrument. The player sits with the cello between his or her knees and reaches around the front to play it. The cello has a low, rich-sounding voice. p. 93 CD 16-23

◀ **Clarinet** A wind instrument shaped like a cylinder. It is usually made of wood and has a reed in the mouthpiece. Low notes on the clarinet are soft and hollow. The middle and highest notes are open and bright. p. 68 CD 16-24

Instrument Key: strings percussion woodwind brass

◀ **Conga** An Afro-Cuban drum with a long, barrel-shaped body. It comes in two sizes, the small quinto and the large tumbador. The conga is struck with the fingers and the palm of the hand. p. 33 CD 16-25

◀ *Darabukah* [dahr-ah-BOO-kah] An hour-glass-shaped drum common in the Middle East and Northern Africa. p. 133 CD 16-26

◀ *Didgeridoo* [DIJ-er-ee-doo] This Northern Australia instrument is made from a termite-hollowed eucalyptus branch after its outer bark is removed. It is a straight natural trumpet that is end-blown. p. 34 CD 16-27

◀ **Dulcimer** A sound box made of wood, with strings across it. The strings are usually plucked. p. 337 CD 16-28

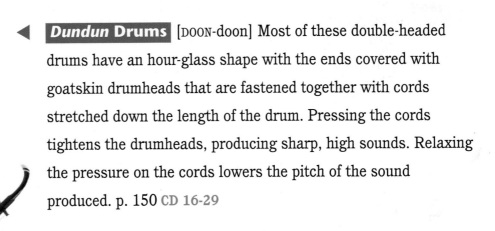

◀ *Dundun Drums* [DOON-doon] Most of these double-headed drums have an hour-glass shape with the ends covered with goatskin drumheads that are fastened together with cords stretched down the length of the drum. Pressing the cords tightens the drumheads, producing sharp, high sounds. Relaxing the pressure on the cords lowers the pitch of the sound produced. p. 150 CD 16-29

◀ *Erhu* [EHR-hoo] A Chinese string instrument played with a bow. p. 303 CD 16-30

Flute A metal instrument shaped like a pipe. The player holds the flute sideways and blows across an open mouthpiece. The flute's voice is pure, clear, and sweet. Its low notes are the same ones children sing, but it can also play very high. p. 68 CD 16-31

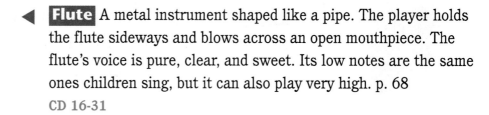

French Horn A medium-sized instrument made of coiled brass tubing. At one end is a large bell. The player holds the horn on his or her lap and keeps one hand inside the bell. The sound of the horn is very mellow. p. 69 CD 16-32

Glockenspiel [GLAHK-ehn-shpeel] A row of metal bars mounted on a wooden frame and struck with mallets. It produces high-pitched bell-like sounds. p. 150 CD 16-33

Guitar A six-string instrument that is a member of the lute family. It has a modified hour-glass shape with a flat back. The strings are strummed or plucked. p. 210 CD 16-34

Harpsichord A keyboard instrument similar to a piano. However, unlike the piano the strings are plucked by a quill, not struck by a hammer. p. 226 CD 16-35

Koto [KOH-toh) An instrument with movable frets and 7 to 17 strings. It is known as the national instrument of Japan. The player sits on the floor, either cross-legged or in a kneeling position. Sound is produced when the player plucks the silk strings with a bamboo, bone, or ivory pick. The sound is similar to that of a harp. p. 106 CD 16-36

Instrument Key: strings percussion woodwind brass

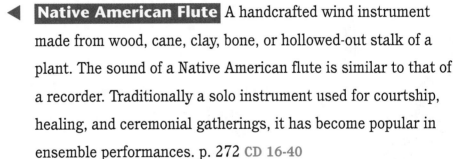

Lute This string instrument usually has a bowl shaped back and is played by strumming or plucking the strings. p. 106 CD 16-37

Maracas Dried seeds or pebbles fill this pair of rattles. They are rhythm instruments. p. 150 CD 16-38

Marimba A large barred instrument. The bars are made of rosewood and are struck with yarn mallets. Below the bars are resonating tubes which help carry the sound. p. 151 CD 16-39

Native American Flute A handcrafted wind instrument made from wood, cane, clay, bone, or hollowed-out stalk of a plant. The sound of a Native American flute is similar to that of a recorder. Traditionally a solo instrument used for courtship, healing, and ceremonial gatherings, it has become popular in ensemble performances. p. 272 CD 16-40

Oboe A slender, woodwind instrument with a doublereed. In its low voice, the oboe may sound mysterious. These are the notes children sing. When it goes higher, the sound is light and sweet. p. 68 CD 16-41

Organ A keyboard instrument with foot pedals and two or more sets of keys called manuals. Forcing air through pipes attached to the organ produces sound. p. 227 CD 16-42

Saxophone A metal-bodied reed instrument with 18 to 20 holes controlled by keys. The saxophone family consists of baritone, tenor, alto, and soprano saxophones. p. 73 CD 16-43

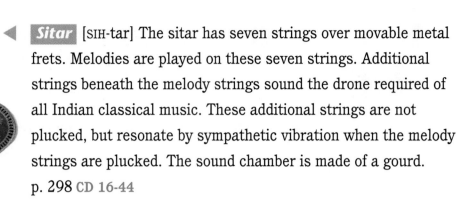

Sitar [SIH-tar] The sitar has seven strings over movable metal frets. Melodies are played on these seven strings. Additional strings beneath the melody strings sound the drone required of all Indian classical music. These additional strings are not plucked, but resonate by sympathetic vibration when the melody strings are plucked. The sound chamber is made of a gourd. p. 298 CD 16-44

Snare Drum A small, metal cylinder-shaped drum. Metal coils are stretched across the bottom of the drum to make a distinctive sound when the top head is hit with sticks. p. 151 CD 16-45

Steel Drum This instrument is made from an oil drum. It comes in different sizes and is played with special mallets. p. 39 CD 16-46

String Bass The string bass is the largest string instrument, and it has the lowest voice. A string bass is usually taller than the average person. The player must sit on a high stool or stand in order to play it. p. 70 CD 16-47

Timbales [tim-BAH-lehs] Round drums, each having a single head, often used in Latin music. p. 150 CD 16-48

Timpani Large, pot-shaped drums, also called kettledrums. Unlike most drums, they can be tuned to notes of the scale. The timpani can sound like a heartbeat or a roll of thunder. The sound can be a loud "boom," a quiet "thump," or a distant rumble, depending on how they are played. p. 151 CD 16-49

Instrument Key:  strings   percussion   woodwind   brass

◄ **Trombone** A large, brass instrument with a rich and strong sound. It has a tubing, a "bell," and a long, curved "slide." The trombone can be loud and brilliant, but its soft voice is mellow. It can play the notes children sing, but also go much lower. p. 69 CD 16-50

◄ **Trumpet** The smallest brass instrument, but one with a big sound. The trumpet's voice can be loud and bright but can also sound warm and sweet. Most of its notes are the same as children sing. p. 69 CD 16-51

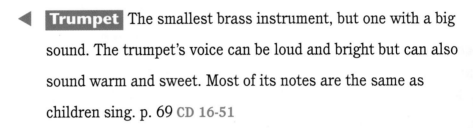

◄ **Tuba** The largest brass instrument, the one with the lowest voice. The tuba's low notes are deep and dark sounding. The higher ones are hearty and warm. p. 69 CD 16-52

◄ *Vihuela* [vee-HWAY-lah] A stringed instrument shaped like a guitar and tuned like a lute. p. 173 CD 16-53

◄ **Viola** A wooden string instrument played like a violin. The viola's voice is similar to the violin's, but deeper, richer, and darker. p. 109 CD 16-54

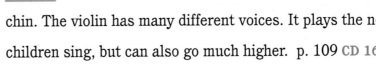

◄ **Violin** A wooden string instrument held under the player's chin. The violin has many different voices. It plays the notes children sing, but can also go much higher. p. 109 CD 16-55

Glossary

AB form A musical plan that has two different sections. p. 56

ABA form A musical plan that has three sections. The first and last sections are the same. The middle section is different. p. 98

accent Indicates to play or sing a note with more emphasis than the other notes. p. 206

accompaniment Music that supports the sound of the featured performer(s). p. 34

aerophones Instruments that produce sound by vibrating air. p. 430

band A group of instruments consisting mainly of woodwinds, brass, and percussion. p. 72

bar line The vertical line drawn through a staff to separate measures. p. 96

beat A repeating pulse that can be felt in some music. p. 12

brass A group of wind instruments, including trumpets, French horns, trombones, and tubas, used in bands and orchestras. p. 69

call and response A musical device in which a portion of a melody (call) is followed by an answering portion (response). p. 18

canon A musical form in which the parts imitate each other. One part begins, or leads, and the other parts follow. p. 345

chord Three or more notes arranged in intervals of a third, sounded at the same time. p. 159

coda A "tail" or short section, added at the end of a piece of music. p. 59

composer A person who makes up pieces of music by putting sounds together in his or her own way. p. 17

concerto A composition written for solo instrument(s) with orchestra. p. 69

contour The "shape" of a melody made by the way it moves upward and downward in steps, leaps, and repeated tones. p. 147

contrast Two or more things that are different. In music, for example, slow is a contrast to fast; Section A is a contrast to Section B. p. 157

countermelody A contrasting melody that is played or sung at the same time as the main melody. p. 155

descant A countermelody that decorates the main melody, often soaring above the melody of the song. p. 358

duple meter A basic pattern in which a measure has one strong and one weak beat. p. 14

dynamics The different levels of loudness and softness of sound. p. 6

ensemble A group of musicians who perform together. p. 188

form The overall plan of a piece of music. p. 18

half step On a keyboard, the distance between one key and the next black or white key. p. 144

harmony Two or more different tones sounding at the same time. p. 158

improvise Making up music as it is being performed. p. 57

interlude A short musical connection between sections of a piece of music. p. 59

interval The distance between two pitches. p. 21

introduction Music played before the main part of a composition begins. p. 59

jazz An American musical style made of traditional Western music combined with African rhythms and melodic contours. p. 72

key signature Tells which notes are to be performed with a flat or sharp throughout a piece of music. p. 144

ledger lines Extra lines for pitches above and below the staff. p. 60

legato A term that describes music performed in a smooth and connected style. p. 86

lyrics The words of a song. p. 196

major scale An arrangement of eight tones according to the following pattern of steps or intervals: whole, whole, half, whole, whole, whole, half. p. 184

measure A grouping of beats set off by bar lines. p. 10

melodic sequence A melody pattern that begins on a different pitch each time it is repeated. p. 223

melody A line of single tones that move upward, downward, or repeat. p. 21

melody pattern An arrangement of pitches into a small grouping, usually occurring often in a piece. p. 22

meter The way the beats of music are grouped, often in sets of two or in sets of three. p. 14

mood The feeling that a piece of music gives. p. 297

movement Each of the smaller, self-contained sections (usually three or four) that together make up a symphony, concerto, string quartet, and so on. p. 151

orchestra A group of instruments usually consisting of strings, woodwinds, brass, and percussion. p. 70

ostinato A repeated rhythmic or melodic pattern played throughout a piece or a section of a piece. p. 74

partner songs Two or more different songs that can be sung at the same time to create a thicker texture. p. 110

pentatonic scale A scale of five notes. p. 23

percussion A group of pitched or nonpitched instruments that are played by striking with mallets or beaters, and by shaking. p. 150

phrase A musical "sentence." Each phrase expresses one thought. p. 114

pitch The location of a tone with respect to highness or lowness. p. 21

pizzicato A term that refers to plucking the strings instead of bowing. p. 88

quartet A composition for four voices or instruments, each having a separate part; a group of four singers or instrumentalists, each playing or singing a different part. p. 68

refrain A section of a song that is sung the same way every time it repeats. p. 57

repeat signs Tells the performer to perform all the music between the signs twice. p. 304

repeated tones Two or more tones in a row that have the same sound. p. 21

rests Symbols for the length of silences. p. 10

rhythm pattern A grouping of long and short sounds. Some rhythm patterns have even sounds. Others have uneven sounds. p. 10

rondo A musical form in which the first section always returns. A common rondo form is ABACA. p. 179

root The tone on which a chord is built. p. 237

round A follow-the-leader process in which all perform the same melody but start at different times. p. 192

scale An arrangement of pitches from lower to higher according to a specific pattern of intervals or steps. p. 23

score The musical notation of a composition with each of the instrumental (or vocal) parts shown in a vertical alignment. p. 386

skip To move from one tone to another, skipping over the tones in between. p. 20

slur A curved line connecting two or more notes of different pitch that tells the performer to play or sing the notes *legato*. p. 88

solo Music for a single singer or player, often with an accompaniment. p. 18

staccato A term that describes music performed in a short and detached style. p. 86

step To move from one tone to another without skipping tones in between. p. 21

strings A term used to refer to string instruments that are played by bowing, plucking, or strumming. p. 106

strong beat The first beat in a measure. p. 12

style The special sound that is created when music elements such as rhythm and timbre are combined. p. 124

suite An instrumental work of several movements, often programmatic or descriptive. p. 364

syncopation An arrangement of rhythm in which important tones begin on weak beats or weak parts of beats, giving an off-balance movement to the music. p. 53

tempo The speed of the beat. p. 46

texture The layering of sounds to create a thick or thin quality in music. p. 32

theme An important melody that occurs several times in a piece of music. p. 219

theme and variations A musical form in which each section is a variation of the original theme p. 220

tie A musical symbol that connects two notes of the same pitch. p. 51

timbre The unique difference or tone color of sounds. p. 28

time signature Tells how many beats are in each measure (top number) and the kind of note that gets one beat (bottom number). p. 54

tonal center A pitch that acts as a resting place or "home" for all of the other pitches that happen around it. p. 24

tonic The key, or home tone in a scale. p. 102

unison The same pitch. p. 192

upbeat One or more notes that occur before the first bar line of a phrase. p. 131

variation Music that is repeated, but changed in some important way. p. 219

verse A section of a song where the melody stays the same when it repeats, but the words change. p. 57

weak beat The second beat in a measure. p. 12

whole step On a keyboard, the distance between any two keys with a single key between. p. 144

woodwinds A term used to refer to wind instruments, now or originally made of wood. p. 68

word painting The positioning of pitch and rhythm patterns to resemble the meaning of words. p. 386

Classified Index

Holiday, Seasonal, and Occasion

450

Poems And Stories

Recorded Interviews

Index of Songs

and Speech Pieces

Credits

Cover Photography: Jade Albert for Scott Foresman

Cover Design: Steven Curtis Design, Inc.

Design and Electronic Production: Kirchoff/Wohlberg, Inc.

Unit Introductions: Steven Curtis Design, Inc.

Photo Research: Feldman & Associates, Inc. and Kirchoff/Wohlberg, Inc. Every effort has been made to obtain permission for all photographs found in this book and to make full acknowledgment for their use. Omissions brought to our attention will be corrected in subsequent editions.

Photograph Credits

ii: (TR) San Diego Museum of Man viii: (BC) Adele Starr/Corbis viii: (BL) Wolfgang Kaehler/Corbis viii: (TL) Ousama Ayoub/(c) AFP viii: (TC) Richard Hamilton Smith/Corbis viii: (TC) Danny Lehman/Corbis viii: (TL) Stephen Johnson/Stone viii: (BC) Astrid & Hanns-Frieder Michler/Photo Researchers, Inc. 1: (TC) Bob Krist/Corbis 1: (BR) SuperStock 1: (BL) Leo de Wys Photo Agency 9: (Bkgd) Laura Farr/TimePix 12: (C) George Lepp/Corbis 12: (CL) David Stover/Stock South/PictureQuest 15: (B) Dean Conger/Corbis 17: (TC) Bettmann/Corbis 22: (BC) Hiroshige/The Granger Collection, New York 22: (L) Orion Press 23: (R) Orion Press 24: (BL) Paul Natkin/Photo Reserve 26: (Bkgd) Rudi Von Briel/PhotoEdit 26: (TR) The Granger Collection, New York 27: (CL) Bettmann/Corbis 27: Linda Twine (CR) 28: (BC) Odile Noel/Lebrecht Collection 29: (BR) Adele Starr/Corbis 29: AP Photo/Christopher Berkey 30: (TL) Deborah Davis/PhotoEdit 30: (BC) Nubar Alexanian/Corbis 30: (T) Melodie Gimple/Warner Bros. Records/Photofest 34: (R) Torsten Blackwood/(c) AFP 38: (TC) Abigail Hadeed/Visuals Concepts 38: (CL) Abigail Hadeed/Visuals Concepts 38: (BC) Teri Bloom Photography, Inc 39: (BL) Abigail Hadeed/Visuals Concepts 40: (BR) Nubar Alexanian/Corbis 40: (T) Melodie Gimple/Warner Bros. Records/Photofest 45: Photofest 46: (Bkgd) Alain Le Garsmeur/Stone 48: (T) Corbis 52: (Bkgd) Lowell Georgia/Corbis 55: (CR) The Granger Collection, New York 56: (Bkgd) David Muench/Stone 58: (Bkgd) Chad Ehlers/Stone 60: (B) Scott Daniel Peterson/Gamma Liaison 61: (B) Scott Daniel Peterson/Gamma Liaison 69: (BL) (c) Jonathan Blair/Corbis 70: (Bkgd) Richard Hamilton Smith/Corbis 71: (TC) Archivo Iconografico, S.A./Corbis 72: (CR) Tim Wright/Corbis 72: (T) Odile Noel/Lebrecht Collection 72: (BL) Arnaldo Magnani 73: (CR) (c) 2000 Scott Saltzman/Barefoot Photography 73: (BL) Arnaldo Magnani 73: (T) Odile Noel/Lebrecht Collection 75: (T) Gerrit Greve/Corbis 76: (C) Bruno De Hogues/Stone 77: (Bkgd) Teri Bloom Photography, Inc. 78: (BL) Jack Vartoogian 78: (Bkgd) Leslye Borden/PhotoEdit 79: (CR) SuperStock 79: (BL) Art Wolfe/Stone 81: (BC) Chad Ehlers/Stone 82: Patrick Bennett/Corbis 82: AP/Wide World 84: Patrick Bennett/Corbis 84: The Purcell Team/Corbis 86: (Bkgd) John P. Kelley/Image Bank 88: (Bkgd) Karl Weatherly/Corbis 89: (TC) Archivo Iconografico/Corbis 89: (T) PhotoDisc 90: (R) Gerry Schneiders/Unicorn Stock Photos 91: (TR) Images Coulour Library 100: (Bkgd) Richard T. Nowitz/Corbis 102: (BC) Robert Gwathmey, "Children Dancing" 103: (TL) Bob Krist/Corbis 103: (CR) Corbis 106: (T) Eyewire, Inc. 106: (BR) Wolfgang Kaehler/Corbis 108: (TC) Francis G. Mayer/Corbis 108: (TC) PhotoDisc 109: (BL) Paul Natkin/Photo Reserve 113: (BR) Ebet Roberts Photography 118: (BL) Grosset Simon/Spooner/Liaison Agency 118: (TR) Grosset Simon/Spooner/Liaison Agency 119: (BL) Ousama Ayoub/(c) AFP 121: (TR) Bob Krist/Corbis 126: (Bkgd) Daryl Balfour 128: (TL) Reuters/Fred Prouser/Archive Photos 128: (Bkgd) Daryl Balfour 130: (TR) Duncan Willetts 131: (BR) Jagdish Agarwal/Unicorn Stock Photos 133: (B) SuperStock 135: (Bkgd) David Muench/Corbis 135: (TL) SuperStock 138: (BL) SuperStock 139: (BR) Greg Gibson/AP/Wide World 140: (B) Robert Freck/Odyssey Productions 141: (TL) Danny Lehman/Corbis 141: (BC) Kevin Schafer/Corbis 142: (Bkgd) Danny Lehman/Corbis 143: (TC) Dan Polin/Lights, Words, and Music 143: (BL) Stephanie Maze/Corbis 143: (Bkgd) Danny Lehman/Corbis 146: (BC) AP/Wide World 146: (Bkgd) Iwao Kataoka/Panoramic Images 148: (Bkgd) Iwao Kataoka/Panoramic Images 150: (T) Chris Stock/Lebrecht Collection 152: (BR) Leo de Wys Photo Agency 152: (CR) Christopher Liu/ChinaStock 155: (BR) Michelle Wood 156: (Bkgd) (c) David Muench/Corbis 161: (TR) Michelle Wood 162: Popperfoto/Archive Photos 162: Culver Pictures Inc. 162: Universal Studios/Photofest 164: Bettmann/Corbis 164: Dagmar Fabricius/Stock Boston/PictureQuest 165: Burke/Triolo Productions/FoodPix 165: Hulton Getty Picture Archive/Stone 165: Phil Banko/Stone 165: Joseph Sohm/Visions of America, LLC/PictureQuest 166: (Bkgd) PhotoDisc 167: (BL) The Granger Collection, New York 168: (Bkgd) (c)Victor Englebert 169: (CR) Bonnie Kamin/PhotoEdit 170: (Bkgd) Jane Gifford/Stone 173: (Bkgd) Robert Freck/Odyssey Productions 173: John J. Van Gool (CR) Photo courtesy of John J. van Gool from his website http://www.lutherie-van-gool.nl 173: (TC) Kenwood House, Hampstead, London/Bridgeman Art Library, London/SuperStock 177: (TR) American David David Gallery, Philadelphia/SuperStock 184: (Bkgd) Donald Nausbaum/Stone 186: (Bkgd) Bob Krist/Stone 186: (BL) (c) Cary Wolinsky/Stock Boston/PictureQuest 187: (TC) Tony Arrzua/Corbis 188: (CR) Kate Mount/Lebrecht Collection 189: (TL) Michael Ochs Archives, Venice, CA 189: (BC) AP/Wide World 192: (TR) Joe McDonald/Corbis 193: (TR) Joe McDonald/Corbis 194: (C) Stephen Johnson/Stone 194: (Bkgd) Stephen Johnson/Stone 195: (BC) Teri Bloom Photography, Inc. 200: (CR) Michael Ochs Archives, Venice, CA 200: (BL) Kate Mount/Lebrecht Collection 200: (BC) AP/Wide World 208: (T) Philadelphia Museum of Art, Pennsylvania/Giraudon,Paris/SuperStock. (c) 2002 Estate of Pablo Picasso/Artists Rights Society (ARS), New York 209: (Inset) Richard Hamilton Smith/Corbis 212: (Bkgd) James L. Amos/Corbis 212: (Bkgd) (c) Mark Segal/Index Stock Imagery/PictureQuest 216: (C) Paul A. Souders/Corbis 216: (BL) Hulton-Deutsche Collection/Corbis 218: (TR) Kent Gavin/Archive Photos 219: (TR) (c) Dorling Kindersley 219: (TL) (c) Dorling Kindersley 221: (TR) Lebrecht Collection 222: (R) Odd Andersen/(c) AFP 224: (TR) Barry Lewis/Corbis 225: (BR) Barry Lewis/Corbis 226: (BL) Eyewire, Inc. 227: (BL) Bettman/Corbis 228: (BR) Mary Robert/Lebrecht Collection 229: (Bkgd) Astrid & Hanns-Frieder Michler/Photo Researchers, Inc. 230: (TL) Michael & Patricia Fogden/Corbis 230: (Bkgd) GAIL SHUMWAY/FPG International LLC 232: (CR) Mauritius/Index Stock Imagery 232: (TR) Tim Davis/Stone 232: (B) GAIL SHUMWAY/FPG International LLC 233: (CR) GAIL SHUMWAY/FPG International LLC 233: (BL) JH Pete Carmichael/Image Bank 233: (BR) Mike Timo/Stone 234: (Bkgd) (c) Hulton-Deutsch Collection/Bettmann/Corbis 235: (BR) (c) Bettmann/Corbis 240: (BL) AP/Wide World 240: (CL) SuperStock 240: (TL) Hulton Getty/Stone 240: (BR) A. Ramey/PhotoEdit 240: (TC) William Lovelace/Hulton Getty Picture Collection/Stone 240: (BC) Gary Holscher/Stone 241: (BR) Barry Lewis/Corbis 241: (TR) Tim Davis/Stone 241: (BL) (c) Dorling Kindersley 241: Sally Rogers (CR) 241: (BL) Mike Wintroath/AP/Wide World 241: (BC) David Sutherland/Stone 241: (BR) Dave G. Houser/Corbis 241: (TC) Aldo Torelli/Stone 252: (TL) David Drew/Corbis 252: (BR) Michael St. Maur Sheil/Corbis 261: (R) The Granger Collection, New York 268: (TR) Bettmann/Corbis 269: (TL) Luca Bruno/AP/Wide World 270: (Bkgd) UPI/Bettmann/Corbis 271: (BR) AP/Wide World 272: (B) SuperStock 272: (TL) SuperStock 273: (CR) North Wind Picture Archives 273: (TC) @2000 John Running 273: (B) SuperStock 275: (BR) San Diego Museum of Man 276: (BL) Hulton-Deutsch Collection/Corbis 278: Joe Viesti/Viesti Collection, Inc. 278: SuperStock 279: F Good 279: B Vikander 279: Paul Chesley/Ston 279: SuperStock 280: ChromoSohm/Sohm/Image Works 281: AP/Wide World 282: (Bkgd) SuperStock 283: (TR) Forbes Collection, New York City/Bridgeman Art/SuperStock 284: (Bkgd) Michael Busselle/Stone 287: (BL) Hulton Getty/Stone 288: (T) Jack Vartoogian 288: (TR) Susan Sterner/AP/Wide World 288: (B) Kyndell Harkness/AP/Wide World 292: (T) Corbis 294: (T) Corbis 295: (CR) Corbis 297: (BR) David Samuel Robbins/Corbis 298: (BR) Seth Kushner/Corbis Sygma 303: Joan Marcus (TC) (c)Joan Marcus 304: (BC) Sarah Stone/Stone 306: (Bkgd) Randy Faris/Corbis 308: A. Ramey/Unicorn Stock Photos 308: A. Ramey/Unicorn Stock Photos 308: Aneal Vohra/Unicorn Stock Photos 312: (Bkgd) AP/Wide World 313: (C) Jack Vartoogian 314: (CL) Steve Gates/AP/Wide World 314: (BL) PhotoDisc 315: Sally Rogers (TL) 316: (T) Flip Schulke/Corbis 316: (B) Tim Mosenfelder/Corbis 325: (C) PhotoDisc 328: (TR) SuperStock 331: (TL) Nancy R. Schiff/Archive Photos 331: (BC) SuperStock 332: (BC) Blank Archives/Archive Photos 332: (B) Gary Holscher/Stone 334: (BL) Bernard Gotfryd/Archive Photos 334: (B) Gary Holscher/Stone 336: (Bkgd) A. Tannenbaum/Corbis Sygma 337: (TR) Joseph Sohm/ChromoSohm Inc./Corbis 338: Chip and Rosa Maria de la Cueva Peterson 340: Corbis 342: (CR) World Perspectives/Stone 342: (Bkgd) Nigel Press/Stone 344: (B) John Fortunato/Stone 344: (TR) Nigel Press/Stone 346: (Bkgd) Bill Bachmann/PhotoEdit 346: (TC) Kim Westerkov/Stone 347: (CL) James Randklev/Stone 349: (TR) MGM/Kobal Collection 353: (T) SuperStock 354: (B) Dave G. Houser/Corbis 355: (T) The Green Bay Chronicle/H. Marc Larson/AP/Wide World 360: James Durst (BL) Photo by Greg Braun, Courtesy of James Durst 360: (Bkgd) John Warden/Stone 362: (TR) Photri, Inc. 363: (Bkgd) World Perspectives/Stone 363: (TR) Photri, Inc. 366: (BR) Lebrecht Collection 372: (TL) Chritsian Pierre/SuperStock 372: (BC) Peter Harholdt/SuperStock 374: (Bkgd) Liam Blake/Panoramic Images 374: (B) (c) Burstein Collection/Corbis 376: (Bkgd) SuperStock 382: (C) AFP/Corbis 383: (TR) SuperStock 384: (TL) SuperStock 384: (TR) Stephanie Maze/Corbis 385: (BC) Aldo Torelli/Stone 386: (TR) Jim Zuckerman/Corbis 386: (TR) Donald Nausbaum/Stone 388: (Bkgd) Sorensen/Bohmer Olse/Stone 388: (Bkgd) Trip/TH-FOTO Werbung 390: (Bkgd) Tom Till/Stone 390: (Bkgd) Bonnie Kamin/PhotoEdit 392: (Bkgd) Myrleen Ferguson/PhotoEdit 392: (Bkgd) PhotoDisc 400: Kolvoord/Image Works 401: Bob Daemmrich/Image Works 402: (TL) SuperStock 402: (CR) Miki Kratsman/Corbi 402: (BL) Archive Photos 403: Reuters NewMedia Inc./Corbis 403: Bob Daemmrich/Image Works 403: David Young Wolff/Stone 405: (BL) Odd Andersen/AP/Wide World 405: (CR) Gavin Wickham; Eye Ubiquitous/Corbis 405: (BC) Richard Vogel/AP/Wide World 405: (BR) SuperStock 411: (T) Mitchell Gerber/Corbis 411: (TL) Victor Malafronte/Archive Photos 412: (Bkgd) FoodPix 416: (TC) A. Ramey/PhotoEdit 416: (TL) AP/Wide World 417: (TR) Doug Armand/Stone 418: (CR) Mike Wintroath/AP/Wide World 419: (BC) David Young-Wolff/PhotoEdit 420: (TR) William Lovelace/Hulton Getty Picture Collection/Stone 420: (B) Hulton Getty Picture Collection/Stone 422: (Bkgd) David Sutherland/Stone 422: (TL) Leland Bobbe/Stone 424: (Bkgd) Brian Stablyk/Stone

All other photos: Pearson Learning and Scott Foresman

Illustration Credits

Rosalind Solomon: viii Steve Barbaria: viii Elizabeth Rosen: 1 Steve Barbaria: 6 Steve Barbaria: 8 Michael Di Giorgio: 8 Ziti Asbaghi: 9 Estelle Carol: 9 Steve Barbaria: 9 Ron Himler: 10 Andrew Wheatcroft: 12 Andrew Wheatcroft: 12 Annoushka Galouchko: 14 Annoushka Galouchko: 16 Tony Nuccio: 16 Eunice Moyle: 18 Antonio Cangemi: 20 Jane Dill: 22 Jane Dill: 23 Kirchoff/Wolberg, Inc.: 24 Kirchoff/Wolberg, Inc.: 26 Andrea Z. Tachiera: 26 Kirchoff/Wolberg, Inc.: 27 Donna Perrone: 32 Eileen Hine: 34 Eileen Hine: 35 Stacey Schuett: 36 Stacey Schuett: 38 Stacey Schuett: 38 Antonio Cangemi: 40 Stacey Schuett: 41 Shawn Finley: 42 Shawn Finley: 42 Shawn Finley: 44 Shawn Finley: 44 Shawn Finley: 44 Kirchoff/Wolberg, Inc.: 46 Michael Di Giorgio: 48 Fian Arroyo: 49 Fian Arroyo: 49 Fian Arroyo: 49 Fian Arroyo: 49 Kirchoff/Wolberg, Inc.: 50 Esther Baran: 51 Kirchoff/Wolberg, Inc.: 52 Elizabeth Rosen: 54 David McCall Johnston: 62 David Diaz: 64 John Hovell: 66 John Hovell: 68 John Hovell: 69 Kirchoff/Wolberg, Inc.: 71 Kirchoff/Wolberg, Inc.: 72 Rae Ecklund: 74 Elizabeth Rosen: 80 David Diaz: 81 Kirchoff/Wolberg, Inc.: 87 Kirchoff/Wolberg, Inc.: 89 Tom Leonard: 90 Tom Barrett: 92 Kirchoff/Wolberg, Inc.: 93 Jean & Mou-sien Tseng: 94 Krystyna Stasiak: 96 John Hovell: 98 Kirchoff/Wolberg, Inc.: 101 Kirchoff/Wolberg, Inc.: 103 Kirchoff/Wolberg, Inc.: 104 Kirchoff/Wolberg, Inc.: 106 Carlos Ochagavia: 110 Carlos Ochagavia: 112 Gerald Bustamante: 116 Kirchoff/Wolberg, Inc.: 118 Gerald Bustamante: 119 Gerald Bustamante: 121 Carmelo Blandino: 122 Carmelo Blandino: 122 Carmelo Blandino: 124 Carmelo Blandino: 124 Carmelo Blandino: 125 Kirchoff/Wolberg, Inc.: 134 John Hovell: 144 Kirchoff/Wolberg, Inc.: 144 Kirchoff/Wolberg, Inc.: 146 Kirchoff/Wolberg, Inc.: 148 Michael Di Giorgio: 149 Kirchoff/Wolberg, Inc.: 153 Linda Wingerter: 154 Nancy Freeman: 158 Tom Leonard: 168 Tom Leonard: 170 Esther Baran: 174 Esther Baran: 176 Kirchoff/Wolberg, Inc.: 178 Kirchoff/Wolberg, Inc.: 179 Kirchoff/Wolberg, Inc.: 180 Kirchoff/Wolberg, Inc.: 181 RosalindSolomon: 182 Michael Di Giorgio: 186 Michael Di Giorgio: 193 Kirchoff/Wolberg, Inc.: 194 David Galchutt: 196 George Baquero: 198 Joel Spector: 202 Joel Spector: 204 Steve Barbaria: 206 Steve Barbaria: 209 Kirchoff/Wolberg, Inc.: 210 Kirchoff/Wolberg, Inc.: 212 Tom Leonard: 214 Joe Boddy: 215 Joe Boddy: 215 Joe Boddy: 215 Tom Leonard: 216 Krystyna Stasiak: 218 Krystyna Stasiak: 221 John Hovell: 226 Michael Di Giorgio: 229 Lane Yerkes: 238 Ralph Canaday: 240 Patti Green: 240 Dave Jonason: 240 T. L. Ary: 241 Nora Koerber: 241 Arvis Stewart: 248 Vilma Ortiz-Dillon: 253 Ralph Canaday: 254 Ralph Canaday: 256 Ralph Canaday: 257 Larry Johnson: 258 Larry Johnson: 260 Tom Leonard: 261 Craig Spearing: 262 Craig Spearing: 264 T. L. Ary: 266 T. L. Ary: 268 Kirchoff/Wolberg, Inc.: 270 Kirchoff/Wolberg, Inc.: 271 Kirchoff/Wolberg, Inc.: 274 Kirchoff/Wolberg, Inc.: 275 Mike Tofanelli: 276 Tom Leonard: 283 John Hovell: 286 John Hovell: 287 John Hovell: 289 Vilma Ortiz-Dillon: 289 Tony Nuccio: 289 Donna Perrone: 290 Jean & Mou-sien Tseng: 296 Fahimeh Amiri: 298 Chi Chung: 300 Chi Chung: 302 Eileen Hine: 306 Eileen Hine: 307 Jerry Tiritilli: 308 Jerry Tiritilli: 310 Jerry Tiritilli: 310 Jerry Tiritilli: 310 Kirchoff/Wolberg, Inc.: 314 Roger Roth: 318 Nancy Freeman: 320 Oki Han: 322 Oki Han: 324 Vilma Ortiz-Dillon: 325 Ron Himler: 326 Bradley Clark: 328 Bradley Clark: 330 Deborah White: 330 Craig Spearing: 334 Vilma Ortiz-Dillon: 335 Vilma Ortiz-Dillon: 335 Vilma Ortiz-Dillon: 335 Kirchoff/Wolberg, Inc.: 337 Kirchoff/Wolberg, Inc.: 343 Kirchoff/Wolberg, Inc.: 344 Kirchoff/Wolberg, Inc.: 344 Kirchoff/Wolberg, Inc.: 346 Lane Gregory: 348 Tom Leonard: 350 Kirchoff/Wolberg, Inc.: 351 Tom Leonard: 352 Kirchoff/Wolberg, Inc.: 352 Alexi Natchev: 354 Alexi Natchev: 355 Alexi Natchev: 356 Alexi Natchev: 357 Bradley Clark: 358 Donna Perrone: 364 Dave Jonason: 366 Dave Jonason: 367 Susan Swan: 368 Susan Swan: 370 Alexandra Wallner: 372 Alexandra Wallner: 374 Tom Leonard: 375 Tom Leonard: 376 Tom Leonard: 377 Jennifer Bolten: 382 Jennifer Bolten: 383 Jennifer Bolten: 384 Jennifer Bolten: 386 Kirchoff/Wolberg, Inc.: 386 Kirchoff/Wolberg, Inc.: 388 Kirchoff/Wolberg, Inc.: 390 Kirchoff/Wolberg, Inc.: 391 Kirchoff/Wolberg, Inc.: 392 Kirchoff/Wolberg, Inc.: 393 Nora Koerber: 396 Nora Koerber: 398 Tom Leonard: 402 Tom Leonard: 404 Cameron Eagle: 406 Robert LoGrippo: 408 Robert LoGrippo: 410 Kirchoff/Wolberg, Inc.: 413 Sally Jo Vitsky: 414 Sally Jo Vitsky: 416 Patti Green: 418 Kirchoff/Wolberg, Inc.: 423 Michael Di Giorgio: 424

Acknowledgments

Credit and appreciation are due publishers and copyright owners for use of the following: 2: "Turn the Beat Around" from the Motion Picture *The Specialist*, Words and music by Peter Jackson, Jr. and Gerald Jackson. Copyright © 1975 by Unichappell Music Inc. This arrangement Copyright © 2001 by Unichappell Music Inc. International Copyright Secured. All Rights Reserved. 6: "Put a Little Love in Your Heart" by Jimmy Holiday, Randy Myers and Jackie DeShannon. © 1969 (Renewed) EMI Unart Catalog Inc. All Rights Reserved. Used by Permission. WARNER BROS. PUBLICATIONS U.S. INC., Miami, FL 3014. 13: "Haul Away, Joe" © 2002 Pearson Education, Inc. 14: "Gakavik" (The Partridge) English words © 2002 Pearson Education, Inc. 18: "Limbo Like Me" New words and new music adapted by Massie Patterson and Sammy Heyward. (Based on a traditional song) TRO-© 1963 (Renewed) Ludlow Music, Inc., New York, NY. Used by permission. 23: "Tsuki" (The Moon) from *Children's Songs from Japan*. Florence White and Kazuo Akiyama. © 1960 Edward B. Marks Music Company. Copyright renewed. Used by permission. All rights reserved. 24: "Waitin' for the Light to Shine" from *Big River*. Words and music by Roger Miller. Copyright © 1985 Sony/ATV Songs LLC and Roger Miller music. This arrangement copyright © 2001 Sony/ATV Songs LLC and Roger Miller Music. All Rights Administered by Sony/ATV Music Publishing, 8 Music Square West, Nashville, TN 37203. International Copyright Secured. All Rights Reserved. Used by Permission. 32: "Sonando" by Peter Terrace. Reprinted by permission of Peter Terrace. English words © 2002 Pearson Education, Inc. 35: "Tie Me Kangaroo Down, Sport" Words and music by Rolf Harris. © 1960, 1961 (Renewed 1988, 1989) Castle Music Pty. Ltd. This arrangement © 2001 Castle Music Pty. Ltd. All Rights for the U.S. and Canada Controlled and Administered by Beechwood Music Corp. All Rights Reserved. International Copyright Secured. Used by Permission. 36: "Pay Me My Money Down" from *Hootenanny Song Book*. Collected and adapted by Lydia Parish. Copyright © 1963 (Renewed) Consolidated Music Publishers. International Copyright Secured. All Rights Reserved. Reprinted by Permission. 42: "We Go Together" from *Grease*. Words and music by Warren Casey and Jim Jacobs. © 1971, 1972 WARREN CASEY and JIM JACOBS. This arrangement © 2001 WARREN CASEY and JIM JACOBS. Copyright Renewed. All Rights Reserved. Used by Permission. 52: "Rock Island Line" New Words and new music arrangement by Huddie Ledbetter. Edited with new additional material by Alan Lomax. TRO - © Copyright 1959 (Renewed) Folkways Music Publishers, Inc., New York, New York. Used by permission. 56: "River" Words and music by Bill Staines. © 1988 Mineral River Music (BMI) Administered by Bug Music. All

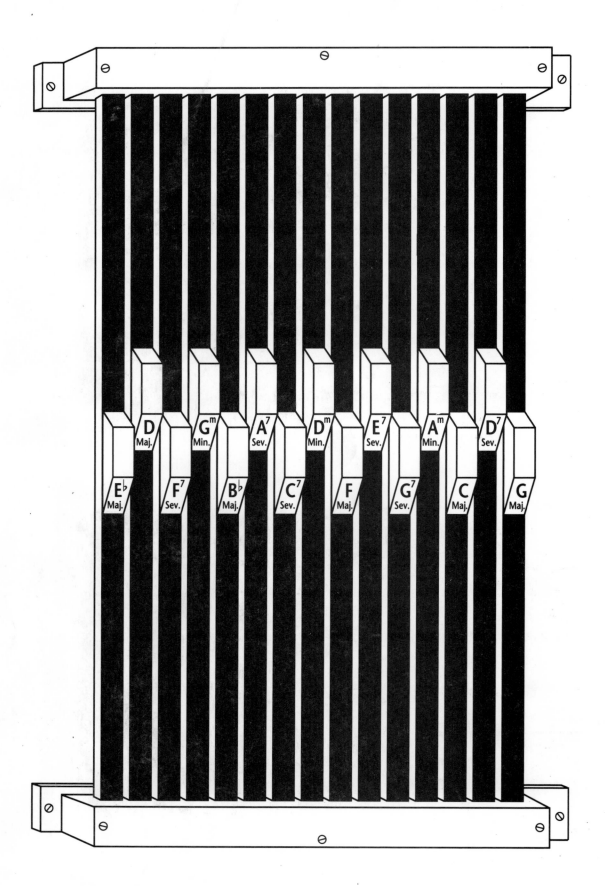